# Kitchen Table Entrepreneurs

# Kitchen Table Entrepreneurs

## HOW ELEVEN WOMEN ESCAPED POVERTY AND BECAME THEIR OWN BOSSES

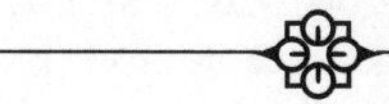

MARTHA SHIRK
ANNA S. WADIA

Preface by
Marie C. Wilson and Sara K. Gould

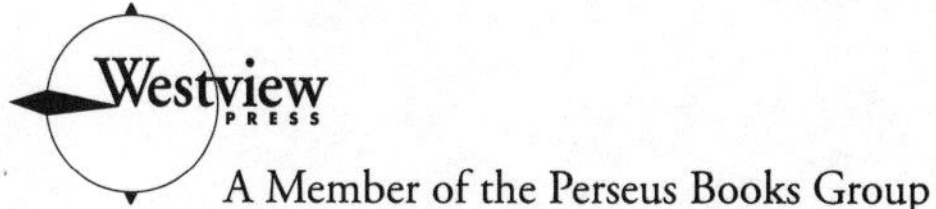


A Member of the Perseus Books Group

Westview Press books are available at special discounts for bulk purchases in the United States by corporations, institutions, and other organizations. For more information, please contact the Special Markets Department at the Perseus Books Group, 11 Cambridge Center, Cambridge MA 02142, or call (617) 252-5298.

Published in 2002 in the United States of America by Westview Press, 5500 Central Avenue, Boulder, Colorado 80301–2877, and in the United Kingdom by Westview Press, 12 Hid's Copse Road, Cumnor Hill, Oxford OX2 9JJ

Find us on the World Wide Web at www.westviewpress.com

Cover photo by Earl Dotter for the Ms. Foundation

Library of Congress Cataloging-in-Publication Data
Shirk, Martha.
Kitchen table entrepreneurs : how eleven women escaped poverty and became their own bosses / Martha Shirk, Anna Wadia.
p. cm.
Includes bibliographical references and index.
ISBN 0-8133-3910-3
1. Self-employed women—United States—Biography. 2. Businesswomen—United States—Biography. 3. Women-owned business enterprises—United States—Case studies. 4. Entrepreneurship—United States—Case studies. I. Wadia, Anna. II. Title.
HD6072.6.U5 S557—2002
338'.04'092273—dc21 2002004337

The paper used in this publication meets the requirements of the American National Standard for Permanence of Paper for Printed Library Materials Z39.48–1984.

Text design by *Trish Wilkinson*
Set in 11.5-point Goudy

10 9 8 7 6 5 4 3 2 1

# Contents

# Photos



### Plates

# Preface

You hold in your hands stories of eleven spirited and resourceful women who—against all odds—pursued the great American dream of launching their own businesses. They represent thousands of low-income women around the country who have taken the same path to financial survival for themselves and their families, with the help of a vibrant network of microenterprise support organizations. Over the years, we have had the privilege of meeting many of these women. We have gone into their dry cleaning establishments; met the children in their day care centers; seen the clients whose hair they braid; feasted on food they've cooked and catered. With every visit, we have been inspired.

It wasn't always like this. We both remember the early days of women's economic development. The year was 1985. We both had come to work at the Ms. Foundation for Women, a leading national women's foundation that raises money to conduct advocacy and public education campaigns and to provide resources to grassroots groups focused on the health, safety, and economic well-being of women, girls, and their families.

Marie came from Iowa. She had been designing employment reentry, minority career development, and flexible work-time programs for women, as well as serving on the city council. She was there when Iowa descended into one of its worst recessions, which devastated farm families. Marie saw firsthand the importance of a woman's ability to produce some additional income "on the side." That small sewing or cooking business might be the only way the woman could keep her family from falling into complete economic ruin. But there were no programs in place to support such efforts.

Sara had grown up in a family business, a machinery company, launched by her great-great-grandfather. She had a deep appreciation for entrepreneurship, a spirit she recognized in the early 1980s among low-income women in three beleaguered urban communities. On the staff of the HUB program for women's enterprise, she conducted one of the first studies in the United States to locate low-income female microentrepreneurs and determine what services they needed to succeed. Sara found that the women were using the profits from their small businesses to supplement paltry wages, public assistance, and other government subsidies, or as the sole source of family income. As in Iowa, the women were running businesses with little or no access to capital; no assistance with marketing, pricing, bookkeeping, or other nuts-and-bolts matters; and often no support.

When we joined forces at the Ms. Foundation, one of our top priorities was to strengthen the organizations that were helping low-income women to start and grow small businesses. At that time, only scattered organizations existed, and there were no funds available to develop their network. Most foundations that supported women's issues did so from pots of money labeled "social services" and "poverty," which saw women as passive victims of systemic oppression, not capable actors who could take steps that would benefit not only them, but the economy too. The most socially conscious foundations with the resources to support this work did not know that this work existed.

Getting the word out and raising money were our first and hardest challenges. At the suggestion of another pioneer in the field—Paulette Meyer, a friend of the foundation—we decided to do what had never been done before: to form a national women's economic development funders' collaborative. It would give funders an opportunity to learn about the work of these microenterprise organizations and the women they served in a hands-on way, by developing program guidelines, visiting the sites, and evaluating projects. It would enable them to pool resources, share risk, and fund programs together, through the Ms. Foundation.

For two long years, we organized, foundation by foundation. We asked funders to donate large sums of money—$150,000 or more—and to give it up front. In response, we were asked if we really could manage that much money. We experienced on a macro level the same distrust that women microentrepreneurs experienced on a micro level when they tried to get a bank loan.

Progressive foundations feared that we wanted to turn low-income women into "little capitalists." Conservative foundations thought that poor women, already overburdened, were incapable of an undertaking so complex as running a business. What both failed to realize was that low-income women were *already* running small businesses—and not because they wanted to become "little capitalists," but in order to feed their families.

We remember one particularly bad evening, as those two years drew to a close, when we were sitting in yet another airport terminal. We had just visited a major foundation where, once more, the reception was cool. As we talked, what gradually dawned on us was that this collaborative might never happen. We flipped mindlessly through magazine pages, tears running down our cheeks. But, as is often the case in life, just as we'd given up hope, the tide turned. The day after we returned from that trip, the first foundation called to join the collaborative.

The rest, as they say, is history. The Ms. Foundation has since organized three rounds of its women's economic development funders' collaborative. To date, forty foundations, corporations, and individuals have generously devoted time, expertise, and funds to this initiative. Together, we have distributed over $10 million to women's economic development organizations, which in turn have helped hundreds of women like those you will read about to plan, launch, and grow all kinds of small businesses. Not only that: These funders have devoted significant *additional* resources to developing their own programs to support low-income women's microenterprise development. Furthermore, our grantees have used Ms. Foundation support to test innovations that have later received millions of dollars from public sources.

The Ms. Foundation also brought together leaders from the growing number of organizations that serve low-income women microentrepreneurs. We organized regional meetings; mounted the first national Institute for Women's Economic Empowerment, now in its thirteenth year; and sponsored attendance by representatives of these organizations at national and international conferences. These activities facilitated an exchange of ideas, the identification of best practices, and the addition of advocacy and public policy work to the direct service agenda. Today, the organizations see their work and the work of the women they serve as integral to the American economic system. The wider world takes the same view, having watched women-owned businesses become the fastest growing segment of the small business community.

At the beginning of the new millennium, the Ms. Foundation was recognized at the highest level for this work. We knew we had come a long way from that airport terminal when First Lady Hillary Clinton presented us with the Presidential Award for Excellence in Microenterprise Development in January 2001.

On a local level, the women and their microbusinesses are now crucial players. In addition to supplying essential income to the women and their families, these businesses provide jobs to other residents and offer useful goods and services. The women themselves—having taken the equivalent of a crash course in economic literacy and, often, self-esteem—are role models for their children and their communities. They are also symbols of hope in tough times. Many give the success that comes to them, however modest, back to their communities a hundredfold.

We should add that we never expected that every low-income woman would—or should—become a microentrepreneur. Starting a business is hard, risky, and realistic only for a small group of women with entrepreneurial drive and a dream. But these women exist at all economic levels. Our goal has been to ensure that all women have an equal opportunity to reach for that dream.

For us, this work has been its own reward. We remember a time when we were called on again and again to be the voice for women's microenterprise. Now there are many voices, from the staff of the microenterprise organizations to the women microentrepreneurs themselves. They speak to other aspiring microentrepreneurs, to foundation boards, city councils, state legislatures, national and international groups, and to all of us here, in this wonderful book.

We know you'll enjoy their stories. We also expect that when you put the book down and walk out your front door, you'll encounter someone just like one of these women. When you do, we hope you'll remember what you read here and give a silent—or maybe not-so-silent—cheer.

Marie C. Wilson, President
Sara K. Gould, Executive Director
Ms. Foundation for Women

# Acknowledgments

The Ms. Foundation and the authors want to thank the many people and organizations around the country that made this book possible. First and foremost, we want to express our gratitude to the nine families who invited us into their homes and businesses and inspired us with their strength and entrepreneurial spirit. We also owe special thanks to the microenterprise development organizations that connected us to the women profiled and that have provided them with invaluable support through the years: the Colorado Enterprise Fund in Denver; the Good Faith Fund in Pine Bluff, Arkansas; the Detroit Entrepreneurship Institute; the Lakota Fund on the Pine Ridge Reservation in South Dakota; the Acre Family Day Care Corporation in Lowell, Massachusetts; West Company in Ukiah, California; the Women's Self-Employment Project in Chicago, Illinois; Appalachian By Design in Lewisburg, West Virginia; and Women's Initiative for Self-Employment in San Francisco, California.

This book would not have been possible without the vision of the W.K. Kellogg Foundation, whose funding underwrote the research and writing. We would also like to thank all of the donors who have come together in the Collaborative Fund for Women's Economic Development over the last ten years to support women microentrepreneurs: Annie E. Casey Foundation, Appalachian Regional Commission, BP America, Pamela T. & C. Hunter Boll, Brico Fund, Citigroup Foundation, Edna McConnell Clark Foundation,

Clio Foundation, Elizabeth Wallace Ellers, Flora Family Foundation, Ford Foundation, French American Charitable Trust, George Gund Foundation, Carol Guyer, Hitachi Foundation, Hite Foundation, Jacobs Family Foundation, James Irvine Foundation, Jean Street Fund, JPMorgan-Chase Foundation, W.K. Kellogg Foundation, Leo Model Foundation, Levi Strauss Foundation, Lindsay Shea, Albert A. List Foundation, John D. & Catherine T. MacArthur Foundation, Bambi MacDonald Estate, McKay Foundation, John Merck Fund, Charles Stewart Mott Foundation, New York Community Trust, Nord Family Foundation, Norman Foundation, Rockefeller Brothers Fund, Alvin and Fanny Thalhiemer Foundation, Turner Foundation, Wells Fargo Foundation, Wendling Foundation, and White Birch Foundation.

We want to express our sincere appreciation for all the people inside and outside of the Ms. Foundation who contributed to the production of this book. Kelly Parisi, the foundation's communications director, reviewed every chapter, helped select the photos, and worked with Westview Press on publicizing the book. Earl Dotter brought a keen eye and deep sensitivity to the lives of the women in his beautiful photographs. Zak Mettger, a consultant to the foundation, helped us write the book proposal and connected the Ms. Foundation with both the authors and the photographer. Angela Bonavoglia worked with Marie Wilson and Sara Gould to recount the history of the Ms. Foundation's economic development work in the Preface. Finally, we'd like to thank Jill Rothenberg for editing the manuscript and shepherding it through Westview Press.

*Martha Shirk*
*Anna Wadia*
*Marie Wilson*
*Sara Gould*

# Introduction

*For years, America Ducasse, an immigrant from the Dominican Republic, struggled to find a job in her new country in which she could earn enough to support her household and pay for child care. Now, with her home-based day care business in Lowell, Massachusetts, she's earning a comfortable living while taking care of her own children.*

*Roselyn Spotted Eagle's $8,000-a-year income from her crafts business on the Pine Ridge Indian Reservation might not seem like much to most people. But for Roselyn and her disabled daughter and grandchild, it has meant being able to move from a tiny cabin with no plumbing into a three-bedroom mobile home with not just a bathroom, but a washer and dryer.*

*Lucille Barnett Washington started an auto parts and repair business in the early 1970s in Detroit that her adult daughter, Sheela Drummer, now helps run. Sheela is working hard to ensure that the business her mother founded will survive competitive pressures from major chains and provide a livelihood for her own children.*

*Kitchen Table Entrepreneurs* tells the stories of America, Roselyn, Lucille, Sheela, and other women who have overcome numerous obstacles to start small businesses that support themselves and their families. The nine stories illuminate their trials, successes, and setbacks. In striving to move their households out of poverty by channeling their creative energies into businesses, the women profiled here demonstrate incredible resilience, strength, and passion. Their stories will resonate with anyone who has ever pursued a dream.

The movement of low-income women into self-employment is part of a larger trend under way in America. The Center for Women's Business Ownership estimated that between 1997 and 2002, the number of women-owned businesses will grow at twice the rate of all U.S. firms, reaching 6.2 million in 2002. Altogether, these enterprises were expected to employ nearly 9.2 million workers and generate more than $1.5 trillion worth of sales each year. One in five of these businesses will be owned by women of color.[1]

Unlike many owners of small businesses, the women you'll read about here are not flying solo. They're benefiting from assistance from some of the hundreds of local organizations around the country that provide training and financing to budding microenterprises—very small businesses, usually owned and operated by one person, that employ five or fewer workers and require less than $25,000 in start-up capital. Assisting these small businesses is now one of many strategies—along with job training, asset building, and organizing for better wages and benefits—that local organizations use to help low-income families improve their livelihoods.

Since 1985 the Ms. Foundation for Women has funded, trained, and networked with these local organizations, increasing their capacity to serve low-income women. Each of the women profiled here has received assistance from a Ms. Foundation grantee.

Having experienced the power of this strategy in changing women's lives, the foundation wanted the American public to hear the story of microenterprise, not through statistics or research reports, but through intimate portraits of women who have started small businesses. The foundation asked Martha Shirk, a journalist who specializes in social issues, to write their stories. She spent about a week with each woman and her family between December 1999 and May 2001, listening to their stories of struggle and triumph and witnessing their passion for their businesses.

## Real Lives, Real Businesses

Not all of the entrepreneurs in this country look like Bill Gates. As a matter of fact, most look more like the women featured in this book. They are individuals with the zeal and sheer determination to create better lives for themselves and their families. Many of the women are fulfilling their lifelong dreams. For Danielle Franklin, it's running a skin care salon in Oakland, California. For Sharon Garza, it's operating a hot dog cart near the convention center in downtown Denver, Colorado.

The stories told in this book illustrate the economic realities, family responsibilities, and business challenges faced by low-income microentrepreneurs throughout the country. They also bear witness to how owning a small business can transform a woman's life, not only in economic terms, but in terms of her self-esteem and her contribution to her community.

Many microentrepreneurs, like Sioux artisan Roselyn Spotted Eagle, use their businesses to supplement government benefits or income from low-wage jobs. Others, such as child care provider America Ducasse, work at their businesses full-time and make a comfortable living. While most don't become rich, a few—like Yasmina Cadiz, who sells imported designer lamps over the internet and from a store in Chicago, and Jeanette Bradshaw, a caterer and wedding planning in White Hall, Arkansas—gross more than $100,000 a year.

Some women have used their businesses as a route off the welfare rolls. When her husband, the family's breadwinner, died suddenly, Danielle Franklin temporarily went on welfare to support herself and her daughter. As she built up her business over three years, she gradually reduced the amount of money she received from welfare and for the last few years has made it on her own. America Ducasse, Sheela Drummer, and Jackie Clark also spent time on welfare.

The social circumstances of many low-income women entrepreneurs present challenges that make starting a business even more difficult than it is for most entrepreneurs. Due to divorce, widowhood, or estrangement from their children's fathers, many of the profiled women are the sole providers for their families. For example, Roselyn Spotted Eagle struggled for years to support her family after fleeing an abusive husband; widowed suddenly, Jeanette Bradshaw patched together income from low-wage jobs and a home-based cake-baking operation to support herself and her teenage son. For many women entrepreneurs, working at home is almost a necessity because they have young children or disabled family members who require their care. America Ducasse is a case in point: Perhaps the greatest benefit of her home-based day care business is that she can care for her own children while earning income. For Ollie Barkley, who makes her living by knitting sweaters and baby items, working at home means that she and her husband can home-school their children, a priority for them.

These businesses that enable the women to provide for and care for their children are often an inspiration to those children. Two of the businesses profiled are mother-daughter ventures. In several others, the children often help out, gaining skills and expanding their horizons. For instance, working in his mother's plant nursery gave direction to Jackie Clark's son, Jackson, and he decided to study horticulture in college. He now brings new techniques to the business, giving it a competitive edge.

Many low-income women entrepreneurs tend to choose businesses in sectors that have been traditionally dominated by women, as the stories of child care provider America Ducasse, aesthetician Danielle Franklin, and caterer Jeanette Bradshaw show. As business owners, however, they have been able to increase their incomes beyond the low wages usually paid in these sectors.

Some pioneering women entrepreneurs, like Lucille Barnett Washington, have broken into nontraditional sectors such as auto parts and repair.

All of the women featured in the book received assistance from local microenterprise programs that understand the economic and personal realities low-income women face and so design services accordingly. These programs work in collaboration with job training programs and welfare offices to best serve women who are patching income from businesses, jobs, and public assistance, or who decide to pursue jobs instead of self-employment. The organizations may provide child care during training, employ social workers on their staffs, and build strong relationships with domestic violence programs to refer women who need counseling or shelter.

## Economic Realities

The reasons why low-income women pursue microenterprise reflect the economic realities of the day.

In the mid-1980s, low-income women were starting small businesses to create jobs where few existed. Even in the boom years of the late 1990s, jobs remained scarce in isolated rural areas and inner cities, and women needed to create job opportunities for themselves. For example, in Pocahontas County, West Virginia, where Ollie Barkley lives, the unemployment rate was 9.8 percent in early 2000, when the country as a whole was enjoying its lowest unemployment rate in three decades (4.1 percent.)

Where jobs existed, they were often low paying and part-time, so some women started businesses to supplement low wages. For instance, Jeanette Bradshaw had moved from one low-wage, low-satisfaction clerical job to another for years, baking on the side to make ends meet, before she took the plunge and began catering full-time. Even in areas where good jobs were available, some women sacrificed the stability of decent-paying jobs to risk starting their own businesses.

In 2001, when the country again entered a recession and jobs were scarce, it became increasingly important for women with entrepreneurial spirit to be able to create new jobs for themselves and others in their communities.

## Making It in Business

Most of the women profiled here brought talent and prior experience in their fields to their new businesses. Lucille Barnett Washington worked in someone else's auto parts store for eight years, Jackie Clark worked in the Northern California nursery she would eventually buy, and Danielle Franklin worked in a beauty parlor. But even with their experience, they needed extensive assistance from microenterprise programs in starting or expanding their businesses.

Some of the biggest challenges for women entrepreneurs are pricing, marketing, bookkeeping, and complying with government regulations, which are particularly complex in fields like food service. In addition, women business owners often underprice their own labor. For instance, caterer Jeanette Bradshaw, desperate for business and afraid to offend customers who were also friends and neighbors, for years took any job she could get, even if the price didn't cover her labor costs. It took her more than a decade before she began to turn down jobs that did not cover her expenses.

Whether they grow plants or fix cars, entrepreneurs in this country must learn how to effectively market their products and services. Small businesses can't compete with large companies for the mass market, but instead must find a niche in which they can gain a competitive advantage. So rather than trying to compete with large-scale wholesale nursery operations, Jackie Clark is working to create a niche for her nursery by specializing in shade plants, which many competing nurseries do not grow. Lucille Barnett Washington and Sheela Drummer are emphasizing the convenience of their neighborhood location, and they are planning to add quick oil-change services to keep established customers coming back to their auto parts and repair shop instead of turning to cheaper national chains such as AutoZone.

Increasingly, microentrepreneurs are experimenting with marketing over the internet. Yasmina Cadiz built up her lamp business through internet sales and only later opened a showroom. Jackie Clark used a programmer in Siberia to design a website that allows her to sell plants at twice the price she charges her wholesale customers. Even though Roselyn Spotted Eagle doesn't have a computer of her own, she sells baby moccasins to customers around the world through the Lakota Fund's website.

While some of the women profiled keep scrupulous books, many find bookkeeping and the timely payment of taxes to be ongoing challenges. As the businesses have grown and hired employees, owners have had to learn the rules governing workers' compensation, workplace safety, and unemployment compensation. Business owners in sectors such as food service and auto repair have to master all sorts of government regulations and invest in bringing their businesses up to code.

Microenterprise programs need to dedicate considerable resources to helping their clients address these challenges. Through classes, one-on-one counseling, and mentoring by established business owners, the programs help microentrepreneurs learn how to keep their books, comply with regulations, and price and market their products and services. Increasingly, the programs themselves are playing a role in marketing entrepreneurs' products. For example, Appalachian By Design, in rural West Virginia, sells high-priced knitted clothing and home accessories to such upscale national stores as Ethan Allen, and then subcontracts with home-based knitters to produce them. In this way, women such as Ollie Barkley can reach markets they would never be able to access on their own.

The programs also advocate for government policies that improve the chances of the women succeeding in business. For example, the Acre Family Day Care Corporation in Lowell, Massachusetts, joined with other organizations to persuade the state to raise the amount of money it pays to family day care providers who care for children of low-income parents, making the women in its network among the highest paid home-based providers in the country.

## Giving Back

Their own struggles have inspired many of the women to give back to their communities. For instance, because of a relative's death while homeless, Sharon and Michelle Garza give a hot dog and a drink to anyone who seems hungry, and they take their left-over food to a soup kitchen. Because she was once in an oppressive marriage, Jeanette Bradshaw has a soft spot in her heart—and often a job in her catering operation—for women who are trying to break out of bad relationships.

For some low-income women, starting and building a business transforms not just their economic circumstances, but also the way they see themselves and their roles in the larger community. Low-income women gain confidence as they overcome the challenges involved in launching a business, from developing a business plan to approaching banks for credit to negotiating with local officials for operating permits. As they learn the rules of the game and what it takes to play, women begin to develop a stake in the way those rules are made. Upon realizing how important location was to the success of her hot dog cart, seventeen-year-old Michelle Garza began to regularly attend City Council committee meetings on zoning and construction plans.

Microenterprise programs can help business owners make their voices heard in policy decisions. Several groups organize visits to Washington, D.C., and state capitals to share their experiences with elected officials and advocate for funding, welfare reform, and other policies that support women's business development. Hearing personal stories from constituents is often very persuasive to policymakers. By sharing their stories, the women realize—often for the first time—that they can influence the political process. Through the Women's Self-Employment Project, Yasmina Cadiz flew to Washington, D.C., to speak at a press conference about the need for federal support for microenterprise programs. This experience showed Yasmina that she was involved in something larger than her own business, and that she could make a difference in national policy.

## Women and the Microenterprise Movement

Of course, starting a small business is nothing new in America. Supporting the creation of small businesses, however, only became recognized as a deliberate strategy to combat poverty in the United States in the mid-1980s.

From the beginning, women have been at the center of microenterprise work in this country, representing the majority of clients and the leading innovators. During the mid-1980s, grassroots women's organizations that helped poor women train for jobs became aware that many women were adding home-based businesses to their strategies to patch together a living. Recognizing the value of these efforts, a few pioneering women's groups in rural states such as West Virginia and in cities such as Minneapolis began to develop ways to help low-income women formalize these businesses, by training them in how to price their goods, write business plans, and market their products, and by helping them obtain microloans. The Ms. Foundation, along with the Ford and Mott Foundations, was among the first foundations to support these fledgling efforts in both rural and urban areas around the country.

At the same time, more information began to reach the United States about the success of microenterprise development as an antipoverty strategy for women in developing countries. An economics professor in Bangladesh, Muhammad Yunus, pioneered the idea of providing the poor with microloans to help them launch, sustain, and expand small businesses. In 1976, Professor Yunus loaned $27 of his own money to several stool makers in a tiny village. With no money for raw materials, the stool makers had to borrow bamboo from exploitative traders and sell the finished products back to the traders at prices far below what the stools commanded in the market. With the tiny loans from Professor Yunus, they were able to buy the bamboo they needed to produce stools and sell them at the local market for a profit. The experience reverberated throughout their lives: Their children ate, the school improved, and the village changed.[2]

From these humble beginnings, Professor Yunus founded the Grameen Bank, which now provides small loans to more than 2 million rural women in Bangladesh. The Grameen Bank and other programs, such as ACCION in Latin America, pioneered the concept of peer lending circles, whose members make joint lending decisions and guarantee each other's loans. With the support of foundations, community leaders from the United States visited Bangladesh and other developing countries in the mid-1980s and began to adapt what they had learned to this country.

One of the first organizations to see the potential of applying Grameen Bank practices to poverty alleviation in the United States was ShoreBank in Chicago, the country's first community bank. After visiting Bangladesh, ShoreBank staff researched the feasibility of setting up a microenterprise program in Chicago. The result, in 1986, was the Women's Self-Employment Project (WSEP), the organization that twelve years later gave Yasmina Cadiz her first loan. Soon afterward, ShoreBank moved into the Mississippi Delta and established the Good Faith Fund, the group caterer Jeanette Bradshaw turned to for technical assistance and a loan.

Over the years, the microenterprise movement in the United States has evolved and grown. Today, there are more than 500 programs that provide business training and credit services to at least 100,000 people a year.[3] Funding from federal and state government agencies, while not enough to meet current needs, has greatly increased, following the lead of private foundations and banks.

Lessons learned overseas have been adapted to U.S. realities. After several years of experimentation with peer lending circles in which members make joint lending decisions and guarantee each other's loans, most microenterprise programs in this country have switched to making direct loans to clients. However, these programs have retained many of the practices associated with peer lending, such as providing gradually larger loans as an entrepreneur repays, creating mechanisms for entrepreneurs to help each other, and securing small loans with nontraditional collateral, such as bicycles and living room furniture.

Because of the sophistication of the American economy, the microenterprise programs have found that entrepreneurs often need training and business counseling as much as or more than they need loans. With a few exceptions, U.S. programs tend to provide entrepreneurs with extensive help in developing a business plan, pricing their products and services to ensure a profit, keeping records, filing their taxes, and developing effective marketing techniques.

The Ms. Foundation supports microenterprise development because it allows low-income women to create their own solutions to the challenges they face in their lives and communities. Not every woman is suited to being her own boss, and building a business can be a slow and difficult process, with frequent setbacks. As a matter of fact, after learning what it takes to start a business, many microenterprise trainees decide to use their new skills in the workforce instead.[4] While not for everybody, business ownership, either on its own or in combination with wage employment, offers an important path out of poverty for those women who choose it. For many, self-employment is a particularly attractive option, allowing women to balance work and family responsibilities, put existing skills to use generating income, and gain self-esteem and self-respect from being their own boss.

We now invite you to enter the lives and businesses of women around the country, who, in the words of hot dog vendor Sharon Garza, are "in charge of our own fate."

## Notes

1. Center for Women's Business Research (formerly National Foundation for Women Business Owners), "Number of Women-Owned Businesses Expected to Reach 6.2 Million in 2002" (Silver Spring, Md.,

December 4, 2001, press release), and "Number of Minority Women-Owned Businesses Expected to Reach 1.2 Million in 2002" (Silver Spring, Md., December 18, 2001, press release), www.nfwbo.org. According to the center, between 1987 and 1999, the number of women-owned businesses more than doubled, reaching 9.1 million in 1999, almost 40 percent of all businesses (source: "Women-Owned Businesses Top 9 Million in 1999," Silver Spring, Md., May 11, 1999, press release). Unfortunately, it is not possible to compare these figures to the more recent data because the Census Department's definition of a woman-owned business changed and became more restrictive. The definition no longer includes businesses in which a woman owns 50 percent or publicly traded women-owned firms.

2. Muhammad Yunus, *Banker to the Poor: Micro-lending and the Battle Against World Poverty* (New York: Public Affairs, 1999), 48–50.

3. John Else, "An Overview of the Microenterprise Development Field in the U.S.," in John Else et al., *The Role of Microenterprise Development in the United States* (Geneva, Switzerland: International Labor Organization, 2001), 5.

4. Of the 57,125 clients served by the 283 programs surveyed in 1997, 42 percent started or expanded businesses. J. Langer, J. Orwick, and A. Kays, eds., *1999 Directory of U.S. Microenterprise Programs* (Washington, D.C.: The Aspen Institute, 1999), xv–xvi.

*Daughter Michelle, center, and mother Sharon Garza are partners who share a passion for their hot dog cart.*

chapter 1

# Moving Up, One Hot Dog at a Time

## Sharon and Michelle Garza

## Heavenly Dawgs

## Denver, Colorado

It came as no surprise to anyone who knew them when Sharon Garza and her teenage daughter, Michelle, announced that they were starting a food service business. The women in their family seem to have food service in their genes.

In the 1940s, a time when few Mexican American women ran their own businesses, Sharon's grandmother owned and operated a hotel restaurant in Rawlins, Wyoming, a town that grew up alongside the old Overland Trail. Following in her mother's footsteps, Sharon's mother ran her own bar and restaurant in Rawlins and, later in life, Denver. When Sharon and her siblings were growing up, a home-cooked meal was usually whatever special her mother was cooking up in her bar that day, be it red chili or Mexican shrimp.

Sharon, thirty-nine, had already spent twenty-two years in the food industry when she and Michelle, then fifteen, decided to start their own food business in 1998. For most of her adult life, she had worked in fast-food restaurants such as Wendy's and

Good Times. To make extra money, she had peddled her mother's burritos outside Denver's Mile High Stadium on autumn Sundays. Grandma Hope's red-chili bean burritos had a following, and Sharon could make $200 in an afternoon.

Even Michelle already had years of food experience behind her. From infancy, she had gone along with her mother to peddle burritos to Broncos fans. They had switched to selling peanuts when Michelle was nine, and Michelle had essentially taken over the operation by the time she was fourteen, becoming known to football fans as "the peanut girl."

For years, Sharon had dreamed of owning her own hot dog cart. She viewed it as a means to an end—a way to work outdoors, be her own boss, and maximize her time with her two children, Michelle and Nikko, who were both old enough to help out. In December 1998, when she and Michelle came into a little money, they bought a used cart for $4,000. In the years since, the cart has served as the family's primary means of support.

Getting the business up and running was often a struggle. The hours are long, and during the winter it's often bitterly cold. In addition, working together as business partners has necessarily caused a shift in their mother-daughter relationship. Even so, Sharon and Michelle Garza love their lives. They're looking for a second cart, and a few years down the road, they hope to begin operating a commissary—a licensed storage area for mobile food carts—to increase the family's income.

"It was my mom's dream, not mine, but once we got the cart, I made it mine too," says Michelle.

## "The Business Will Engulf You"

Since she'd grown up in her grandmother's and mother's restaurants, food service was the only kind of job Sharon even looked for when she left high school in 1974 after completing eleventh grade. "When I told my mother I was going to work for a restaurant, she warned me, 'The restaurant business will engulf you,'"

Sharon recalls. "She was right. It became my life. And within a year, I began to be promoted—assistant manager, then night manager, then finally store manager. I've had all the titles."

Advancement came with a price—long hours and wear and tear on her body. After Sharon married and gave birth to Michelle, her first child, in February 1983, she decided that she couldn't be both a restaurant manager and a good mom.

So instead, she went back to being an hourly worker, even though it meant trading a decent salary for a wage just over the state's minimum. "I chose not to be the robot, the person who put in fifty or sixty hours a week to make a bigger salary," she explains.

She gave birth to a second child, Cameron, in October 1984. Tragically, he died of Sudden Infant Death Syndrome (SIDS) when he was just four months old. His death shook an already fragile marriage, and soon afterward, Sharon and her husband, a floor layer and part-time rock band drummer, separated.

They got back together just long enough to conceive a third child, but were separated again by the time Nikkolus (who's called Nikko) was born in January 1987. Sharon has been a single mom ever since, supporting Michelle and Nikko on her fast-food wages and their father's intermittent child support checks.

No one in this close-knit family can remember a time when money wasn't tight. Attending elementary school in Northglenn, a middle-class suburb north of Denver, Michelle was embarrassed by her family's modest circumstances. "Even though my mom seemed to work all the time, we never had very much," Michelle says. "As I got older, I began to realize how big a problem money was, because whenever I'd ask for things, she'd say, 'Let's just wait.'

"I was nine or ten when I really began noticing the difference between what other kids had and what I had," she continues. "I was going to school with girls whose dads owned car dealerships or worked as CEOs of companies, and my mom worked at Wendy's. They lived in big houses, and we lived in a little one-bedroom apartment. When my friends asked, I'd make up stories about where my mom really worked. Only my best friend knew the truth."

### A Sickly Child

Sharon's ability to bring home a paycheck big enough to support the family was hampered by Michelle's poor health. Michelle suffers from severe allergies and asthma.

"A lot of times, my mom would be at work and they'd call her from school and say, 'Michelle's sick. She's had an allergic reaction again,'" Michelle recalls. "I'd be having trouble breathing. My tongue would swell really bad and my lips would turn blue, and she'd have to come and pick me up and give me a shot of epinephrine. If I was well enough, she'd take me back to the restaurant with her, and I'd sit in a corner and color or work on my homework. On her breaks, she'd come out and have lunch with me, and sometimes I'd help clear the tables.

"I spent a lot of school days at Wendy's. But if I was too sick, she'd have to call in sick herself and stay home with me."

Despite her frailty, Michelle helped her mother however she could. Besides selling peanuts on game days, while still in elementary school she talked her paternal grandfather, Vicente de la Garza, into giving her a job in his home-based business, the Sobriety Training Institute, a drug and alcohol prevention program for reservation-based Indian children.

"He let me package orders, check invoices, and send them out," she recalls with pride. "Eventually I graduated to doing other things for him. He let me make phone calls to customers, and keep his books, and make reservations for the seminars he was giving around the country. Sometimes we'd have deadlines to meet, and I'd have to show up at 5 A.M. on a Saturday so we'd be able to get everything ready before the postman came at noon. Just me and my grandpa, that was the whole staff."

Michelle's grandfather paid her $10 an hour—a grand wage, even for an adult, in the early 1990s. (Paying her so well was apparently his way of making sure that Michelle didn't lack for school clothes or supplies.) "He'd give me bonuses for silly stuff, like 'Star Employee,'" Michelle recalls. "And he'd take me out to lunch so we could talk about the business."

## A Setback in School

In the mid-1990s Sharon moved the family to the Sunnyside neighborhood of Denver. Michelle attended seventh grade at the Kunsberg School, a private school for children with serious asthma or other chronic illnesses. Kunsberg is located next to the National Jewish Medical and Research Center, one of the nation's leading treatment centers for respiratory problems. Kunsberg students receive medical supervision and instruction in illness management, along with a rigorous academic program. Michelle flourished there.

Midway through eighth grade, her second and final year at Kunsberg, an uncle took Michelle and some of her cousins on a mini-vacation to a hotel in Aurora, Colorado. While there, Michelle slipped on a wet floor and fell, chipping two discs in her lower back. The injury left her in constant pain. When she reentered the public school system for ninth grade, she found the stairs at her local high school, Denver North, difficult to navigate. "I tried to go to school, but I was in too much pain," she says. "Because of my asthma and the back injury, I missed a lot of days."

Michelle tried to keep up with her class by working at home, but ended up falling short of credits for the year. When she returned to North in the fall of 1998, she had to start ninth grade over again. She was placed in the school's Welcome Center, a self-paced program designed for students who are at risk academically. The program met Michelle's needs perfectly, because it only required her to be at school for four hours a day, which, at the time, was about all her back could take.

Despite the academic setback it caused, the injury to Michelle's back had an unanticipated benefit. Late in the fall of 1998, she learned that she would be receiving a small cash settlement from the hotel's insurance company. About the same time, Sharon also received a small cash settlement from workers' compensation for an injury to her back in a fall at a restaurant where she had worked a few years before.

## "I Felt Like a Robot"

By this time, Sharon was growing tired of working in fast-food franchises. Like her grandmother and mother before her, she dreamed of operating her own food business. One reason was that she yearned for the opportunity to develop personal relationships with her customers. "At Wendy's, I felt like a robot," she says. "You do the same thing every day. You greet your customers, give them their food, and then they're on their way. Six years in one store, I'd build a relationship with my customers. But there was always pressure to push them along, to not stop and talk to them. It was inhuman.

"I decided there needed to be another way of me being comfortable at work and being able to interact with people. But I didn't feel too comfortable with the idea of buying a hole-in-the-wall restaurant, which was all I'd be able to afford, because I knew I'd be stuck there every day just waiting for someone to walk in the door."

Another thing propelling Sharon was worry about money. "Michelle was in seventh grade when she asked me one day, 'Mom, how am I going to be able to go to college? Do you have a college fund for me?'

"I laughed, and said, 'What about the Army?'

"Then she said, 'No, really, Mom, how are we going to do this?'

"I said, 'Well, I guess your father and I are going to have to have a talk.' And I began to think more about starting my own business. I didn't see myself being able to put Michelle through college on $8 an hour."

Sharon had first seen a mobile cart vendor in Juarez, Mexico, when she visited relatives there a few years before. "I had seen a little man pushing a cart," she said. "He sold tacos as he walked up and down the street. He kept his food hot with hot lava rocks. So the concept started coming together.

"I thought, 'There has to be some way of doing this in Denver, with more variety of food.' I had worked inside for twenty-some years, and I wanted to be able to work outside, where I could get a suntan, and my kids could come along, and I could get to know my customers. I told myself that one of these days I was going to have enough money to have one of these built. So in my spare time, I would make drawings of carts, which pretty much looked like boxes on wheels.

"Then when the Sixteenth Street Mall really took off in the mid-nineties, all of these carts showed up there, and I realized the idea could work. I would go out and watch the vendors on the mall, and it seemed to me an easy way to make money—and a lot of it. They'd come in with their carts loaded with product, and at the end of the day it would be all gone."

Since Michelle had grown up with her mother's dream, it didn't take much persuading to make it her dream too. "Mom had been talking about getting a cart forever," Michelle says. "Every time we'd see one on the street, we'd have to drive around the block and come back again to get a better look. We'd get out and ask the vendor, 'Where did you get that? Where do you store it? How much do you make?'"

Sharon and Michelle decided to pool their settlements, pay off all of the family's outstanding bills, and go shopping for a hot dog cart.

### "This Is Meant to Be"

After several false starts, Sharon and Michelle learned in late 1998 of a cart that was for sale.

"I waited a couple of days to call, because I didn't want to be disappointed," Sharon recalls. "Then I had a reason to drive out that way, and I drove by and looked at it and just loved it. The lady who was running it was in her sixties, and I watched as she closed it up for the day. I thought, 'If she can do it, I can do it.' I brought Michelle back the next day, but the lady wasn't there. So we went back a third day and got out and bought a soda. We stood by the side and watched her interact with her customers. Then I asked her, 'What do you want for your cart?'"

The woman wanted $4,000, which, as it happened, was just the amount they had to spend (Sharon was contributing $1,000 and Michelle $3,000). Then and there, they decided to buy it and gave the woman a $1,000 check as a deposit, promising the balance in thirty days when Michelle's settlement check came through.

The thirty days turned into thirty-five when their bank insisted on holding the insurance company's check until it cleared. Sharon and Michelle worried that the cart would be sold out from under them. "When we finally got there with the rest of the money, she told me that the day after I'd make the offer, she'd been offered $5,500 cash, and she'd told the man, 'I'm sorry, but I gave my word that I would sell it to someone else.'"

Sharon still marvels at the seller's honesty. "That was my first major experience with somebody who had kept her word," she says. "I was really thrown off by it. I couldn't imagine that somebody in her situation had given up an extra $1,500 to honor her word."

Sharon and Michelle learned that day that the reason the woman was selling the cart was that she was facing bankruptcy and the loss of her home as a result of unpaid medical bills. "It was hard for me to feel so excited when the reason she was selling was so sad," Sharon says.

Mother and daughter took the whole experience as an omen. "My mom said, 'This is meant to be,'" Michelle says.

## What Next?

So now they had a shiny stainless steel cart, the realization of Sharon's dream. But they had no idea what to do with it. They didn't know what sort of licenses might be required to operate it, let alone where they could get the best prices on food, where they could store the cart and their inventory, or where they could set up to sell. They parked the cart in a rented storage unit while they figured out what to do with it.

Michelle had just finished the first term of her freshman year in the Welcome Center at North. A good student, she had been cleared for enrollment in regular ninth grade classes. The first day of the new term, during her Spanish class, she was called into the office.

"There was a group of girls around a table, and a lady named Stephanie Herrera, who was going to be teaching a class called B!ZWORK$," Michelle recalls. "She explained that this class was only going to be offered to a select number of kids who they believed would do well. Our principal was there, and he said, 'You guys are going to be the first ones ever to do this. It's going to be great.' So we all signed up. And suddenly I was out of Spanish and into B!ZWORK$."

B!ZWORK$ is a three-course entrepreneurship sequence developed in 1996 by the Colorado Enterprise Fund with a three-year, $150,000 grant from the Ms. Foundation's Collaborative Fund for Women's Economic Self-Sufficiency. The Colorado Enterprise Fund is a nonprofit financial institution whose main mission is to lend money to the kind of entrepreneurs that conventional for-profit lenders scorn—those with spotty credit histories or low incomes.

In the early 1990s the Colorado fund had moved into microenterprise development. To further expand its impact on the community, it had been looking for a way to support teen entrepreneurs. When the Ms. Foundation sought proposals for a second round of microenterprise grants, the Colorado Enterprise Fund proposed developing an entrepreneurship curriculum suitable for high school girls.

The fund launched B!ZWORK$ in 1997 as a regular academic offering at Denver West High School for both boys and girls. The next year, the course was offered at Manual High School and at Denver North, Michelle's school.

North is located in a predominantly Hispanic, low-income neighborhood near downtown. At North, school administrators saw the course as ideal for students like Michelle who, for one reason or another, had spotty school attendance records and hence were at risk of becoming dropouts.

Stephanie Herrera, hired by the Colorado Enterprise Fund to teach the course at North, couldn't have been better suited for the job. She grew up in a low-income Latino family, like most of the students at North. Now in her early thirties, she remembers wondering why no one at her suburban Denver high school ever encouraged her to consider college.

"Their attitude was that I was just going to have babies, so why go to college," she says. She put herself through Front Range Community College with the help of an employer and later earned a bachelor's degree from Regis University. Today she operates several small businesses, teaches college part-time, and is working on a doctorate. But just about every minute of her spare time is spent mentoring Latina teenagers. "I had to learn on my own, so if there's anything I can do to help them have an easier life, that's what I want to do with my time," she explains.

From the beginning, Michelle loved the B!ZWORK$ class, even though she resented being labeled at-risk.

"I never considered myself at-risk, and when they used that term, I'd be insulted," she says. "But I can see where the rest of the kids were. Three of them were in a gang, and some were immigrants. There was one who was engaged to a guy who was always beating her up."

Soon after Michelle started the B!ZWORK$ class, she confided in Herrera about her family's dream of operating a hot dog cart. "I told her, 'We have this cart, but what do we do now?'" Michelle says.

## The Birth of Heavenly Dawgs

From their first encounter, Herrera says, it was clear that Michelle was different from the other girls in the class. "She had all these wonderful ideas," Herrera recalls. "A lot of the other students had an interest in being entrepreneurs, but Michelle was really ready to go. I said, 'OK, let's sit down and focus these ideas of yours so you can get working on them.'"

Michelle had already come up with a name for the business—"Heavenly Dawgs"—in honor of the brother who had died of SIDS. "I know he's up there in heaven watching over us," she explains. Herrera told Michelle that writing a good business plan was the next step toward launching a business. So that's what Michelle worked on.

In the first draft of her initial business plan, Michelle wrote that Heavenly Dawgs would sell "quality American and Mexican products." She asserted that it could be successful because "this is a growing industry in Colorado and has great opportunities for expansion."

As the B!ZWORK$ class progressed, Michelle's view of the cart business grew too. "As we were going through the B!ZWORK$ curriculum, every chapter would give me a new idea," Michelle says. For example, after learning about the importance of marketing, she came up with the idea of a "frequent patron card" that regular customers could use to earn free meals.

Among the other things Michelle learned was the necessity of obtaining the proper legal authorizations to operate a business. She took on the responsibility of navigating the city bureaucracy, calling a half-dozen city departments before she finally found the one that issued licenses to mobile cart vendors. And there, for the first time, she ran smack into the legal barriers against someone her age opening a business.

"My mom and I went down there together to apply," she says. "My mom gave her fingerprints and agreed to a criminal check, and then I asked them, 'Can I do it, too?' They said not for two years, when I turn eighteen."

Michelle was devastated. The license could be issued only in Sharon's name.

At the city Health Department, Sharon and Michelle learned that food-service carts needed to be stored overnight in licensed commissaries, but they got no advice as to how to find one. Apparently fearful of more competition, the vendors they approached for information weren't any help.

Finally, Sharon resorted to following a vendor to his commissary at the end of the day. "My mom stalked him," Michelle jokes. "She followed him and lost him, and then the next day she followed him more carefully and watched this big wooden cart go into a garage. She went in and explained that she needed a commissary for our cart. He said to her, 'We're just opening. You can have a space.' She came and picked me up from school and handed me the receipt for $250 for the first month's rent. She was so proud of herself."

With their business license about to be issued and their first month's commissary rent paid, Sharon and Michelle were raring to go. "We thought, 'Let's go get some stock,'" Michelle recalls. "We didn't have our license yet or a corner to park on, but we were so thrilled that we had our cart and a place to store it that we went and spent $1,000 on stock."

They bought dozens of varieties of candy and chips and soft drinks and arranged and rearranged them on their cart.

"Then the license came, and we had to think again, 'Now, what do we do?'" Michelle remembers. Back at City Hall again, she learned that she still needed to schedule inspections by the health, fire, and zoning departments.

"I skipped school on the day the health inspector came to check it," Michelle recalls. "He was the first person outside our family to see it, and he looked at it and said, 'This is gorgeous.' We were so happy.

"Then we asked him, 'What do we do now?' He told me to go to the Annex Building to the Right-of-Way office. We asked him, 'What do they do there?' He said, 'They'll approve your location.' And here we'd thought we could just set up anywhere!"

Michelle and Sharon had different ideas about what kind of corner they should choose. Michelle wanted to be in front of a Starbucks outlet at the corner of Eighteenth and Broadway, close to downtown's banks and office buildings. Sharon wanted to set up at Fourteenth and Stout, right in front of Currigan Hall, an exhibition hall across the street from the Colorado Convention Center.

Both had scouted their favored sites, counting cars and pedestrians and developing an absolute certainty in their minds that that particular spot was the only place to be. Since they couldn't agree on a site, they listed both of their choices on their application.

"Right-of-Way called us back and said, 'Starbucks says no. But the one on Fourteenth and Stout is okay. Do you want it?'" Michelle remembers. "My mom said, 'I'll be right in to pay.' So she went in and paid $300 for our corner, and that's how we ended up at Fourteenth and Stout."

Finally, mother and daughter thought they had cleared all the hurdles. "We were like, okay, the fire department has checked us out," Michelle says. "The health department has checked us out. We've got a license. We've got a corner. But it still took us months to start the business.

"At first they told us we had to go to zoning, but it turned out we didn't need to. Then they sent us to a couple of other departments, but we didn't need to. It dragged on and on, and finally we got the okay. We set up on our corner for the first time in April [1999]."

### A Slow Start

Sharon and Michelle decided that Sharon would keep her four-day-a-week job at Good Times, a drive-through fast-food restaurant, while they built their clientele. Although Sharon was only making about $8 an hour, it was money the family could use for living expenses until the business was established.

Because she worked Mondays, Wednesdays, Fridays, and Saturdays at Good Times, Sharon could only take the cart out on Tuesdays, Thursdays, and Sundays. On Saturdays Michelle would take the cart out by herself, or with her brother's help. That meant that the cart sat idle in the commissary three days a week, not producing any revenue.

The cart's unpredictable hours made it difficult to establish a following; not knowing whether they could count on buying lunch, workers in nearby buildings kept bringing their lunches from home or patronizing their usual haunts. "Business was so bad at first," Michelle remembers with a shudder. "Hardly anybody would stop."

Early on, there were many weekdays when the cart grossed less than $20; one memorable day, Sharon took in only $9. "And some weekends, there was no event going on, so nobody at all would come by," Michelle says. "My brother and I would be out there working, and we'd have ice fights just to keep from getting bored."

As the weeks passed, business finally began improving. Since Michelle and Sharon treat anyone who buys anything from them—even a pack of gum—like a lifelong friend, they soon had regulars.

"We'd get lots of advice from the people who work at the convention center," Sharon says. "They told us we needed to be here at 10 A.M., and we needed to be here every day, not just the days I didn't have to work at Good Times." But Sharon wasn't yet ready to give up the security of a regular paycheck.

One convention center worker began bringing them the monthly schedule of conventions and special events, enabling them to stock up on inventory and stay open late when warranted. Their regular customers began asking for lunch items besides hot dogs, which led Sharon and Michelle to expand the cart's menu to include nachos with cheese sauce, burritos, and tamales.

Health regulations require that unpackaged food served by a mobile food vendor be prepared in a licensed kitchen, and it fell to Michelle to figure out where to buy tamales and burritos. She found what she believes to be the best tamales in town at La Casita, which is owned by the brother of her high school principal. La Casita sells her red and green tamales for fifty cents apiece, permitting a 100 percent markup. "They are not only the best tamales in Denver, but in the entire world," Michelle gushes, in characteristic teenage hyperbole.

Michelle located a source for burritos just a few blocks from her house. The burritos are terrific, she says, but the restaurant's owner won't give her a break on the price, so she makes virtually no profit on them. "But that's okay, because the people who buy them usually buy a drink too," she rationalizes.

By May 1999 the hot dog cart still wasn't producing enough revenue to pay the family's household expenses. Finally heeding the advice of their customers, Sharon and Michelle decided that Sharon should quit her job at Good Times so that she could take the cart to its corner every day of the week. To make up for her mother's lost wages, Michelle took a job after school with TicketMaster of Colorado, where she made $9 an hour.

## Up Before Dawn

Dawn is just breaking over the eastern horizon when Michelle's mother and brother drop her off in the parking lot at North High School one Friday morning in September 2000. The sky looks like a painter's palette, with broad swaths of purple, lavender, and midnight blue. One leg of a rainbow is reaching out of the clouds toward the mountains, but Michelle is too nervous about the lecture she's about to give to even notice. This fall, Michelle is serving as the teaching assistant for Entrepreneurship 101, the name North gives to the introductory B!ZWORK$ class.

Michelle has spent most of the ten-minute drive from her home combing out her wet waist-length hair and putting on eye makeup. Like any teenager, she tries to maximize her sleep, and she had rolled out of bed at 6:30 A.M. to get to school by 7 A.M. She's missed her goal by fifteen minutes.

By the time the bell rings at 7:20 A.M., seven girls and one boy are sitting in desks arranged in a semicircle in front of a lectern in the B!ZWORK$ classroom. "Where is everybody?" asks Stephanie Herrera, the businesswoman and community activist who is again teaching the class.

Twenty students are enrolled, but today, fewer than a dozen have shown up. "It's Friday," one girl says, as though that explains everything.

Not only is it Friday, but it's the Friday before the big homecoming game and dance, it turns out. Several class members have received excused absences to prepare for the festivities; several more have just chosen not to show up. In honor of homecoming, a few of the girls who did come to class are wearing purple and gold ribbons in their hair.

Sensing that this is not a day on which to be a firm taskmaster, Herrera lets the students chat among themselves for a few minutes before calling the class to order. "Today, Michelle's going to be talking to you," she tells them. "You know we do this periodically so you can get a different point of view instead of just mine. Michelle's been through this class, and she now operates her own business, so you can learn a lot from her."

This is Michelle's first lecture to the class, and her topic is the importance of a business plan, precisely the lesson Herrera had hammered home in her first discussions with Michelle nearly two years before. Michelle starts the day's lesson by defining a business plan.

"A business plan is like a road map for your business," she explains. "It contains everything about your startup. It's the map you want to follow, the direction you plan on going, what you hope is going to happen, the money you think you're going to bring out of it.

"People write business plans to prove that their idea could be successful, that they know what they're doing. If you start a business without doing a business plan, you're not going to know what you need to do. When you go to a bank for your loan, it will show them that you know what you're doing."

By now, four other students have arrived and taken seats. Michelle becomes more animated as she begins to talk about the importance of her own business plan.

"A business plan isn't a short five-pager," she says. "Mine's twenty-two pages long. It took a year and a half to finish my final business plan. And it's not something you just write and then file away. It's good to periodically look at it so you know if you're following it.

"Now that my business is seventeen months old, I can go back and see how well I followed my business plan. Did I make the $150,000 that I said in my business plan I would make in my first year?" She breaks into a big smile. "No, I didn't make $150,000. I made $60,000. So it kind of burst my bubble to look back at my plan and see where I'd fallen short."

Michelle instructs the class to turn to page twenty-four in the workbook, which contains a series of questions designed to help students write concept statements for their business plans. "You need to write down a detailed description of your proposed product and service, not just, 'I'm going to have clothes for men and women,' but details like whether they're going to be name brands or custom clothing," she says. "When someone reads it, he needs to know exactly what you're going to be doing.

"You also need to know what sector of people you're going to offer it to and why people need your service—for instance, a beauty salon—when they already have four in the area. Who's going to be involved in your business? You solely, or are you going to bring in partners? What's your target market? Who will your customers be? Your unique niche: What's different about your service? Maybe you're going to make home calls so that people don't have to come to your salon.

"So if you guys want to take a stab at writing up your concept statement, that's the assignment for today."

Michelle looks relieved to be finished with her lecture. The students spend the next half hour working on their concept statements. Then Herrera goes around the room and asks each student to share his or her concept for a business.

Among their ideas are several clothing boutiques, a restaurant, a Mexican bakery, a boxing club, a string of McDonald's franchises, and a nightclub. One sixteen-year-old boy, whose girlfriend is expecting a baby, wants to start a recreation center for youth. "I'd like to help kids stay out of trouble and stay off the streets," he explains.

After the class ends, Herrera talks about the challenges the students face. "A lot of these kids have really low self-esteem, but they have a lot of potential," she says. "Quite a few of them have families that own businesses, and they help out in their stores, so they have a lot of interest in business. But some of them have families that are real traditional. They don't want their daughters to be thinking about finishing high school or going to college or starting a career because they want them around to take care of them.

"I'm ashamed to say that in the Mexican culture, there are still a lot of people who don't believe that their daughter's education is as important as their son's."

On the way out of school, Michelle stops to talk to her counselor, Luisa Vigil. Mrs. Vigil gives her a big hug and asks her how she's feeling. Although Michelle is serving as the teaching assistant for the B!ZWORK$ class, she's not enrolled at North this year for health reasons. Her back pain is less disabling than it was a few years ago, but other health problems have popped up.

In April 1999, after more than a year of stomach pains and countless visits to doctors, Michelle had her gallbladder removed. More recently, she was found to have a heart condition. Shortness of breath makes the steps at North difficult for her, so she decided to study at home through an internet-based curriculum.

Mrs. Vigil tells a visitor that she's very sorry not to have Michelle as a student at North this year. "It was really hard to accept that she wasn't going to be here this year, because she has so much going for her," she says. "But she has to take care of herself. Her health comes first."

Although she has more than 400 students in her caseload, Mrs. Vigil knows Michelle better than most because of all of the difficulties she's encountered in the last few years. "She's really had a lot of obstacles to overcome," Mrs. Vigil points out. "The things she's had to go through are really incredible. She's had to work on just surviving.

"But even when she was going through all those hard times last year, she was very positive, and she always took the initiative to mentor other kids. She has such a big heart."

*Taking Stock*

By the time Michelle gets to the corner of Fourteenth and Stout, it's almost 9:30 A.M. and her mother has just about finished opening up the cart. "How's business?" Michelle asks.

"Pretty slow," her mother answers. "I've sold a couple of drinks and a few breakfast burritos."

Michelle grabs a piece of hot dog paper to write on, and mother and daughter put their heads together to come up with a shopping list. Michelle is going to make the rounds of the local discount stores this morning to stock up on staples like Gatorade, sodas, chips, and hot dogs. Over time, Michelle and Sharon have learned that if they shop the sales at stores, they can save money. "What kind of burritos do you want today?" Michelle asks her mother.

"See if he'll do the special price still for green chili, and get a bunch of steak," Sharon answers. "There are a lot of construction workers in the area today."

While they talk, Michelle is pawing through the drinks that her mother has already iced. She sees that they're short of Pepsi and Mountain Dew. "Oh, and we need more Coke," her mother adds. "If you can get it from Safeway at $4.99 for two, go ahead and buy four cartons."

"At Albertson's, it's two twelve-packs for $4," Michelle points out.

"Oh, well, then get it there," Sharon answers. "And how about a bag of mixed fruit from Sam's, you know, apples and oranges? And maybe some more fruit snacks? But we just need one flat of Gatorade. Don't go crazy on me. Remember that we've got to unload it."

Her grocery list complete, Michelle climbs into the driver's seat of the family's leased Chevy Blazer, which is equipped with a hitch so it can pull the cart. Her mother comes over to the open window, leans in, and kisses her good-bye. "Drive safely," she urges.

As she's backing into the street, Michelle sees a regular customer approaching from the convention center. She leans out the car window to instruct her mother. "Here comes Charles. Tell him his tab is $36. It was $35.75, and I threw in a quarter tip."

A customer running a tab at a mobile food cart? "He's a regular," she explains. "He likes me to bill him for his food because he doesn't always have the cash on him. I know he'll pay."

*Browsing for Bargains*

As she pulls into traffic, Michelle tunes the radio to a station that plays Spanish-language pop. She sings along with the late pop star, Selena, as she drives across the Platte River, past her high school, to her first stop: the burrito place.

It's 10:55 A.M., too late to get the early-bird price ($1.20) for green chili burritos, so she just orders ten steak with chili burritos. The tab comes to $29.20, which means that if she sells the burritos for $3 each, as she usually does, she'll make just about a ten-cent profit on each of them. Michelle has tried to talk the owner into giving her a wholesale price, but he won't. Michelle tells him that she'll be back in an hour to pick up her order.

The next stop is Grocery Warehouse, where she spends $41 on cans and bottles of Pepsi, Hawaiian Punch, Country Time Lemonade, 7UP, and Mountain Dew, along with a couple of packages of Polish sausage and sauerkraut and few packages of hot peanuts. "I've got a bus driver who only eats the hot ones, so I get them for him," she explains.

For consumption at home, she picks up two boxes of Air Crisps, a few cucumbers and avocados, a pomegranate, a bag of carrots, and a package of vermicelli. "We try to have dinner together as much as we can, but it's really hard with our schedule," she says. "We haven't had a day off in four months. We work all day and go home and sleep."

The next stop is Sam's Warehouse, where she spends $130. Then it's on to King Soopers, the only place in town where Michelle has been able to find Stokes green chili sauce, with which she smothers the burritos, allowing her to charge an extra $1.

"Our customers think we make it ourselves," she confides. "We tried that for awhile, but the Health Department made us stop. This is as close as we could find to Grandma's recipe. It even passed her taste test, though she'd never serve canned chili at home."

The sale prices this week at King Soopers are great. She buys several twelve-packs of Coke and Minute Maid grape and orange soda, as well as one of Welch's grape soda, since one customer prefers that to Minute Maid. Although it wasn't on her list, Fruitopia, at sixty cents a bottle, turns out to be too good a buy to pass up. "We'll sell those for $1 each," she says.

The twenty-four-ounce bottles of Pepsi and Dr Pepper are favorably priced too. "We can make $6.50 off a six-pack," she explains as she loads four six-packs into her cart.

In the checkout lane, she looks at the candy display to see what bargains are to be had. Nestle's Crunch and BBs are each four for $1, so she puts four of each in her cart. The bill initially comes to $65.92, but after the weekly discounts are deducted, the total is reduced by $22.01 to $43.91. "You've got to watch the sales, that's for sure," Michelle comments.

Michelle swings by the burrito stand to pick up her order and then drives over to the commissary to drop off the excess inventory. From the outside, the commissary looks like an ordinary two-car garage. Inside, the floor looks clean enough to eat off of, and the walls are lined with shelves that hold an assortment of canned and bottled items and dry goods.

About a half-dozen carts are stored here each night. In a room attached to the garage, there's a small kitchen equipped with a sink and counter area that carry the Health Department's seal of approval. There's also a large refrigerator, several freezers, and a commercial ice machine—all certified sanitary by the Health Department.

As Michelle is leaving the commissary, two homeless men start walking down the alley toward her. Although she's normally a very trusting person, Michelle looks nervous. She tries to break the tension with a smile. "Hi, guys," she says to the men. "Sorry for blocking the alley." As she's getting behind the driver's seat, she explains the reason for her nervousness.

Earlier this year, as her mother was unloading the cart after a good day on the corner, she was held up at gunpoint in the alley and robbed of $900 in cash and money orders. "That's the only thing that really worries me about this commissary," Michelle says. "It can be scary at night."

### *Back on the Corner*

Back at Fourteenth and Stout, Sharon is fixing a customer a luncheon special—a hot dog, chips, and a drink, which sell for $2.25. "How's business been?" Michelle asks as she puts the burritos into the steamer to keep them warm.

"There've been a few people," Sharon responds without much enthusiasm.

Neither is too hopeful about doing much business today, since the theme of the exhibition at the convention center is holistic living, and the kind of people attending are probably not going to be very interested in hot dogs or burritos.

With seventeen months of business under their belts, Sharon and Michelle have learned what kinds of conventions are most likely to bring customers to their cart. "Computer shows are the worst," Michelle observes as she makes room in the coolers for some of the drinks she's purchased. "Everybody who's attending them just wants to go out and have a nice expense-account lunch, and if they do buy anything from us, it's just a bottle of water, and then they want a receipt.

"The Great American Beerfest is the best, and that's coming up again next week. The tips are great."

As she's talking, two Currigan Hall female security guards pull up in a golf cart. "Where've you been keeping yourself?" Sharon says in greeting. "I haven't seen you in a while."

"Whatcha got to drink?" one of them asks Sharon, as they begin pawing through the coolers, chatting away the whole time. One settles for a large bottle of Pepsi and the other for a can of V-8 juice, which seems to be the beverage of choice today. Michelle wipes off the melted ice before handing them over.

"What are you making for Richard tonight?" Sharon asks one of the guards as she gives her change.

"It's payday, so we're going out," the guard responds. "I don't cook on Fridays. Nooooo, ma'am."

Engaging in friendly banter with their regular customers is the favorite part of the job for both Sharon and Michelle. "I was never allowed to have this kind of interaction in my previous jobs, and I really like it," Sharon says. "But I think it's Michelle that people come to talk to. They just love her."

"I'm a people person," Michelle says in agreement. "I like to be around people, to know what's going on in their lives, to have people tell me that their daughter was born or that they got engaged. That makes me feel special. I've really bonded with our customers."

Even as she's finishing the transaction with the security guards, Michelle is greeting a convention center employee who's crossing the street and approaching the cart. "Hi, how ya doing today?" she calls out.

"Oh, tired, tired," he answers, before ordering a Polish sausage.

Ever the saleswoman, Michelle asks, "Anything else?" But a Polish sausage is all he wants today.

Just then, a car pulls up to the curb, and a passenger leans out and asks for directions to the Denver Athletic Club. Lost tourists are one of the banes of the corner business, but Sharon cheerfully provides them with directions and then turns to Michelle and jokes, "We need to put a sign up here: 'Information Extra.'"

"Where's the Mint? Where's the Oktoberfest? Where's the baseball stadium? Do you know if there's a Rockies game today?" Michelle quips, mimicking the most common questions they get from tourists. Then she turns to greet her next customers with a smile.

Three construction workers have ambled over and are looking through the cooler full of bottled drinks. They're interested in trying a Sobe for the first time, one of them says. "Sobes are good for you," Sharon says encouragingly.

"They taste like an Orange Julius," Michelle adds.

Each of the workers buys one. As the money changes hands, one of the workers says to Sharon, "You need to sell cigarettes."

She's ready with a retort: "You're the only one who'd buy them."

As the men sit down on a concrete planter to enjoy their drinks, Michelle says to her mother, "Great. Now we've turned three more people on to Sobes." She buys a case of sixteen for $20 and sells them for $2 apiece—for a profit of $12 a case.

"Can I get two all-beef hot dogs?" another customer asks. She's wearing a name badge from the convention center.

"Are you with the convention, may I ask?" Michelle quizzes the woman as she extracts two dogs from the cooker.

"Yes, but they're all in there eating holistically, and I need meat," the woman says conspiratorially.

"That must be why I've sold so many V-8s today," Sharon comments. "We hardly ever sell any of those."

"Hi, how ya doing?" a male customer calls out. Michelle knows before he even asks what he's going to want.

"I'm out of sour cream and onion chips today," she says apologetically.

"I bet you ate them yourself," he responds good-naturedly.

"I'm sorry," she replies. "I'll have them next week."

As he walks away, Michelle explains that his usual lunch order is for one bag of sour cream chips, two all-beef hot dogs, and a Coke. "Every day he walks here from Eighteenth," she says. "He could stop at another cart along the way, but he likes us. That makes me feel really good, to know that someone will walk four blocks because he likes us."

Two more people come by wearing badges that identify them as convention exhibitors. As she prepares a burrito and two tamales for them, Sharon asks them what the convention is all about.

"They have all types of workshops—energy healing, muscle therapy, relationships, vegetarianism," explains a woman in her fifties.

"All the good stuff," Sharon comments. "I'm glad I asked, because I was thinking it was just organic foods. That sounds like our kind of show to check out. We like that kind of stuff."

While they eat, the conventioneers sit on one of the concrete planters in front of Currigan Hall. It's a glorious fall day, and with so many people taking advantage of the weather and eating outside, the plaza in front of Currigan Hall resembles an outdoor café.

"That's one of the reasons I wanted this location," Sharon comments. "We could have had a lot of corners, but this one just felt so right with the planters here. I liked the idea that people could buy food from us and sit down and enjoy their lunches under the shade trees. After twenty-two years in the fast-food business, I needed a site that was relaxing."

### *Handouts for the Homeless*

As Sharon and Michelle are packing up, another regular customer approaches the cart, a homeless man known as Mayfield, who appears to suffer from a mental illness.

One of the things Sharon and Michelle spent a lot of time talking about in the early days of the business was how much food they could afford to give away. Denver has a large population of homeless people, and on any given day, a few would inevitably find their way to the cart. Sharon and Michelle agreed not to give out cash, but to give a hot dog and a drink to anyone who seemed hungry. "We think we have it rough, but our lives are a walk in the park compared to what some people deal with," Sharon explains.

Michelle offers Mayfield a Polish sausage, which she knows from past encounters that he prefers to hot dogs. He declines, but pulls out a $1 bill and says, "I want to buy something from you." He chooses a fruit drink and sits down on one of the planters near the cart to drink it. Since there are few potential customers, Michelle goes over to chat. He tells her his troubles, from his childhood in Boston to his two tours of duty in Vietnam to the death of his mother two weeks ago. "I'm from good people," he says over and over again.

After a few more minutes of conversation, he admits to Michelle that he's hungry. She returns to the cart to prepare a Polish sausage with ketchup and pickles and onions for him. "God is good," Mayfield tells her as she hands it to him. "God is great."

One reason for Sharon's and Michelle's sensitivity to the homeless is that Sharon's brother, Archie, lived on Denver's streets for several years. "I'm hoping that when he was hungry, there was somebody there to feed him," Sharon says.

Michelle reminisces about the first day her uncle showed up on the corner of Fourteenth and Stout, about two weeks after they started the business. "He was sitting here as we pulled up," she recalls. "He was homeless, and he was poor, but he was clean. He said to my mom, 'Hey, Sis, what's up?' just as though he'd seen her yesterday, instead of more than a year ago. We got to talking, and I told him, 'You'd better make sure you check in with us at least once a week. Don't you make us worry.'

"So for a long time, every week he'd check in, and we'd talk. He never panhandled, but when he came by, I'd give him something to eat. He made sure that other homeless guys knew who my mom and I were and didn't mess with us."

In February 2000 Archie died while sleeping on a heating grate near Denver's courthouse. "That was one of the worst things my family's ever had to bear, that he died alone on a heat grate," Michelle says, her eyes brimming with tears. An autopsy showed that the cause of death was cirrhosis; he also suffered from epilepsy and a brain tumor. He was forty-two years old.

So now, most days after they close down the cart, Sharon and Michelle take their leftover hot dogs, sausages, and burritos to a soup kitchen that feeds the homeless. Sharon often makes Nikko run the food in.

"I want him to see the effects of alcohol," she explains. "I want him to see what happens if you go down that road. Him seeing that side of it, hopefully he'll make different choices in life."

Seeing her uncle's life destroyed by alcohol has turned Michelle into something of an anti-alcohol activist. Even before Archie's death, Michelle had led a protest against a neighborhood business association's plan to accept a $10,000 donation from the Coors Brewing Co. to underwrite a neighborhood festival. In May 1999 Michelle took a group of her B!ZWORK$ classmates to a meeting of the Highland Business Association at which the donation was to be put to a vote.

"We're told not to drink, and to have a brewery come in and support our community event would say that it's okay if money is involved," Michelle argued at the meeting, according to a newspaper account.

When it seemed likely that the association would vote to accept the donation, Michelle offered the contents of her savings account—$600—as an incentive to the group to decline Coors's offer.

In the end, the group accepted Michelle's offer and kept the event alcohol-free. "This is an example of our youth voicing what is valuable to them," Shelly Garcia, who facilitated the meeting, told the newspaper. "It's wonderful to have this young leader say, on behalf of so many other youth, that alcohol is not where their future is."

## The Corner Is Threatened

Michelle is extraordinarily self-confident for her age, as well as politically savvy, as the experience with the Highland Business Association demonstrated. Her poise and curiosity came in handy in 2000 as the fate of Currigan Hall was discussed by the Denver City Council and its committees.

In November 1999, just six months after Sharon and Michelle started doing business in front of Currigan Hall, Denver voters approved a proposal to replace it with a state-of-the-art annex to the convention center.

When Sharon heard the news, she says, "I felt sick for days. It was like a hole in my gut. When I was looking around for a corner, I didn't just pull the location out of thin air. I stalked the area. I sat there and counted the number of people who got off of buses, the number of cars that parked across the street, the number of people who walked by on their way to the convention center, and the number of people who went in and out of Currigan if there was a show. This corner was a good corner."

In the six months that followed the vote, bookings at Currigan declined noticeably. "It was really depressing," Sharon says. "No one had any reason to go into Currigan Hall anymore. We'd see people park across the street and then walk diagonally across the street to get to the convention center, without even walking past our cart."

Fortunately, early in the summer of 2000, a construction project down the street began sending scores of hungry workers to their corner every day. "Thank God, during these three months when nothing has been going on in Currigan, there's been all this construction going on," Sharon says. "These construction workers are big boys. They eat a lot. So even though Currigan is retired, there's still life on the corner."

Michelle and Sharon debated about whether they should try to get permission to move the cart to a new location, and if so, where and when. Michelle decided that rather than act on the basis of rumors, she and her mother needed facts. She began attending meetings of the City Council's special projects committee, which had been charged with superintending the shutdown of Currigan and the construction of its replacement.

Her attendance at these meetings paid off late in September 2000, when she was present for a discussion of the timetable for the project. She learned at the meeting that the entire block would have to be cordoned off during demolition. When she heard the plans, she raised her hand.

"I said, 'If you do that, where am I going to park my cart?'" she recalls. "The councilwoman asked me where I wanted to park it. I said, 'Show me a map.' I pointed to it, and I said, 'Here's where I am now, and here's where I want to be. It's the corner right in front of the convention center.' There was a lot of talking back and forth, but in the end they said fine."

Since she had the floor, Michelle decided to take the opportunity to secure the cart's long-term right to the location. "What about when construction's over?" she asked. "Do I get to stay?" She was told, "You can either stay on your new corner or move back to your old one."

That was great news. Since she was on a roll, she decided to press her luck.

"I've been thinking about getting a second corner, too, at Fifteenth and Welton," she told the committee members. That corner, one block from Michelle and Sharon's current location, was the designated site for a new convention hotel. Michelle wanted to secure the right to it then and there so she could place a second cart there once construction began.

"It turned out the owner of the land was sitting next to me," she says. "On the spot, he wrote out a letter authorizing Heavenly Dawgs to set up a hot dog cart on his corner. He told me that he was so impressed with me that he wanted me to have his corner. He said, 'I don't know what will happen once the hotel is open.' And I said, 'I don't care about that. I just want to be there for the construction.'"

## Sunday: Another Day of Work

It's a September Sunday, a potentially big day for Heavenly Dawgs. The Denver Broncos are playing the Boston Patriots, and as on every other Sunday during football season, Heavenly Dawgs will be selling food and soft drinks on a prime corner just two blocks from the stadium. Sharon has been selling food to football fans in the vicinity of Twentieth Street and Federal Way since she was a teenager herself.

"Even before I was married, I used to come over here on game days to sell burritos that my mom had made," Sharon says. "After Michelle was born, I brought her along in her carriage, all dressed up in Broncos outfits, because I didn't have anyone to leave her with. The customers loved her."

Sharon sold her mother's burritos all through Michelle's childhood, until she narrowly escaped getting a citation from a health department inspector when Michelle was nine. He told Sharon she needed a peddler's permit, but that it would only allow her to sell dry goods, such as peanuts and licorice ropes. She got the permit and reluctantly switched to peanuts. To her surprise, she found she could make even more money, with less trouble, than she had with burritos.

Over the years, Michelle became known to game regulars as "the peanut girl." "I had a bullhorn and I would scream through it, 'Peanuts, peanuts. Get your peanuts here,'" Michelle recalls. "I was a cute little kid, and everybody bought from us because of that. We could make $300 profit in a day."

Typically, Bronco Sundays are the biggest day of the week for Heavenly Dawgs. Today, the Garzas are hoping to gross $450.

"Every day before we leave the house we pray, 'Lord, we need to make this much today,'" Michelle says. "Nikko may say $100, my mom may say $150. I usually say $250. Nobody else goes as high as I do, but today we all agreed on $450."

Sharon and Nikko got up around 7:30 A.M. in order to arrive at the commissary by 8:30. In deference both to her health and her age, Sharon let Michelle sleep in. Michelle had been out late the night before doing some last-minute shopping at three different stores. By 10:10 A.M., Sharon and Nikko have finished loading the cart and hauling it over to the corner of Twentieth Street and Federal Way. The proprietor of Santos Muffler Shop lets them sell from his parking lot, charging them just $30, the same rate he charges people to park.

When Michelle arrives at 11:15 A.M., she takes over. "It's $100," her mother says as she sees Michelle starting to count a wad of bills. "I've already counted it." Michelle keeps counting anyway, and after she finishes that task she takes a squirt bottle and paper towels and disinfects the back of the cart, a chore her mother has also completed.

After seventeen months in business together, Sharon has come to expect that Michelle will redo nearly everything she does. "That's just the way she is," Sharon shrugs. Because Michelle is a take-charge kind of person, she pretty much functions as the chief operating officer of the business.

Today's first customers are three men in their thirties. "Got any brats today?" one asks.

"Nope," Michelle answers. "We didn't have any beer at home, so I couldn't make them."

"What happened to the beer?" the man asks playfully.

"I don't know," Michelle replies. "My mom was up late last night. Maybe she drank it."

"Blame it on your mom," he teases. "That's an old excuse."

"Well, I know for sure it wasn't me, because I'm allergic to beer," Michelle says, flashing a smile.

Michelle's bantering earns her a $1.25 tip on an $8.75 sale. She takes it as a good omen for the day. "The more you joke around with the customers, the more likely you are to get a tip," she explains. "That's one of the things I've learned over the years.

But if they're with their wives, I always make a point of talking to the wife, because they don't like you joking with their husband. You do this long enough, you learn what works."

It's still two and a half hours before kickoff, so there's not much pedestrian traffic yet. Half an hour later, it's noon, the time the gates open, and now there's a nearly constant stream of fans heading to the stadium. "Peanuts, get your peanuts here!" Michelle yells every time she sees a cluster of people begin to cross Federal Way. "Burritos, tamales, hot dogs!"

A couple and their two sons are about to walk by without buying anything when the husband notices the peanut display and stops. Yesterday, Nikko's job was to separate about ten one-pound bags of peanuts into seven or eight separate servings. The peanuts cost $1.70 a pound, and the Garzas sell a medium-sized Ziploc bag full of them for $1, so they make a nice little profit.

At the request of several regular customers, they recently added pistachios to their offerings. They buy them for $8.15 a pound and sell a small Ziploc bag containing about one-quarter pound for $3, which gives them a profit of almost $1 a bag.

Taking advantage of a lull in customers, Sharon fixes a hot dog for herself and scans the approaching crowd. "See those ladies walking down the street carrying a cooler?" she asks. "I bet they've got illegal product in there. There's no way they have a license. It makes me so mad to see them."

Moments later, Sharon spots several other burrito vendors heading toward the corner diagonally across the street, a spot that will give them first dibs on most potential customers.

"Look at them," Sharon says, pointing to the group of three teen-age girls and one boy. "They're carrying two cold-food coolers, and they've got no heat source. Plus, they're putting the coolers right down on the ground. That's clearly illegal. And they're in our territory! Michelle, can you just go over there and tell them to leave?"

Michelle doesn't want to get involved in a dispute. "No, Mom, I'm working," she says, as she continues to wait on customers.

But when she sees the teenagers sell six burritos to a family a few minutes later, she begins to share her mother's frustration, and now she urges her mother to do something. Sharon crosses Twentieth to ask the traffic officer who's controlling the stoplight to summon a health inspector.

"So what did the cop say?" Michelle asks when Sharon returns.

"He said he'd call somebody," Sharon says.

"But meanwhile, they've had four more people stop to buy their burritos!" Michelle complains.

"We've done all we can do," Sharon says. "Just chill."

As Sharon waits on customers, she continues to eye the illegal vendors. "I hate to turn them in, but I'm paying $75 for my license, $500 a year for insurance, and $250 a month to park my cart in a commissary," she says. "And they're out there underselling me! I hope they get a ticket. For every burrito they have in the cooler, it's a $5 fine. That should teach them their lesson big time."

Ten minutes later, a white sedan pulls up at the curb near the illegal vendors. Three of them hurriedly cross the street, leaving one behind with the cooler. "Oh, thank you, Lord, he did his duty," Sharon says as she watches a patrolman get out and approach the sole remaining vendor. Two uniformed police officers join him in conversation with the vendor. They talk for a few minutes, and a cloud crosses the vendor's face. As the inspector and police officers turn to leave, she picks up her cooler, crosses the street, and sits down in front of a service station, looking disconsolate.

Once again, the intersection belongs to Heavenly Dawgs.

## "You Go, Girl"

It's now 2:35 P.M., thirty-five minutes past kickoff, and there's very little foot traffic anymore. Michelle has been counting the money they've taken in. It adds up to $400, about $50 less than they'd hoped. "But we sold sixty-seven burritos, all but three," she announces. "And there's thirteen bucks in tips!"

"You go, girl," her mom responds.

"Do you want to go home or go to the corner?" Michelle asks, referring to their spot in front of the convention center.

"You told people we'd be there, didn't you?" her mom responds.

"Yeah, about six of them asked," Michelle says.

"We don't have to go," Nikko interrupts. Most weekends, Nikko works alongside his mother and sister, as he's been doing today. As a reward, he's hoping his mom will take him to see a movie at the IMAX theater. "They can eat somewhere else," he says, referring to the convention center workers.

"We'd better set up on the corner," Sharon answers. "We have a lot of product left."

Nikko looks crestfallen. There's no discussion about him going to the movie himself. If the cart's going to the corner, so is he.

"One of the ideas behind operating the cart was that I'd have my children working it with me, so I'd always know where they were," Sharon explains. "If they're with me, I know they're not off with their buddies doing who knows what."

By 3:30 P.M., they're all set up on their regular corner. Since it's a Sunday, there are no construction workers to feed, but people are trickling in and out of the convention center for the last day of the holistic living show. A few of them stop by the cart to buy bottles of water or hot dogs.

In between customers, Sharon and Michelle lie down on the stone planters to rest. "This is when the tiredness hits," Michelle laments. "My body was ready to go home. Now it wants to know what I'm doing here again."

She pulls out her Nebulizer and takes a couple of quick puffs. Her asthma has been acting up; this is the third time today she's had to use it. Then she gets out the convention center's schedule for the month of October so she and her mother can discuss the coming week.

Michelle notes that movers will be arriving at 6 P.M. to move out the holistic living convention. "That means we ought to stay until seven," she says. "Then tomorrow morning they start moving in the Beerfest, which will be here all week. That ought to be a great week for us."

Perhaps a dozen more customers stop at the cart over the next three hours. By 7 P.M., the cart has taken in $44 more, bringing the family close to its goal of grossing $450 for the day.

Long ago, Michelle and Sharon figured out that they needed to sell an average of $90 worth of products every day of the month in order to pay all their business-related expenses. Whatever they took in above that, they viewed as profit. "The games are what help us do it," Sharon says.

Dusk is in full bloom by the time they've finished closing down the cart. Sharon takes a few moments to look at the sky before she gets into the car.

"The city looks so beautiful as dusk falls," she observes. "Just look at how the light is changing. I wouldn't be seeing any of this if I was working inside. This kind of work is so much better than being in an office."

## Lessons Learned

Although their business is still young, Sharon and Michelle have already learned a lot, both about their relationship and about how to run a business.

Being in business together has meant that they've had to renegotiate their mother-daughter relationship. Early on, they agreed that Michelle would take care of the books, because she's more attentive to detail. But starting with the choice of a location, they've have had differing opinions about many aspects of the business. "We're completely opposite," Michelle says. "We think totally differently."

For one thing, they approach inventory differently. "She likes to run out and get things as we need them," Sharon says of Michelle's approach. "I like to minimize the number of trips. I'm thinking things like time management, standing in line, driving from one store to another.

"But she keeps me grounded, too. More and more, I'm realizing that I don't need to have all that product sitting on the shelf if we're not going to use it right away. We're learning to compromise as partners."

Michelle agrees. "I think we balance each other," she says.

Sharon has to be careful not to permit Michelle's dominating role in the business turn into a dominating role in the household. "Working together has added a lot more frustration to our relationship," Sharon says. "That's the word I have to use. She's just a teenager, and sometimes I have to say to her, 'I am the mother twenty-four hours a day.' Then she tells me, 'That's not fair,' and I'll tell her, 'It has to be this way because I say so. I've had twenty-two years in the fast-food business, and I know what I'm doing.'"

Perhaps the most important lesson they've learned about running a business is that in an enterprise like theirs, location is everything. Because the revenues they bring in on the convention center corner aren't enough to pay all their bills, they're constantly looking for additional locations where they can set up for the evening. They haven't always chosen well.

Agreeing to a six-month evening stint outside one of Denver's bus stations turned out to be a costly error. "They charged us $1,000 a month just to sell there, and we lost $10,000," Michelle says. (By comparison, the Sixteenth Street Mall, which has a constant stream of foot traffic, charges mobile food vendors only $130 a month.) Business was often so slow that Sharon and Michelle would make Nikko wander through the station with a smothered burrito in hand, with hopes that the aroma would cause people to ask him, "Where'd you get that?"

Another location-related mistake, which took them two months to recognize, was setting up outside an alternative nightclub every Tuesday night. It turned out that the attendees didn't have much appetite for food.

Another time, they made the mistake of agreeing to provide food service for a crew shooting an experimental film. "That was a real bust," Michelle laughs. "We made $19."

Still, both mother and daughter are willing to learn from their mistakes and move on. "I hooked up with a guy who's sponsoring a rave in a couple of months, and I'm going to set up outside," Michelle says. "People who go to raves don't eat much, but they'll buy lots of drinks."

She's also thinking about putting together a flyer aimed at car dealerships. "They could promise people a free hot dog and soda for coming out during a sale, and pay us to serve their customers," she says. Setting up at birthday parties, family reunions, and liquidation sales are other possibilities.

Sharon and Michelle realize that they need to increase their gross revenues if they're going to be able to improve their lifestyles measurably. Midway through their first year in business, after a few big events at the convention center resulted in a couple of particularly lucrative weeks, they had made a mistake characteristic of many novice business owners, especially those with cash-based businesses.

"We started acting like we were rich before we were," Michelle says. "We were blowing the money on stupid things. We were going out to dinner all the time, spending $200 when we really didn't have it to spend. It was all so new to us to suddenly have all this money, and we blew it on various forms of enjoyment."

Mother and daughter were forced to confront reality in July 2000, when the bank repossessed the 1999 VW Passat that Sharon had leased for Michelle. A few weeks later, Sharon's 1996 Mitsubishi Galant was also repossessed. With Currigan Hall's closure, foot traffic around their corner had fallen off, and they had gotten behind in their payments. Fortunately, they were able to lease another vehicle, without which they would have had no way to transport their cart.

Sobered by the repossession experiences, the family has been trying to live more frugally. "We're keeping up with most of our bills," Michelle says. "The phone, the utilities, the rent, and the commissary bills are paid, and we're not going out to dinner as often anymore. Luckily, my mom's never had a credit card, like a

MasterCard or Visa. If we had one, our business would be down the tube by now, because I like nice clothes and shoes. I listen to Oprah, and I can't believe the trouble people get into with credit cards."

Another step they've taken to firm up their finances is to meet with their accountant to talk about how to minimize their tax liability. "Our first year, we didn't know all the tricks of the trade," Michelle says. "The tax lady told us that we could write off all the burritos we were donating to the shelter. We didn't want to do it, because we considered that our tithe. But the tax lady talked us into it."

They've also learned to be more scrupulous about writing down all of their business-related expenses, keeping their receipts, and paying their taxes on time. "My grandma lost her restaurant because she didn't realize she had to pay taxes for the mariachi bands that played there, and we don't want anything like that to happen to us," Michelle says.

In 1998, Sharon's last full year in a fast-food job, she earned $6,435, barely enough to pay the family's rent. In 1999, in the cart's first partial year of operation, the business grossed $60,000. After paying their business-related expenses, the family ended up with about $20,000 in income, elevating them above the poverty threshold for the first time since Sharon had divorced eleven years earlier.

By the end of 2000, the cart's first full year of operation, the Garzas say, the gross was up to $90,571, with the net profit perhaps a third of that. Income from the cart enabled the family to meet all household expenses, plus put aside $6,000 toward expansion of the business.

Sharon, the worrier in the family, still misses the certainty of a regular paycheck. "When I was working at a job, I would anticipate my check," she says. "I miss being able to add up my hours and figure out what's coming in, the certainty of it. I would know exactly what I would be getting and how much I'd have to spend after I paid my bills.

"The uncertainty of running a cash business is scary, though I wouldn't admit it to my kids. The car, the business, the house, all run off what we make. But in a way, knowing that is also exhilarating. We're in charge of our own fate."

## Expanding the Dream

Although owning a hot dog cart was initially Sharon's dream, now it's Michelle's too. And in her imagination, the dream is expanding.

First, in Michelle's expansion vision, comes a second cart, to be parked at the construction site for the new convention hotel. Sharon would continue to staff the original cart, and Michelle, or a cousin, would run the second cart. The cart they're eyeing is smaller than their current one, but affordable, they think, at $8,000, including financing costs. Their payments on it would be $174 a month, which they think they could easily afford once the hotel site is crawling with construction workers.

Then, maybe, they'll buy a third cart. The cart they both yearn to own is a beautiful, custom-made wooden walk-in model, complete with refrigerator, freezer, microwave, air conditioner, and heater, and a price tag of $17,000. "It's absolutely gorgeous," Michelle gushes. "The man who owns our commissary builds them from scratch. If we can buy one like that, my mom won't have to be outside in the elements all winter. This way she'd be in a heated unit, with a hookup in which she can plug in a TV. I won't have to worry about her so much."

Then, maybe five years down the road, they'd like to start their own commissary.

Ever practical, Sharon isn't sure either a third cart or a commissary makes sense for them. "I said to Michelle once, 'You know if we have three carts, we're going to have to have employees,'" she says. "At first, she was tickled at the idea of being a boss. But then she had the same thought I had: How are we going to find employees we trust?"

When Sharon thinks about Michelle's desire to own a commissary, her thoughts turn to how much work it would be. "The owners of our commissary, I watch how hard they work," she says. "They make it look easy. But if Michelle were to actually sit still long enough to see what it takes to run it, then maybe she'd have second thoughts about getting into that."

Michelle acknowledges that her timetable for expanding the business is ambitious, but she thinks her mother is worrying excessively. "The people who own our commissary have only been in the U.S. for four years," Michelle points out. "When they first came here, they were on public assistance, and now they own a house, four carts, and a commissary, and they've put two sons through college. I figure if Russian immigrants can do it after coming here with nothing, we can too."

Sharon is trying to moderate her innate cautiousness and let Michelle take the business as far as she can. "We both learned from Mom and Grandma to visualize something you want," Sharon says. "You have to feel it and be in it. Michelle can do it better than I can. I can visualize it and know in my heart that it will happen one day, but along the way I get hung up on all of the expenses and all the little things that can go wrong. Whereas Michelle sees the bigger picture and doesn't get hung up on the little things."

Somewhere in the bigger picture, Sharon hopes, is college for Michelle. Michelle has been told she's a good candidate for a full scholarship to Regis University in Denver, and neither she nor her mother wants an opportunity like that to slip through their fingers.

"Michelle loves being involved with the business, but I don't want her to feel stuck with this," Sharon says. "I want her to have the wings to go on to other ventures. I keep worrying that if we have three carts, she'll be stuck, which would be a shame.

"She has the potential to do so much," Sharon continues. "She could get out of the food industry totally. She has the ability to do anything she wants."

Not to worry, Michelle reassures her mom. "I want to go to college," she says. "But I know that whatever I do after that, I'm always going to have to have a hot dog cart. I may not be running it, but I always want to have one, because it was my first business, and it will always be special to me."

*Jeanette Bradshaw, who has more than 125 different styles of wedding cakes in her repertoire, can often be seen doing two—and sometimes three—things at once.*

chapter 2

# An Artist with a Pastry Knife

## Jeanette Bradshaw

## Elegant Traditions by Jeanette

## Whitehall, Arkansas

Jeanette Bradshaw's customers think of her as the Martha Stewart of Arkansas.

Her three-layer chocolate raspberry cake looks like a work of art.

Her "cotton blossom" appetizers disappear within moments of being served.

And her wedding cakes, garnished with thousands of handmade confectionery flowers, can top five feet.

In just a few short years, Jeanette has become one of the most sought-after caterers and wedding planners in eastern Arkansas. From 1999 through 2001, her annual billings topped $200,000.

Jeanette hasn't always been a successful businesswoman. Married at eighteen and the mother of three children by age twenty-one, she has had to overcome numerous obstacles on her way to becoming the wedding planner of choice to eastern Arkansas society.

Her first husband didn't want her to work outside the home. That marriage ended, and after years of being a single mother, she found happiness in a second marriage. But in November 1985, her second husband died suddenly, leaving her a forty-two-year-old widow with no life insurance, a new mortgage, and a fifteen-year-old son to raise on her own.

With Arkansas's economy in seemingly perpetual recession and prevailing wages well below the national average, Jeanette moved from one low-wage, low-satisfaction job to another for several years. To help make ends meet, she made and sold handicrafts, took in sewing, and baked custom birthday cakes, often staying up all night to tend the oven.

In 1991 she took a leap of faith into full-time self-employment. With the aid of the Good Faith Fund, a nonprofit organization that provides training, technical assistance, and loans to low-income women entrepreneurs, Jeanette started her own home-based catering business.

Since then, her annual billings have grown more than eightfold. In 1998 she graduated from her home-based kitchen into a 5,000-square-foot party facility. She no longer relies on relatives and friends to help her fill orders: She now employs four people full-time and about twenty people part-time, making an important contribution to the economy of her small town.

Jeanette Bradshaw's story shows how innate talent and drive can serve as the launchpad for a successful business. It also shows how difficult it can be for some women to overcome their own self-doubts and confront their inadequacies. Even now, the prospects of growth for Jeanette's business are hampered by her difficulties in delegating responsibility.

"I know I'm a perfectionist," says Jeanette, a petite, impeccably groomed woman in her late fifties whose insecurities are betrayed only by her bitten-to-the-quick nails. "It's okay to call me that. Just don't call me hyperactive."

## An Early Marriage

Jeanette was born in Helena, Arkansas, in the Mississippi Delta, in 1943, the second of five children. Throughout her childhood, her father, a sixth-grade dropout, changed jobs frequently and periodically attempted to follow his own entrepreneurial dreams. He owned a series of neighborhood grocery stores, none of which ever generated enough income to make life very comfortable for the family of seven.

Even as a child, Jeanette loved to bake. "Cookies and candies were my specialty, because I have a real sweet tooth," she says. She took over the family kitchen when she was a junior in high school. "My mother was going through the change, and she couldn't cope," Jeanette says. "She was an emotional wreck, and she just stayed in bed all the time. So I cooked dinner for the family every night for two years."

During her senior year in high school, Jeanette fell in love with a young man who bagged groceries at the neighborhood Safeway store. She was seventeen and he was nineteen when they married, two months after she graduated. "That's just what girls in Pine Bluff did then," she explains. "There was no expectation that we would go to college."

The couple lived with his parents for a few months and then took out a mortgage to buy Jeanette's grandmother's house in Pine Bluff for $1,500. It had three rooms and an outdoor toilet.

Less than a year into their marriage, their first child, Sherri, was born. Eleven months later, Buddy was born, followed by Carolyn Jeanine thirteen months after that. By this time, Jeanette's husband was working as an engineer with the Cotton Belt Railroad and was often away. Jeanette threw herself into full-time homemaking.

The young couple didn't have much money. "But I was very efficient with the little bits of money we had," Jeanette says. For example, the couple's first house had unfinished ceilings, with the studs showing, and the walls were covered with a shabby precursor to Sheetrock. Jeanette flattened out large cardboard packing boxes, stapled them to the studs and walls, and then rolled wallpaper over them. Visitors never guessed what was beneath the pretty paper.

Despite Jeanette's best efforts to be the perfect homemaker, the marriage was unhappy. "My husband was always putting me down, telling me I was ignorant and stupid and worthless," Jeanette says. "Sometimes I'd start feeling that way, even though I knew I wasn't. I kept an immaculate house. I sewed all our clothes. I was raising wonderful children. I was really good at everything I did."

When her two oldest children reached school age, Jeanette began taking knitting classes at Sears. She proved so good at it that she was soon asked to teach the classes. At first, her husband didn't want her to work even a few hours a week. "He wanted me home waiting for him," Jeanette says. But the family needed the money, so he relented. That job eventually led to part-time sales jobs in the fabrics and drapery departments. An aunt babysat the young children.

In 1970, about three years into her job, Jeanette unexpectedly found herself pregnant again. After Brian's birth, the marriage deteriorated further. Early in 1971, Jeanette decided to move out.

"I had been putting aside what money I could," she recalls. "I knew I had to leave. I just prayed and prayed and prayed that something would happen that would enable me to get away, and that's when a job came along. God showed me the way out of the marriage."

The job was a minimum-wage position as a secretary to a middle school principal in Pine Bluff. Without telling her husband, Jeanette applied and was offered the job. She left him while he was on one of his extended railroad trips.

"I was so scared," she says. "I didn't believe in divorce myself, and I knew that most of the people around me didn't, either. In those days, in Pine Bluff, women just didn't leave their husbands. If you got divorced, it meant you were a bad wife and a bad mother. I was worried that people wouldn't want their children to play with mine. I was even afraid that the other parents wouldn't let their daughters stay in the Girl Scout troop I was a leader of."

## Building a New Life

Jeanette settled into her new job and began to build a life for herself and her children.

"When she first started, she had a real confidence problem," recalls Terry Smith, the former principal at the school. "But the longer she worked for me, the more confidence she got. She really grew into the job."

With her wages and court-ordered child support, Jeanette was able to support herself and her four children. Most people had no idea that the family was poor. "If you make sure you look nice everywhere you go, nobody ever has to know," she says.

Late in 1971, the divorce was finalized. A year later, she started dating Bob Bradshaw, a former coworker at Sears. He too had recently been divorced. They married in August 1974. Brian was almost four years old, and her other children ranged from eleven to fourteen. From the start, Bob treated Jeanette's children like his own four, who continued to live with their mother.

Soon after the marriage, the family moved to Atkins, Arkansas, 120 miles from Pine Bluff. Bob, an insurance agent, transferred to an agency there. When Brian entered kindergarten a year later, Jeanette went to work organizing Tupperware parties. After just six weeks, she was promoted to regional manager. For most of her six years with the company, she was among Arkansas's top ten managers.

"In my first marriage, I was so beaten down that I didn't think I could do anything. But now I was happily married, and I had a job I loved and a good income," Jeanette recalls. "I felt like I was on top of the world."

In 1980 the couple bought country property in Conway, Arkansas, closer to Little Rock, where Bob had taken a new job. They installed two mobile homes side by side and built a utility room to link them. "It was on the side of a mountain overlooking a valley, just a beautiful place," Jeanette reminisces. "And it was really lovely inside. I carpeted and wallpapered everywhere."

After a year in Conway, Jeanette gave up the Tupperware job and took a new job managing a restaurant attached to a Kroger supermarket. She made $10 an hour, a good wage for rural Arkansas. When Bob's employer offered him a buyout, he took it. The buyout provided him with a modest lump sum, which he put into his own small-business dream: a traveling funnel-cake operation. He and Jeanette hoped that once the children were grown, they could travel the Southern county fair circuit together. Meanwhile, Bob took the truck on the road himself.

In the fall of 1985, the couple bought a new house in town for $56,000. They sold their country property for $18,000 and took on a $450-a-month mortgage, which was just barely affordable on Jeanette's income from Kroger and Bob's income from the funnel-cake business. They moved in just in time to celebrate Thanksgiving with their blended families.

The day after Thanksgiving, Jeanette went to work and Bob went on a deer-hunting trip with his grown son, Mike. Bob never came home. While hunting, his heart failed, and he died. He was fifty-six.

## A Wrong Turn

Bob's funeral cost $3,500, just about wiping out the couple's savings, which had already been reduced by moving expenses. Although Bob had once sold life insurance as a livelihood, it turned out he had none of his own.

For two weeks after his death, Jeanette stayed home. She was barely able to get out of bed. "My dad had died the year before," she said. "My mother had just been diagnosed with terminal cancer. And now Bob was gone."

She went back to work for the pre-Christmas rush, but began cracking under the strain. On a doctor's advice, she took a medical leave. "What I really needed was the time to grieve," she says.

Jeanette spent several months in counseling, trying to figure out how to live the rest of her life without her soulmate. Early in the spring of 1986, she went back to work at the restaurant, but found that the job had lost its appeal. "Everybody who came into the restaurant would want to tell me how sorry they were about Bob, and I'd start feeling bad all over again," she said.

By then, too, she was driving 150 miles round-trip every week to visit her mother, who was dying. She would leave Conway on Tuesday afternoon after work, spend that night and the next with her mother in Pine Bluff, and then return Thursday morning in time to report to work at 7 A.M. Brian, by now a high school freshman, would stay behind and fend for himself. The stress on the family was enormous.

By chance, one day Jeanette made a wrong turn off the highway in Whitehall, a suburb of Pine Bluff, and saw a "For Sale" sign in front of a cozy-looking white frame house sitting on nearly two acres of land. "This may have been the craziest thing I ever did in my life," she says. "I drove into the driveway, got out of my car, and looked into the windows. It was totally filthy inside, and the yard was a real mess. But I said to myself, 'This is where I want to live for the rest of my life.'"

Jeanette offered $46,500 for the two-bedroom house. A local bank approved her application for a mortgage, contingent upon the sale of her house in Conway. The owners agreed to let her rent until her other house sold.

Jeanette's mother died in May 1986, before Jeanette and Brian could move to Whitehall. They moved a few months later, in time for Brian to start his sophomore year at Whitehall High School. But it was fourteen months before the house in Conway sold, putting added strain on Jeanette's finances. During that time, she had to pay $450 a month for her mortgage in Conway, and $350 a month to rent the house in Whitehall.

Jeanette had planned to transfer to the Kroger restaurant in Pine Bluff. But before she could begin work there, the chain closed its Pine Bluff store. She took a $5-an-hour job—half her restaurant pay—as a receptionist in the doctor's office in which a sister-in-law, Jane, worked as a nurse. The job didn't pay nearly enough to cover her bills, so to supplement her income, she began taking in sewing and making and selling crafts, with the help of another sister-in-law, Mary. "It seemed like every time I turned around, somebody was asking me to do something," Jeanette says. "Whether or not I'd ever done it before, I'd say, 'Sure, I can do that.'"

Mary remembers countless nights sitting with Jeanette at her dining room table piecing together crafts. "I'm kind of craftsy too, and we'd burn the midnight oil together," Mary says. "Jeanette's sister, Linda, worked for a company that always gave Christmas gifts to its customers, and she got us the job of making them two years in a row. One year we made Christmas wreaths, maybe seventy-five of them, and shipped them all over the country. The next year we made little Christmas trees out of cone-shaped Styrofoam and eucalyptus leaves. Jeanette was doing everything she possibly could to support herself and Brian, and sometimes it seemed as though it wasn't going to be enough."

"Looking back, I don't know how we made it," Jeanette says. "Just the will to survive, I guess."

## A Business Is Born

About a year and a half after she moved to Whitehall, Jeanette's best friend from high school asked her to coordinate her daughter's wedding. "She had been in an accident and wasn't up to doing it herself," Jeanette says. Although Jeanette had helped a few friends plan their weddings, she had no previous experience coordinating the whole event. Nevertheless, she willingly took on the job.

"I had always loved doing cakes, and I thought it would be fun to organize the wedding for her," she explains. "I did all the planning and made all the food for the reception. Brian helped me serve, and she paid us $700 cash for our work. At the time, it seemed like really good money, though if I had figured out how much time Brian and I had put into it, we probably only made $1.50 an hour."

About 200 people attended the wedding, and soon some of them asked Jeanette to bake cakes for other special events. "Probably three months later I did another wedding," Jeanette says. "Word just got around."

At first, Jeanette didn't even have sufficient cash reserves to buy ingredients in bulk, which would have saved her money. "I would get an order for a wedding cake, but I wouldn't have enough money in my account to pay for the ingredients," she remembers. "So I'd go to the store after 2 P.M. on a Friday, which is after the banks stop posting checks for the weekend, and write a check, even though I knew I didn't have enough money in my account to cover it. I'd stay up all Friday night making the cake and get paid for it on Saturday or Sunday. Then I'd get to the bank first thing on Monday morning and deposit the payment to cover my check."

Jeanette priced the cakes at $1 a serving, about twice as much as the ingredients cost her, which made for a nice profit. "I thought I was doing good with that," she says. Pretty soon, people began asking her not just to bake wedding cakes, but to serve them. So she'd dress up and stand by the cake during the reception, charging customers $10 an hour extra. On days when she had two weddings at which servers were needed, she'd send Brian or Mary to the second.

Throughout these early days, Brian was a big help. "I can't draw, but Brian is really good at it," Jeanette says. "He'd still be sleeping, and I'd go in and beg him to get up and draw a Mickey Mouse on a cake for me."

Brian was good-natured about it. "I can remember spending many hours, either very late at night or very early in the morning, helping her with her cakes," says Brian, now in his early twenties and working at a bookstore in Fayetteville. "I'd barely be awake, and I'd trace a design on the white icing with a toothpick, which she'd outline and fill in with colored icing."

That wasn't all Brian did to help out. As soon as he was old enough, he began working up to thirty hours a week at after-school and weekend jobs to help pay household bills. Jeanette tears up with pride as she recalls her son's desire to help. "After I was widowed, there was never enough money," she says. "Without my asking, Brian would bring home his paycheck and hand it over to me and tell me to pay whatever bills I needed to."

### The Final Straw

Although Jeanette was devoting an increasing amount of time to baking and cooking for other people, she was still working full-time at the doctor's office. However, in 1987 the doctor relocated to another state, and she was out of a job.

It turned out to be the beginning of almost four years of intermittent and unsatisfactory employment. All through the late 1980s, the unemployment rate in Arkansas hovered around 9.5 percent, more than two percentage points above the national rate, and jobs were hard to find.

Jeanette's next job was with a dentist; that lasted for a year and a half, when she took a better-paying job at the Pine Bluff Convention Center. But that job didn't work out. She left after three months and collected unemployment benefits for a few months while she looked for another job.

She finally found one as an administrative assistant and bookkeeper for a moving company. "That turned out to be another mistake," she says ruefully. A year after she went to work there, federal authorities shut down the company and arrested fifteen of its employees for operating a drug ring. "So I was unemployed again," she says.

After that, Jeanette and Brian spent a few months in Dallas with her daughter, Sherri, and her family. Jeanette kept her hand in her emerging wedding planning business, consulting with Arkansas clients by telephone and flying back for weddings. Because she was frustrated with the Arkansas job market, she considered relocating to Texas. "But it turned out that in the Dallas job market, I had no marketable skills," she says. "You have to understand computers to work in an office there, and I had no computer skills."

Jeanette and Brian returned to Whitehall in time for him to pack up and leave for the University of Arkansas at Fayetteville. She soon found a job with a law office and, for a year and a half, combined what she regarded as an unfulfilling day job with the increasingly satisfying cooking and wedding planning that she was doing at night and on weekends.

Again, misfortune struck. In early 1991 one of the firm's partners was prosecuted in connection with a local savings and loan scandal, found guilty of fifteen counts of fraud, and sent to prison. The firm was forced to retrench. "They laid off some attorneys, and they couldn't afford to keep me either," Jeanette says.

That was the final straw for Jeanette. "I thought, 'If I'm going to starve to death, I may as well do it working for myself,'" she says. "I decided to go into business for myself full-time."

## The Neighbors Pitch In

Without a day job, Jeanette now had no steady source of income. She hadn't had health insurance since she worked for Kroger, and simply continued to go without, praying that she and Brian would remain well. Brian's college costs were being covered by a combination of scholarships and Pell grants, so she didn't have to worry about that. All her new business had to do was generate enough income to pay her mortgage and homeowner's and car insurance bills and buy groceries. Any way she looked at her expenses, though, they added up to a lot of cakes.

Jeanette was a natural as a baker and a wedding planner, but she didn't know much about running a business. She had about ten weddings under her belt, almost all for relatives, friends, and friends of friends. She had credit problems left over from her first year in Whitehall. She didn't have a business plan or any real concept of how to grow her business. "But I always knew where I was going, even if I didn't know how I was going to get there," she says.

One of her first decisions was choosing a name for the business. "My sister [Linda] told me, 'Whenever I think of you, I think of the word *elegant*. You should think of a name that includes *elegant.*' So I came up with Elegant Traditions by Jeanette, and I've been that ever since."

Having a name for her business didn't make an immediate difference, since she couldn't afford business cards. "And advertising was out of the question," she says. "It cost too much. I had to rely on my cakes as my advertising."

Initially, Jeanette worked out of her home kitchen, which contained a single conventional oven and family-sized refrigerator. She turned her laundry room into a storage room for pots and pans and serving dishes, most gleaned from garage sales. Her combination living and dining room was now dedicated to meetings with clients. "I always met with my clients right here at my dining room table," she says. "They loved coming here because it was always decorated for the season." Her living room looks like an illustration out of *Victorian Home* magazine, with many unique decorative touches, such as an antique trunk upended and opened as a display area for quilts and tatted doilies.

Early on, one of the services Jeanette offered to her wedding clients was custom-tailored wedding gowns and bridesmaids' dresses. She's an expert seamstress and could make her own patterns that were reproductions of gowns pictured in *Modern Bride* magazine. But she soon discovered that she couldn't make enough money to compensate her for her time. "People want to pay you just $20 to sew a dress that it might take you fifteen hours to make," she says.

Jeanette thinks that in her first full year of business she made about $2,500 in profit, clearly not enough to meet her household expenses, but enough to make her think she had a good concept. (To pay her bills, she maxed out her credit cards, creating credit problems that lasted for years.)

In the second year, her income doubled. "I couldn't believe it," she says. As the orders for wedding cakes and bridal showers and anniversary parties and retirement parties started coming in, she began needing to bring in helpers to get all the cooking and serving done. "Just about all of my relatives and everyone in my neighborhood worked for me at one time or another," Jeanette laughs.

Larry Bradshaw (no relation), a former Navy cook who lives down the street, was exceptionally helpful. "I just volunteered to help out because I could see that she really needed it," he says. "There were times when she had so much food to cook and so little room in her kitchen that I'd cook the vegetables over in my kitchen."

Gloria Connell, whose yard adjoins Jeanette's, was also indispensable. Gloria had become friendly with Jeanette when their children were singing in the Whitehall High School Choir. Even though Gloria works full-time as an elementary school teacher, she'd pitch in whenever Jeanette had a big wedding to prepare for.

"I'm a logistics-type person," Gloria says. "Jeanette would handle the cooking, and I'd make sure we had 240 candles, or twelve tables, or twenty centerpieces—whatever the hostess wanted. At one time, I think all four of us in my family were working for her—my husband playing the piano at a reception or putting a design on a cake, and my children dressing up in tuxedo shirts and black ties and serving. Every now and then, she might force some money on me or bring me a cake. But I wasn't doing it for money. I just loved doing it."

Mostly, though, Jeanette did the actual cooking herself, staying up all night long many Fridays to bake her Saturday orders. If she was lucky, she'd catch a few minutes of sleep in the thirty-five minutes it took each cake to bake. "There were times when I was so busy that I'd go without sleep for two or three nights in a row," she recalls.

## Looking for Money to Grow

Sometime late in 1991, Jeanette's sister, Linda, read an article in the Pine Bluff newspaper about the Good Faith Fund, which was offering business skills classes and loans to low-income people who wanted to start their own businesses. Linda had recently been laid off, and she and Jeanette decided to sign up for one of the organization's courses, which was a requirement for anyone who wanted to apply for a loan. "She only lasted a few sessions, but I was reaching out for any help I could get, and I kept going," Jeanette says.

Iris Garza, a former loan officer with the Good Faith Fund, remembers Jeanette initially expressing skepticism about the program. "She called the Better Business Bureau to see if we were legitimate," Garza recalls. Jeanette explains, "There were a lot of scams going on, and I didn't want to get caught up in one."

Jeanette was attracted to the peer lending program that the fund had recently started based on the model of the Grameen Bank in Bangladesh, which pioneered the provision of microloans to entrepreneurs too poor to qualify for traditional bank loans. "I needed to borrow money if I was going to grow, and I didn't have good credit, so there was no other place to go," Jeanette says.

After completing a class in basic entrepreneurial skills, Jeanette joined one of the Good Faith Fund's first peer lending groups. It included a man with a floor-laying business, a woman who wanted to start a hair-bow business, a man who owned a convenience store, and a woman who provided child care in her home. The Good Faith Fund's two dozen peer lending groups met twice a month to listen to a speaker on a topic of general interest and then broke into their own peer groups to talk about their businesses.

"Through both the classes and the discussions, we learned that we all had pretty much the same problems," Jeanette says. "We all needed to learn how to manage our money. It was really helpful to know that I wasn't the only person out there in the world trying to build a business from the ground up." Each participant put about $10 a week into their personal savings, and then, as a group, they decided how much of their savings to lend each other for business development.

Ron Wales, the floorer, marveled at her energy. "She was pumping hard to get her business going," he recalls. "She was all business, just push, push, push. I was really impressed with the way she set her mind on it." Jeanette was everybody's favorite, he remembers, because she'd often bring in cakes for them to sample.

While she was enrolled in the peer lending group, Jeanette applied to the Good Faith Fund for a $1,200 direct loan to buy a used walk-in freezer from the Pine Bluff Police Department. There was no doubt that the freezer was a bargain. A new one would have cost $6,000. But in retrospect, the purchase spoke volumes about Jeanette's lack of business experience. She hadn't budgeted for the $1,000 it was going to cost to install the freezer at her home—to pour a concrete pad, upgrade her electrical system, and infuse the condenser with refrigerant—so she couldn't use it.

Jeanette paid back the loan on schedule, but to this day, the freezer remains in storage. "I'm going to use it someday, as soon as I buy my own building," she insists. "There are just so many other things to take care of first."

## A Knock on the Door

One day in 1992, as Jeanette decorated a cake in her kitchen, a man knocked on her door. He introduced himself as Dan Smith, an inspector for the Arkansas Department of Health. He said he had come to investigate a complaint from a commercial baker that Jeanette was illegally operating a bakery out of her home.

"It put the fear of God in me," Jeanette says. "I almost died on the spot. I thought he'd come to take me to jail. All I could think of was the embarrassment of seeing my name in the paper, arrested for baking cakes."

Years later, Smith still remembers his first meeting with Jeanette. "What really struck me about her was her determination to do things right," he recalls. "She also had an air of discipline and purpose about her, which is very important in that kind of business. She was very focused, and I thought that was kind of a unique trait. She's a real detail person."

Fortunately for Jeanette, Smith viewed his job as being as much an educator as an enforcer. "I like to think of myself personally as a supporter of people who are operating small businesses, because I think that's one of the foundations of our country, something that makes it successful," Smith says.

Over the next year, Smith helped Jeanette work out a plan to bring her home-based business into compliance with Arkansas law, which requires a separate kitchen to produce baked goods intended for sale. The health department allowed her to continue using her home kitchen as long as she showed progress toward compliance.

At first, Jeanette considered building an addition to her house. But when she found out it would cost $25,000, she decided instead to enclose a 10-by-14-foot screened-in porch. Her brother, Jim, and his teenage son, Joe, agreed to do the carpentry work for $8 an hour. Because Jeanette had by now given up her credit cards, Jim charged the materials on his credit card and let her pay him back as she could.

By this time, Jeanette was dating Frank Lightfoot, a widower who owned Whitehall's weekly newspaper. The two had met at a Republican Party fund-raiser in 1990. He helped her obtain cabinets and plumbing work through a trade agreement with his advertisers. And in what may have been the most unusual courtship gesture of all time, Frank bought her a used commercial six-burner stove, at a bargain price of $600, for her new kitchen.

In 1992 Jeanette married Frank, just as the commercial kitchen in her home was being finished. (Characteristically, she spent a day of her honeymoon giving cake-decorating lessons to the owner of the Branson, Missouri, bed-and-breakfast where she and her husband stayed.) After the wedding, Frank moved into Jeanette's house. Then came another scare. The commercial baker who had lodged the initial complaint against Jeanette accused her of a zoning infraction. "That bakery owner in Pine Bluff was riding me hot and heavy," Jeanette says. "The really bad thing is that when I'd send a client there to buy a cake topper, the owner would ask her who was baking her wedding cake. When she'd tell her it was Jeanette Bradshaw, the other baker would tell her, 'Well, you're really taking a risk hiring Jeanette, because she's about to be shut down and you may end up without a cake on your wedding day.'"

To bring her business into compliance with her county's zoning regulations, Jeanette had to seek a conditional use permit. "I called up the Southeast Arkansas Regional Planning Commission, which handles zoning for Whitehall, and a man there told me that I'd never get a permit because I was in a residential area," Jeanette says. "I just about lost it. I told him, 'I'm a widow. I'm trying to raise a child on my own. I have enough pride that I won't go on government assistance. What do you want me to do?'"

Determined to get the permit, Jeanette came up with a plan. "I got it in my head that it would help me to get a petition together and get all my neighbors to sign it in support of what I was doing," Jeanette recalls. "So I went all through the neighborhood talking to people about what I wanted to do with my business. I'd made choir gowns or birthday cakes for most of their children, and a lot of them had even helped me in my business, so I had no trouble getting their support. But I worried right up until the end of the hearing that I wouldn't get my permit." She got the permit.

Being ignorant of health department rules and zoning regulations wasn't the only mistake Jeanette made in the early years of her business. Initially she paid her employees in cash and didn't bother to withhold federal taxes or Social Security. "I didn't know any better," she admits. The Good Faith Fund helped her straighten out her tax mess.

"And it wasn't until 1994, I think, that I started buying workmen's comp coverage for my employees," she says. "That was about the same time I started carrying product liability insurance.

I had to do it to get the jobs I wanted. There's a museum in Little Rock, which has lots of parties, that requires $1 million in product liability coverage before I can even walk in the door."

## A Romantic at Heart

From 1992 through 1998, Jeanette's business continued to grow steadily, particularly the wedding planning side of it. A profile in the *Arkansas Democrat-Gazette* in 1995 helped her more than double her billings, from $22,000 to $48,000, which, in turn, earned her a business development award from the Good Faith Fund. Descriptions of her elaborate wedding cakes began appearing regularly in the accounts of society weddings that fill several pages of the *Democrat-Gazette* almost every Sunday. "The all-white bride's cake, on a table swagged in Italian ruscus accented with silver bows, featured alternating vanilla and amaretto layers and was iced with rolled fondant with gum paste flowers and ribbons," reads a typical newspaper description of one of her cakes. "The table for the bridegroom's chocolate cheesecake was heaped with assorted Godiva chocolates and champagne grapes." The publicity brought her clients like the Dillards, the department store owners who are among Arkansas's most prominent families.

Most of Jeanette's wedding-related work occurs in the months before the actual nuptials, beginning with an initial two-to-three-hour planning session with the bride (and usually her mother). Over the next few months, she helps the bride select invitations that reflect her personality; choose a site for the ceremony; arrange for flowers, a photographer, and a videographer; audition bands; decide on church decorations; choose the music for the ceremony; hire limousines; and plan the reception from start to finish.

Then there are the many hours Jeanette spends with the brides, and often their mothers, just providing an empathetic ear and calming nerves. A lot of what Jeanette does for her clients actually amounts to premarital counseling. "By the time I work with someone on a wedding, I can tell if their marriage is going to work or not," she says. "There have been many couples that I wanted to beg not to marry each other."

On the day of a wedding, Jeanette functions as the major-domo. "I'm coordinating anywhere between twenty and forty people who are directly involved in the wedding," she explains. "I have to make sure the bride is dressed, the photographer and the musicians are on time, the wedding party knows what they're supposed to do, the minister's there. In the meantime, my staff is setting up the reception. There's a lot of responsibility in wedding planning that nobody ever sees."

At a wedding, she's all business. She never cries. "Except once," she says. "I knew this family really well. The mom was very sick and went into the hospital the week before the wedding. The doctors hoped the mom would be able to leave the hospital for two hours to come to the wedding. But she died on a Thursday, the day before the wedding rehearsal. The wedding went on, because that's what the mom would have wanted. But I sent the bride down the aisle and just stood in the back of the church bawling."

Jeanette loves working with clients throughout the planning process. Her favorite part, though, is designing and decorating the cake, which, after the bride's dress, is what most guests remember. She has more than 125 different styles of wedding cakes in her repertoire. Her scrapbooks bulge with color photos of cakes decorated with real tropical flowers, gum paste flowers, and fountains spilling water between the layers; there's even a cake topped with a replica of the Eiffel Tower, a nod to the city where one bride and groom met. "The more complicated the cake, the more I like it," she says.

Her most memorable cake, made in 1995 at a cost of $1,600, was five feet tall, just an inch shorter than she is, and decorated with 874 gum paste roses and 5,800 confectionery lilies of the valley. "We made all of them petal by petal," recalls Jeanette's sister-in-law Mary. "I couldn't even begin to tell you the number of hours it took."

Jeanette's least favorite wedding cake was topped, at the bride's insistence, with a Mickey Mouse with pink and purple ears. "My opinion is that if you're that immature, you're not ready to get married," Jeanette says, still disapproving years later.

And then there are the "groom's cakes," which are an Arkansas tradition. These are cakes decorated with full-size, edible sculptures of mallard ducks or wild turkeys; topped with edible replicas of the groom's hunting cabin; made to replicate a favorite golf hole; or crafted to look like a ball and chain.

"Whatever they want, I make," Jeanette says, "except I draw the line at body parts. There's a big demand for them, but I won't make X-rated cakes."

### A Building of Her Own

As her business grew bigger, working at home began to strain her marriage, at least from Frank's point of view. "She had always made time for her clients—days, nights, weekends, whatever," he says. "The client always came first, and it was difficult for me to accept that. I used to joke that I was the only man in town who had to get fully dressed in the morning before he went to the bathroom because there might be five or ten people I'd have to walk by."

Jeanette began looking around for a freestanding facility into which she could move her business. "I was stagnating in my home," she says. "There was no way I could make my business what I wanted it to be operating out of such a small space. I was having to turn down jobs because we couldn't get them done there."

In the fall of 1998, she learned that a Mexican restaurant in Whitehall had closed and that the 5,000-square-foot building it had occupied was vacant. Dan Smith, the health inspector, went with her to help judge its suitability as a catering facility.

The building included a commercial kitchen, seating space for 125, and ample parking. It also sat in a highly visible spot on the main route through Whitehall. "I knew the minute I went into it that it was perfect," Jeanette says. Smith assured her that after it was cleaned up, the kitchen would have no trouble meeting the Health Department's regulations.

The owner was asking $150,000. Jeanette applied for a loan from the Good Faith Fund, but the loan officer recommended that she lease the facility for a year or so until she could be sure that her revenues would be sufficient to cover her loan payments. She took his advice. She moved her business in October 1998, just in time to book a series of holiday parties into the facility.

That year, she billed $186,000. By the end of 1999, her first full year of operating out of the new facility, her billings had grown to about $220,000.

Moving allowed her to expand her business, but there was an additional benefit. "It's been the greatest thing for our marriage," her husband says. "I don't feel like I'm living in a place of business anymore."

## The Nose Knows

It's a typical day in the kitchen of Elegant Traditions by Jeanette. It's mid-December 1999, and it seems as though everyone who's anyone in Pine Bluff wants to entertain, and they all want Jeanette Bradshaw to cook for them. This week, she's catering ten private parties, along with the three annual madrigal dinners staged by the Whitehall High School choral group, to which Jeanette gives a bargain price because of Brian's long association with it.

Her new kitchen is immaculate and attractive to boot. Jeanette inherited the striking—and now spotless—green-and-white-tiled floor. Most of the equipment is hers, bought here and there (often at yard sales) whenever she's had some cash to spare. More than 1,000 cookbooks line the shelves of a bookcase in a side room. Near the front of the building, there's a separate storage area for all of the linens, crystal, and serving pieces that she uses at parties and wedding receptions. She has artfully transformed the décor in the dining rooms from a Mexican hacienda motif into something reminiscent of a Southern garden setting.

Jeanette has been here since 5:30 A.M., after rising at 4:30 A.M., following just four hours of sleep. Her employees began trickling in at 7 A.M. Like most service workers in rural Arkansas, they earn anywhere from $5.50 to $7 an hour.

"I'd love to pay my staff $10 an hour, but I just can't do that and make it," Jeanette laments. "On the plus side, they don't have to buy expensive clothes to work in, like they would in an office, and they get a free lunch every day."

Jeanette has an unconventional hiring philosophy. Probably because of her own life experiences, Jeanette lets her heart guide her hiring decisions. She doesn't even require prospective employees to fill out application forms.

"I guess you could say I hire by intuition," she says. "And for some reason, I seem to have a lot of people working for me who have a lot of serious hardship in their lives."

In her current workforce, she's got at least one battered woman, one woman with an alcoholic husband, one with a severely disabled son, one who suffers from clinical depression, and an epileptic. "I guess everybody who works for me is needy in one way or another," she says. "It's probably because I get pleasure out of building up the people who work for me, helping them feel better about themselves."

No employee would ever accuse Jeanette of leaving the grunt work for her staff. For the last hour, Jeanette has been standing at a counter cutting dough into silver dollar rolls—or "little lady" rolls, as she calls them—for a luncheon she's catering the next day for 115 senior citizens, mostly women. Four trays are sitting on a counter, awaiting a free oven, and two others are already baking. The smell of yeast-raised dough wafts through the kitchen air.

"I've got to have 300 rolls by tomorrow, and I'm making plenty of extra so I'm prepared if I get an order," she explains. "You can't make 'em just like that."

Once the rolls are all cut out, she starts spreading cream cheese icing on an 8-inch-tall double-layer Italian cream cake. She had first shaved the layers to rid them of brown edges, a true perfectionist's touch. The cake, which contains ground pecans and coconut, is one of her specialties. She charges $35 for it. "Up in Little Rock, they'd charge $45 or $50 for it, but the people in this area won't pay that much," she says.

As she's adding decorative rosettes, Betty, one of her employees, comes across the kitchen to consult with her about the grocery list. Betty wonders how many boxes of strawberries she should pick up, given how expensive they've become. As it turns out, Jeanette needs lots of strawberries this week, both to garnish her chocolate raspberry tortes and to serve to partygoers to dip in chocolate fondue.

As they're conferring, the phone rings, and Betty answers. "Mr. Elegant wants to speak to Mrs. Elegant," Betty says, referring playfully to Jeanette's husband, who's on the other end of the line. Crunching a portable phone to her ear with her shoulder, Jeanette talks with her husband as she carries the now-finished cake over to a helper for boxing. It's one of hundreds of times today that she'll be observed doing two and sometimes three things at once.

As she hangs up, she calls out to her employees, "Would you check the ovens? Something smells ready to come out." Unlike most cooks, Jeanette doesn't use a timer. She uses her nose.

Sure enough, the first batch of rolls is ready to come out. Now Jeanette is icing another cake, this one a strawberry layer cake, prepared, uncharacteristically, from a mix. "I don't do this very often, but this family loves a mix," she says. "It's for their daughter's seventeenth birthday. I've been making this cake for her since she was four. I used to make all of her Halloween costumes too."

Jeanette then moves on to a chocolate raspberry torte, which a family plans to serve at a holiday dinner. She still decorates all the cakes that come out of the kitchen herself. "I haven't had a good cake decorator for some time," she explains, "but I really need one bad. A lot of times I end up staying up all night just to get them all done."

Amazingly, Jeanette has never taken a cake-decorating course. She's entirely self-taught. For years, she was too poor to buy presents for her children's friends on their birthdays, so she'd send a cake as a gift. "I got a lot of practice making free cakes," she says.

Jeanette laughs as she recalls some of her earliest efforts. "The first wedding cake I made was for my sister-in-law, Mary, and I didn't even know how to make flowers then," she says. "I used those hard little premade flowers that come stuck to cardboard."

Elsewhere in the kitchen, five other employees are engaging in friendly banter as they prepare food for 100 for a party tonight at Southeast Arkansas Community College. The menu features molded salmon mousse with crackers, sliced pork tenderloin on rolls, honey walnut chicken, garden veggie pizza, onion soufflé and pita chips, chocolate fondue and strawberries, and bar cookies and fudge.

There's also a small happy hour party to prepare for at the Pine Bluff Chamber of Commerce. The menu for that one is simpler: frozen grapes, honey walnut Brie, assorted cheeses, and a small salmon mousse and crackers.

Because it's the holiday season, Jeanette's staff is hoping for tips. "Pine Bluff people don't tip all year long, but they do at Christmas," Jeanette says.

Vanessa, who's working tonight, confirms this. "I got in on two tips last week: $20 a night, two nights in a row, both at doctors' houses," she says. "It was wonderful."

Jeanette's staff will serve at both events tonight, without her supervision. She's tied up training the parent and student volunteers who will help serve at the madrigal dinners. She'll pay her neighbor, Larry Bradshaw, to come in for a few hours to cook the prime rib, and one of her newest hires will spend a few hours in the afternoon chopping and slicing. Otherwise, Jeanette likes to do the cooking for the dinners herself, both to keep her labor costs down and because of a sentimental attachment to the high school's choral program, which is regarded as one of the best in the state.

Searching in the refrigerator for some of the ingredients she'll need for another batch of silver dollar rolls—since she's just figured out that she's short—Jeanette realizes that she's out of milk.

"Can somebody make a phone call?" she calls out. "See if you can catch Miss Betty at the store. And don't fire me for forgetting."

When possible, Jeanette does most of her purchasing at the local grocery, Brookshire's, which is where she's hoping to catch Betty. "It costs us more, but they let us go into the back room and pick out our own produce, and they'll special-order things for us too," she explains. "They treat us like royalty, because they really appreciate our business."

As she's preparing the dough for the additional rolls, one of her most labor-intensive products, she ruminates on how much work they are. "We tried—didn't we, girls?—to not have to make our own rolls," she says to the room in general. "For a while, I used a prepared roll. No client complained, but my girls said, 'They just don't taste the same.' So we went back to homemade."

Vanessa and another helper, Ann, are packing up a lunch delivery, and before they head out the door Jeanette stops them for a pep talk about the event they'll be working this evening.

"I want to caution you girls about something tonight," she says. "You're going to think that the woman who's giving the party is real persnickety, but she's not. She's real sweet. You'll run into much more persnickety people in this business. But she gets real nervous when she has parties. Her husband has a big job, and there's a lot of pressure on her. She comes across as demanding, but she's really nice. She just loves that catering magic.

"Oh, and by the way, we're doing really great today, guys. The timing is working out just perfectly. Coming in so early makes a big difference."

Just then, a customer arrives to pick up a groom's cake with a ball and chain design. "It smells so good in here," she says as she walks in the door. "How do you all stand it?"

## "I Can't Be Everybody's Friend"

In a 1995 interview with the *Arkansas Democrat-Gazette*, Jeanette told a reporter that her goal over the next five years was to have "a huge kitchen with lots of help."

She's got that now, so she's expanding her vision. By 2004, she hopes to more than double her billings, which would put her at the half-a-million-dollars-a-year mark.

How will she do it? She doesn't have a comprehensive plan for growth, just lots and lots of ideas that involve both cutting costs and increasing revenues.

For starters, she plans to apply for a loan to buy the building she's leasing. With monthly payments at $1,500 and climbing, the new facility has added significantly to her overhead. She calculated that a monthly mortgage payment would cost her less, and she would build equity.

In 1999, her first full year in the new building, she was forgoing a salary for herself after drawing $500 a week in the previous two years. "With my new place, I wanted to give the business a chance to show how much it could grow," she says. "There's so much new overhead, I didn't want to take money out for myself until I knew I was going to make it."

But she's beginning to realize that she might have to spend more money to make more money. She really needs a good right-hand helper, someone just like herself, who will work tirelessly to please her customers and never let a cake that's less than perfect leave the kitchen. "And I'm also going to have to get someone to be a full-time baker and decorator," she says. "I've got to give up trying to do every single thing myself."

Most of all, Jeanette has to start increasing her revenues. Throughout her nine years in business, she's wrestled with a problem that plagues many women entrepreneurs: how to price themselves. "I can remember nearly fainting with embarrassment when I first told someone a cake cost $57," she says, laughing at her insecurity. The trick is raising prices enough to cover her costs and provide a nice profit, but not so much that she loses customers.

The event she's hosting today is a perfect example of the difficulty of balancing those competing values. She has 115 largely well-off senior citizens in her dining room eating a festive holiday dinner—turkey with all the trimmings, plus a flaming dessert—and they're complaining about the $9.50-per-person price. "The lady who organized it told me that her people really liked the lunch, and they'd like to start coming here every month, but they don't want to pay this much," Jeanette says. "I'd already lowered my price to try to get their regular business. That's a meal I've charged other groups $15 a person for."

Jeanette is working up the nerve to tell the organizer that she not only can't offer a meal like this for less, but that she can't even offer it again for as little as she charged today.

"It used to be that I would accept any business that came over the telephone," she says. "If I gave someone a price and they told me, 'Oh, that's a little high,' I'd juggle my figures and come down so I could get the job. But I'm learning that I can't be everybody's friend. I've turned down a lot of business this year because they didn't want to pay enough. I've learned to say, 'I'm sorry, but that's my bottom line.'"

One thing Jeanette knows she definitely needs to do is to start billing brides for more of the time she spends planning their weddings. She now charges a flat rate of $500 to plan a wedding. But for some very elaborate weddings, that has translated into pay of just a few dollars an hour. She wants to raise her basic fee to $600, with regular increases every year. "I know my time is worth $100 an hour or more," she says, "but I don't know many people I can charge that much."

Whether she can stick with her resolution to begin charging more for her services is a big question mark. "Just today, a little girl came in with her mother-in-law to plan her wedding," Jeanette says. "We went through all the details, and just as she was getting ready to leave, she turned to me, with tears in her eyes, and said, 'My mother has cancer.' I immediately started thinking about how I could cut my charges to her. But I know I have to start thinking with my mind and not my heart. Dillard's doesn't give me a break on a dress because I'm going to wear it to a funeral."

Besides raising her prices, she's thinking about how she might utilize her party space more regularly in order to increase her billings. One of her ideas is to begin to offer weekday lunches. "There's no place close by for people to go to lunch, and I know that would succeed," she says.

That would also enable her to expand one of her recent innovations—"casseroles-to-go," a line of meals packaged for take-out and easy warm-up by harried parents after work. "People could order them at lunch and then pick them up on the way home," she says.

She's also going to get more aggressive about marketing herself. She has already learned about the power of referrals. For example, she had baked a $200 cake for one client and received a referral from that for what turned out to be one of her most expensive wedding receptions yet. At that reception, she distributed a few dozen business cards and is confident she will hear from someone in the future. "Word of mouth is my best advertiser," she says. "But I've got to expand into other areas of the state where people are more willing to pay for quality."

Among her other goals for the future is to publish a cookbook—not just a loose-leaf binder filled with favorite recipes, which is what many clients tell her she should put together, but "a coffee-table type book, with beautiful pictures."

As of winter 2000, the prospects for her business looked good. She already had nine weddings booked for the following June, more than ever before this far in advance. "At the rate I'm going, I'll have all my June wedding dates booked by February," she says. Bookings for parties in January, usually a slow month, were also uncharacteristically heavy. She also learned that President Bill Clinton might show up at a party she would be catering at the dedication of a new federal toxicological research center in Pine Bluff. It would be quite a feather in her cap to be able to tell clients that she cooked for the president.

And if he showed up, she might be able to request a moment of his time to tell him about another goal of hers. "I want to bake Chelsea's wedding cake when she gets married," she says.

*Sheela Drummer knows her destiny: "I don't care what I do or where I go. I will always want to be up under someone's car, figuring out a problem."*

chapter 3

# "God Gave Me the Knowledge" Lucille Barnett Washington Sheela Drummer F & S Auto Parts Detroit, Michigan

Lucille Washington got into the auto parts business by accident.

One day in 1961, she stopped at an auto parts store in her Detroit neighborhood to buy a gasket for her '54 Buick. Impressed by the initiative she showed in wiping up some spilled oil, the store's owner offered her a job as a parts clerk. Although she knew little about cars, she found she loved doing a job that at the time was considered man's work.

When her boss died eight years later, Lucille used $8,000 in savings to open her own auto parts store. Five years after that, she bought her own building and added an auto repair shop, doubling her annual revenues. In May 2002, F & S Auto Parts celebrated its thirty-second anniversary.

"When I was young, I never would have dreamed that I'd make a life out of cars," Lucille says. "I knew how to drive a car, put in gas, and change the oil, and I knew what the parts of the car did. Beyond that, God gave me the knowledge."

Lucille, an energetic sixty-eight, and her daughter, Sheela Drummer, thirty-six, work together to make sure that the business survives the market pressures that have forced thousands of independently owned auto parts stores and repair shops around the country to sell out or shut down. With the help of the Detroit Entrepreneurship Institute, a nonprofit organization that provides training and technical assistance to low-income entrepreneurs, Sheela is trying to nudge her mother's business practices into the twenty-first century so that the enterprise can improve its profit margin while still retaining its emphasis on customer service.

Sheela is determined that the business will still be around when her children, now nine, ten, and thirteen, are old enough to run it.

"I've always told my children that they have to do well in school so they can get a good job," she says. "But with businesses downsizing and laying off people, it's made me realize that there's no guarantee there will be a job for them even if they do well. That's why I want to make sure that this business is still around for them."

## "There's a Reason for Everything"

A deeply religious woman who punctuates nearly every paragraph with "God is great," Lucille describes an almost unimaginably hard childhood growing up in the post-Depression South.

Born in 1933, Lucille spent her early childhood in Washington, Georgia, in a two-room house with an outhouse in the backyard. Her parents were both farmworkers. "My mother would have a baby, and two days later she'd be back in the field," Lucille recalls. Only eight of her mother's seventeen children survived infancy.

As a little girl, Lucille often helped her mother wash other families' clothes. They earned fifty cents for doing a week's laundry for a family of five, with a tomato sandwich for a tip. By high school, Lucille was working three different jobs to help her family make ends meet. "I'd get out of high school at 3 P.M. and ride the bus to one home, where I'd clean up, and then the woman would take me to her sister's house, where I'd work until seven or eight, and then I'd go to a restaurant and work until 11 P.M.," she remembers.

After Lucille graduated from high school in 1952, her family joined the migration of African Americans from the rural South to the industrial cities of the Midwest and Northeast. Their destination was Detroit, where they had relatives. Lucille had high hopes for a better future than Georgia offered. But with no local references and most good-paying jobs effectively closed to black women anyway, the only work she could find was as a domestic.

Lucille worked for one family for a year and a half and left when the husband of the house made suggestive remarks. She worked for another family for more than six years, but quit in disgust after her employer refused her holiday pay.

"The lady told me that if I took off for a holiday, she would have to dock my pay," Lucille recalls, "and sure enough, when I took off for Memorial Day, she docked me $5 for the day. That's when I determined I was going to do something different.

"My brothers were already on me about my work. They'd say, 'Lucille, why do you work domestic? You have a high school education. You can do better.' But it takes faith. I was afraid to try something new."

Lucille took the summer of 1961 off to stay home with her son, Frederick, whom she'd been raising herself since his birth in 1955. They lived off the proceeds of a settlement that she had received from an accident involving her Buick.

Toward the end of the summer, Lucille went into a neighborhood auto parts store to buy a part for the damaged car. When she noticed a puddle of oil on the shop's floor, she instinctively bent down to clean it up. "Oh, don't do that," the owner told her. "You'll get your hands dirty."

"That doesn't bother me," she responded. "And I'll tell you something else I'm not afraid of either. Hard work."

The owner, a Canadian named Ed Clark, was impressed. A week later, he called someone who knew her and asked him to tell her to stop in.

"At first, I didn't want to go, because I thought he was going to ask me to be his wife's maid," Lucille recalls. "But I'm a very spiritual person. I think there's a reason for everything. So I went in, and he said to me, 'I understand you're looking for a job.' I hesitated before I said yes, because I didn't want to work as a maid again. But then he told me he was looking for someone to work in the shop.

"I asked him, 'How much are you willing to pay?' He said, 'Let's start you off at $50 a week.'

"I couldn't believe it. When I quit the job as a domestic, I was making $35 a week. And here it was, a better job, plus a $15 a week raise."

Though she knew little about cars, she said yes. "I was broke," she explains. "I needed a job." With that, she became one of very few African American females working in the auto parts business in Detroit.

"I was blessed," Lucille says. "I give Him praise, to be able to be exposed to the opportunity and grasp it. God is good."

## Chasing Parts

Lucille became what's known in the business as a parts chaser. "I put the stock up on the shelves when it came in, and got it down for the customers," she explains. Her boss taught her the business from the ground up.

"He was a beautiful guy, the nicest man I ever met," she says of Ed Clark. "He always told me, 'Learn as you handle the parts. When you bring the merchandise in to put it away, always look at it so when you go back to retrieve it, you know where it is.' So I just put my shoulder to the wheel and worked really hard. I got to know the business so well that people would come from all over the city to see that black chick who knew about auto parts.

Especially the black guys would come from all over the city to see this black chick."

By 1964 she was making $125 a week, a good living for the mid-1960s. That year she gave birth to Sheela. Before her daughter turned one, Lucille was able to put a $5,000 down payment on a $12,500 house in a nice neighborhood, a dream that would have been impossible on her wages as a maid.

In her eighth year on the job, Clark made her a proposition: He would set her up in her own auto parts shop. "He was going to finance it, and I was going to run it," Lucille recalls. "He would pay me *x* amount to run it, and at the end of the year, whatever was left, we would split it.

"I couldn't believe it. I'd been on my knees cleaning floors a few years before, and here he was giving me an opportunity to be independent."

To Lucille's sorrow, Clark became ill with prostate cancer, which forced him to put their plans on hold. Six months later, he died.

After taking a few months off, Lucille took a job at another auto parts store. But Clark had planted a dream in her mind: that she could run her own shop. She got encouragement from some of Clark's longtime customers, who followed her to the new shop. "A gentleman used to come in and say to me, 'I don't see why you beat your brains out for this man when you could go out on your own,'" Lucille says.

So Lucille went looking for a suitable building in her price range. She found a storefront on Linwood Avenue, a few blocks from Clark's shop. The inside was filthy, but at $125 a month, the rent was cheap. "The previous tenant had had an egg business, and there was litter and broken eggs everywhere," she recalls. "The owner told me, 'If you clean this up, I'll give you three months free rent.' God is good."

Lucille used $8,000 in savings to remodel the shop's interior and purchase inventory. She named her store F & S Auto Parts, after her children, Frederick and Sheela. She opened for business on May 20, 1970.

## "You've Got to Keep Going"

Compared with other parts shops, her initial inventory was sparse, so for the first year she put all of her profits into building it up. "I'd buy one item, and when I'd sell that I'd buy two more," she explains. "When I sold those, I'd buy three more, and when I sold those, I'd buy five more. That's how I financed my business."

The store was a success from the start. "Things just took off," Lucille recalls. "The customers I used to take care of at Clark's came to my shop instead. The business provided a good living."

A year and a half after opening, Lucille took over the storefront next door so she could begin to sell exhaust systems. A distributor agreed to put them on consignment, and she hired her first employee, who encouraged her to think even bigger.

"He told me the future of F & S was in the building across the street," Lucille recalls. "He was pointing to this building that we're in now, which was occupied by an old 'bump and paint' shop. Oh, my God, I couldn't imagine operating a business in here. This building was so big. I thought, 'No way.'"

But then Providence intervened. A businessman had made inquiries about buying the building for use as a beer store, and the building's manager, a minister, appealed to Lucille to buy it instead. "Reverend Kinney came to me and said, 'We don't want a beer shop coming in here. You've got to buy it.'

"I said, 'Buy it? How can I buy it? I don't have the money.'"

The asking price was $50,000, but to keep out the beer store, the owner was willing to sell it to Lucille for $36,000. She had no qualms about taking on such a big debt, because she was confident that business would be even better at the new location.

"I had seen how successful I could be," she says. "Once you step out, you've got to keep going. With that I was able to put everything under one roof. And with that big service area back there, we could start a service bay right away."

## From Boom to Near-Bust

By offering auto repairs along with auto parts, Lucille doubled her gross almost immediately. She learned the repair business the same way she'd learned the parts business: on the job.

"It's not really as difficult as it sounds, when you know how cars work," she says. "A person comes in, and they know they have a problem, but they can't describe it. They'll say, 'I need a thingamajig for the doohickey.' So, I'd ask them some questions like, 'What is your car doing? How does it sound? How long has this been going on?' And I'd talk to the mechanics about what it might be and learn from what they had to say."

Business was good through the 1970s. At its peak, F & S had three clerks working in the parts shop and six mechanics working full-time in the back, including Lucille's husband, Jeff Washington, whom she'd married in 1971, around the time she opened the bigger shop.

The business became the center of family life for Frederick and Sheela and their numerous cousins. The waiting area served as the de facto living room, and the adjoining kitchen even enabled Lucille to prepare the family's meals.

"When we were thinking about opening a shop together," Lucille recalls, "Mr. Clark told me, 'You make sure it has all the comforts and conveniences of home, because it's going to be your home.' And, boy, that's a fact. We've always had children around here. God is so great that he's given us a job we can do and still be involved with the children, with no need for a babysitter."

Both Frederick and Sheela began working in the store in their preteens. "My mom let me ring up sales on the register from the time I was little," Sheela recalls. "That's how I learned my math. Collecting the money. I just loved that part of the business."

And there were always jobs for Lucille's siblings and her many nieces and nephews, as well as for countless young men who lived in the neighborhood and had few other prospects for work. "There were so many young people whom I was able to give a job to, whether I really needed a new employee or not," Lucille reminisces. "I had one man call me and say he needed a job to get out of county jail. I told him, 'I don't need you, but I'll hire you.' He's straightened himself out now and is driving a truck.

"I guess growing up in the South made me a sentimentalist. There's a famous writer named Edgar A. Guest, who wrote a poem about wanting to live alongside the road so he could be a friend to man. To me, that's what life boils down to."

Says Sheela of her mother's hiring practices, "I think that one reason my mom gives people chances is because Mr. Clark gave her a chance. Most people would have said to her, 'What do you know about cars? You've been scrubbing floors.' But she was willing to learn, so he was willing to hire her, and she's never forgotten that."

The business began changing not long after Ronald Reagan was elected president in 1980, ushering in an era of middle-class flight from many of the nation's Rust Belt cities, as well as federal disinterest in urban revitalization. Lucille watched the neighborhood around her shop deteriorate.

"We used to have more homeowners, more older people who were stable customers," Lucille explains. "And there wasn't an unoccupied storefront in this neighborhood for two miles. But in the eighties, we started to get a lot of blighting here. Even today, there are more unoccupied homes than occupied."

The flight from the neighborhood diminished her customer base. In addition, many of the people who stayed in the neighborhood were too poor to own cars, and many of those who owned cars lost their jobs, making it hard for them to afford car repairs. As a result, both the auto parts and auto repair businesses declined.

"It wasn't easy for us to stay in business," Lucille says. "I was using my fingernails to hang on, and we almost closed."

## Sheela: Different Plans

Although Lucille wanted Sheela to join her in the business after she graduated from Friends School in Detroit in 1982, Sheela had other plans. She wanted to be a photographer. She received about $2,500 in back payments from the Social Security Administration because of the death of her father in 1981. (Although Sheela's parents never married, she says he played an important role in her life.) She used the money to enroll in the Art Institute of Atlanta.

Sheela stayed in school for about a year, until the money ran out, and then took a succession of jobs, including one as a portrait photographer for Sears. She found the work unfulfilling.

"I had been spoiled," Sheela admits. "I had always worked for my mom before, and I didn't have to fear losing my job if I didn't do something right. Working for someone else in Atlanta taught me a lot, especially about the way you talk to employees. You have to treat your employees with respect and be willing to do what you expect them to do."

Sheela became pregnant in 1987. Six months after daughter Amber's birth, she decided to go home to Detroit. Unmarried and estranged from Amber's father, she knew she'd need the help of her extended family to raise her baby. She and Amber moved in with her mother and stepfather and drew welfare benefits. Sheela helped out at F & S when she could, but she was busy raising her daughter and, a few years later, a son, Jordan, so she couldn't spend as much time in the shop as she would have liked.

In 1992, when Jordan was two, Sheela decided to go to work in the shop full-time. She took Jordan and Amber along to the shop with her, and they'd often ride along with her uncle when he picked up parts. "He was my mobile babysitter," Sheela quips.

As she spent more time at the shop, Sheela was shocked to see how much the business had declined since its heyday. "My mom is a very private person, and she hadn't shared her problems with me," Sheela says. "She doesn't like to talk about stuff like that. But once I started working there full-time, I could see that the business was almost at a standstill. We were still making money in the repair shop, but the stock in the parts store was down, and customers stopped coming in because we often didn't have the parts they needed. Plus a lot of the people who had been longtime customers had moved out of the neighborhood, closer to the suburbs."

By this time, competition from chain stores was also becoming a big problem. The 1990s saw the emergence of several megachains, all seeking dominance in the $75-billion-a-year auto parts and repair industry, which brought about the closure nationwide of thousands of independent shops like F & S. By the end of the decade, the dominant parts chain was Memphis-based AutoZone, with 2,565 stores (up from 1,515 just two years before and growing at a rate of one a day).

The increased leasing of cars was also affecting the repair business. "Up until the nineties, leased cars weren't so available," Lucille explains. "Right now, it seems like everybody has a leased car, and they don't bother to maintain them. I had a young woman come in the other day and ask me the price of new pads and rotors on a '99 Caddy. When I told her $70, she said, 'Oh, forget it, I'll just trade it in.' All they have to do is come up with a down payment and keep the payment going and they've got a new car every few years."

Without much discussion, Sheela and Lucille settled on a division of labor that made sense and pretty much continues to this day. "I do the parts chasing, and Sheela works behind the counter," Lucille explains. "Before Sheela came, I was behind the counter and someone else chased parts."

With as many as 6,000 parts in each individual vehicle and almost fifty different models and styles being added by auto manufacturers every year, no auto parts store, even one of the megastores, can stock every part that a customer might need on any given day. So a lot of parts have to be special-ordered from nearby warehouses and picked up. Because the parts warehouse that used to be a few blocks from F & S is no longer there, pickups have often required a fifteen-mile drive to the far suburbs.

A year or so after she took over the counter operation, Sheela began to think that she could benefit from learning more about cars. When Hunter, an alignment company, offered a class on its alignment machine, she took it and passed the certification test with ease. She decided to sign up for other auto-related courses at Wayne County Community College, where she'd already taken a few business courses.

"From growing up around the shop, I knew more than most people, but I didn't have formal training," she explains. "Seeing the respect my mom got because her customers knew she knew her stuff, that made me want to know more too. When I started going to school and learning why things work like this or that, I thought, 'Wow, that's really amazing.' I found I liked the learning experience. And now, when I talk to my customers and my mechanics, I know what I'm talking about. To me, that's very important. I used to feel bad standing up here and telling a customer he needed a really expensive repair when I didn't have a good grasp on why."

Sheela has since taken courses in basic automotive knowledge, automotive electrical systems, brakes, manual transmission and engine rebuilding, and air-conditioning service. She's certified in several subspecialties of automotive repair.

## "Something Had to Change"

Sometime in 1995, Sheela started hearing radio advertisements for a nonprofit organization called the Detroit Entrepreneurship Institute, which was recruiting low-income entrepreneurs for business classes.

"I just kept hearing the ad over and over and over, and then there was a discussion on a talk show about it," Sheela remembers. "It just kept coming up, and I thought, 'Hmmm. Maybe that's something I should do.'

"I knew something had to change here. This business was being run the old mom-and-pop way, where you come in and make money and put it in your pocket at the end of the day and pay the bills as they come in."

The Detroit Entrepreneurship Institute traces its origins to the Detroit Self Employment Project (DSEP), a microenterprise development program started in 1989 at Wayne State University in Detroit. DSEP was part of a national microenterprise demonstration project initiated by the Washington, D.C.-based Corporation for Enterprise Development to test whether self-employment was a viable economic alternative for welfare recipients. The four-year pilot found that self-employment held promise, and in 1996, with financial support from the city of Detroit and several foundations, DSEP had metamorphosed into the Detroit Entrepreneurship Institute (DEI), a freestanding nonprofit.

Sheela couldn't afford the $300 fee for the class, but qualified for a scholarship. She enrolled in the institute's eleven-week "Introduction to Business" class and found it more helpful than the business courses she'd taken at Wayne County Community College.

"DEI made it specific," she says. "The instructors taught us what we needed to know to run our particular businesses. They taught me the steps I need to take to make our business run more successfully."

After completing the introductory course, Sheela went back to DEI periodically for computer training and short courses on select topics, such as certification as a city vendor. In 1998 DEI gave Sheela an Entrepreneurial Spirit Award in recognition of the economic contribution of F & S to its neighborhood.

In 1999, DEI became one of ten organizations from throughout the United States selected for a study on the effectiveness of advanced-level business-consulting services to entrepreneurs who formerly received welfare. The study is sponsored by the Aspen Institute's Microenterprise Fund for Innovation, Effectiveness, Learning and Dissemination (FIELD.) One of FIELD's missions is to increase the sustainability of microenterprise development efforts. Sheela was asked whether she'd be interested in being one of about two dozen DEI clients who would receive technical assistance for up to two years as part of the study. She jumped at the opportunity to get one-on-one consulting from experts on the kinds of problems small business owners face every day.

"When I had finished my course at DEI, I had lost my way," she says. "It was easy to get back into a rut and just let things run the way they always had."

## A Typical Day at F & S

As soon as you walk through the door of F & S, you know you're in a place that services automobiles. The smells of grease, oil, and rubber permeate the air. In the front room, which serves as the parts shop, there are auto parts everywhere—stacked on the floor, perched temporarily on the sales counter, or hung from hooks high up on the pegboard-covered walls. Thousands more parts are stacked neatly on rows of shelves that fill a back room. Dog-eared catalogs of auto parts and automobile specifications line the counter.

Sheela is by herself in the shop this morning, since her mother is out chasing parts. It's shaping up as a typical day. The phone rings every minute or so, and a customer comes through the door about every five minutes. Some are looking for parts so they can repair their cars themselves. Others want to leave their car for repairs or get an early estimate on a future repair so they can start putting money aside. F & S serves a mostly low-income clientele, most of whom drive cars that were manufactured in the '80s or early '90s. The mechanics are even willing to take a crack at cars from the '70s.

Although Sheela is alone in the front room this morning, the three mechanics are all at work in the repair shop.

There's Joe, seventy, a mechanic with more than fifty years' experience who came to work at F & S after retiring from a job at Firestone about eight years earlier. The income supplements his

Social Security check. He specializes in suspensions, brakes, alignments, and air-conditioning repairs. There's Mike, thirty-one, a certified mechanic's assistant who's worked for F & S off and on for ten years. "He's gifted in all aspects of auto repair," Sheela says. Some of his six children sometimes hang out in the shop after school and on Saturdays. And there's Keith, who's also worked for F & S intermittently over the years as a mechanic's assistant. Forty years old, he receives disability payments because of a seizure disorder. But he can earn up to $700 a month at F & S without jeopardizing his benefits.

As Sheela is leafing through the paperwork on the counter, Joe brings a customer in from the front lot, where he's been looking under the hood of a customer's car. "This gentleman needs a tune-up, and possibly a rotor and cap," Joe tells her. "And a new heater core. It's an old Buick. It's been sitting in a body shop for two years."

Sheela begins writing up an estimate. "If you get a major tune-up, it'll probably run you about $195," she tells the customer, who's drinking from a bottle wrapped in a brown paper bag. "That includes the cap rotor and an oil change. With the heater core, altogether you're looking at $445."

The customer looks shell-shocked. "You need all that in cash up front?" he asks.

"No. Let's say $200 in cash," Sheela responds. "And then I can charge the balance."

"You short of cash or something today?" the customer asks playfully.

"No," Sheela responds. "We just want to make sure you come back for your car." A few months ago, F & S began requiring a cash deposit on repair work since so many of the cars it services have such a low book value. Otherwise, the shop risks putting parts and labor into a car that an owner fails to reclaim.

The customer says he'll be back after he stops at an ATM, and he drives off.

A few minutes later, a woman comes in to pick up an alternator that Sheela had special ordered for her '84 Renault. Like many of F & S's customers, she plans to install it herself. "I took it out myself, so I figure I can put it back in myself," she tells Sheela, as Sheela writes out a receipt for $95.

"Just remember to disconnect the battery," Sheela advises. "And be sure to put your receipt in your glove box. That's your warranty."

As she's heading out the door, the customer suddenly does an about-face and returns to the counter. "Hey, how much it would cost me to get a used battery for my car?" she asks.

"I'm not crazy about putting a used battery in with a new alternator because it could blow it," Sheela tells her as she looks through her stock of batteries. "Let me see what my cheapest one is. It's $59." She pulls out a parts manual and leafs through it. "Hmmm. It looks like this one I have here won't work for you. There's another auto parts store down the street, Broadway Transmission. Try there."

Although Sheela may be losing a potential sale to a competitor, it doesn't bother her. "I don't think of them as competition," she says. "We're part of the same community. If I don't have something, I send people to them. And if they don't have something, they send people to me." (Sheela's mother has even been known to drive a customer to another shop if F & S didn't have the needed part. "If he didn't need it, he wouldn't have come here," she has said. "God gave me this responsibility. I feel where I go when I leave is going to be determined by what I did when I was on the earth. This is the final before the final.")

Next in the door is Sheela's brother, Frederick. Over the years, he has periodically worked as a mechanic at F & S, but right now he's a "street mechanic," working on people's cars in front of their homes. "He's got a gift," Sheela says of her brother. "He can listen to a car and tell right away what's wrong with it. And he's a good truck driver too." He has brought along the owner of the car he's working on to pay for the part.

"I need an alternator hose for an '88 Cutlass," Frederick tells Sheela.

She uses a long pole with a grabbing device on the end to pluck the correct alternator hose from its place on a pegboard wall.

"That's $7.37 with tax," she tells him.

"Where's Mother dear?" Frederick asks.

"She had to pick up a part," Sheela responds.

"Tell her I'll probably see her later," he says, as he and his customer head out the door.

Next in the door is a man in his late seventies who's been a customer for years. "I want Joe to check my exhaust," he tells Sheela.

"Gonna leave it with us?" she asks, as she begins to write up a work order.

"Yup," the customer replies. "How's your mama doing?"

"She's doing real well," Sheela says. "What is it, a '75?"

"No, it's a '78, a '78 Lincoln Town Car."

"My mom will be in here later," Sheela tells him as she hands him a copy of the work order. "I'll tell her you were here."

"Maybe I can see her when I come back," he answers, tipping his hat toward Sheela as he turns to leave.

The next customer has a harried look about him. "Is the owner here?" he asks Sheela, who simply shakes her head, since she's on hold on the phone with a warehouse.

"You got a mechanic here?"

"Yup," she answers.

"I'd like him to take a look at this car I got out here," the man says.

Sheela summons Keith from the repair shop, and they accompany the man out front to look at an old GM compact. This will turn out to be the shop's first moral quandary of the day.

### *The Importance of "Idiot Lights"*

The car's owner, a frazzled-looking woman in her early twenties, is standing next to the hood. She's got a sleeping baby and three giggling preschoolers in the car.

The man explains that the woman is his granddaughter's niece, and that the week before she had paid a street mechanic $220 to replace the flywheel on her car. "Now the car's engine is shutting off after she drives it for an hour, and she can't find the guy who worked on it," he says.

Sheela and Keith peer under the hood and ask the owner to start the engine. There's a knocking sound, which they can't immediately diagnose. They ask for the car's history, and the owner tells them she's had it for about a year and has never changed the oil. Keith shakes his head, and Sheela gives her a disapproving look.

"I know, I know," the woman says sheepishly. "I didn't do right."

Keith takes a closer look at the equipment under the hood, and after a few moments tells the woman, "There ain't no new flywheel in here. You got swindled." The woman looks as though she's about to burst into tears.

Her companion asks Sheela what F & S can do for her. "I've known your mother for a long time," he tells Sheela. "I know she'd want to do something nice for this girl."

Sheela doesn't know whether this man is really an old friend of her mother's or not. Plus, if she gave a break to everyone who asked, the shop would be out of business by the end of the week. So she tells the man that it will cost $50 for F & S to diagnose the problem, with the $50 charge to be applied to the repair bill if the woman has F & S fix whatever problem is found. While the man and the woman confer about what to do, Sheela returns to the shop.

A few minutes later, Lucille comes back from a parts run. Sheela tells her mother about the car in the parking lot and asks her to go out and talk to the man who says he knows her. The man greets Lucille with a hug and then he pleads with her to authorize a mechanic to diagnose the car's problem at no charge. "She's already out $220 because some other guy cheated her," he explains.

"I'll see what I can do," Lucille responds. Then she, too, goes over to the car and looks under the hood.

Keith gives her a quick rundown on the car's history and recent problems. She thinks for a moment and then goes into the shop to get a broom. She takes the handle and places it against the water pump, the alternator, and the valve cover, and puts her ear to it, listening as a doctor would a heart.

"Nothing unusual there," she tells the man. "The problem's got to be in the lower section. She probably needs an engine.

"Let me finish my lunch, and then I'll come out and talk to you about what we can do for her."

In the waiting room, which is furnished with a couple of old armchairs draped with floral sheets, Lucille, Sheela, and Keith eat lunch while they talk about what to do. Because he sympathizes with the young woman, Keith wants to do the diagnostic work at no charge. "She's got all those kids with her," he says. "I can't stand to see her stranded."

But Sheela wants to stick with the shop policy of requiring customers to pay for diagnostic work. "Otherwise, you'll put in all that work, and she'll take the car back to another street mechanic to fix," Sheela argues.

Lucille is silent on the subject of what to charge, but from experience, Sheela knows she's probably inclined to give the woman a break.

In the end, they come up with a compromise. If the woman will leave the car with them for the rest of the day, Keith will push it into the service bay and let the engine run until it stops, at which point he'll attempt to diagnose the problem and just charge her $25 for his time, half the usual charge. They head back out to the front lot to tell the car's owner.

Still angry about being cheated by the street mechanic, the woman doesn't want to pay F & S anything. Keith warns her she's not going to get far in the car, given the shape it's in, and urges her to call him on his cell phone if it breaks down. Fighting back tears, she rounds up the preschoolers, who have been playing in the parking lot, and takes off, her tailpipe spewing black smoke.

As she drives off, Lucille shakes her head about the folly of failing to change the oil regularly. "I've had a lot of customers come in here who've told me they've never changed the oil," she says. "All they do is add to it. You really need to try to change it at least every 3,000 miles unless you're using synthetic oil. The oil is the lifeblood of the car. If you don't change it, you blow the motor every time. In this area, we have a lot of blown engines, because people don't maintain their engines. They don't watch the idiot lights."

### *"Life Is Full of Bad News"*

The next customer has been in and out of the shop several times in the last few days. This time, he's come back to see whether a part he ordered for his alternator has come in. In his mid-forties, he suffered a stroke at age twenty-nine and never quite recovered. As usual, he's on foot. His truck seems to be perpetually broken down.

"I've got bad news for you," Lucille tells him. "This part you brought in is the wrong part for your truck. Yours has a nut instead of the press on top."

The man looks as though the news comes as no surprise. "Oh, well, life is full of bad news," he says. "You've got to roll with the punches. I learned a long time ago not to let everything upset me."

With his plan to work on his truck dashed for the moment, he sits down in the waiting room to rethink his day. "I know you want to get it back on the road," Lucille says sympathetically. "It's no fun walking everywhere."

A man in his sixties who teaches at the local elementary school comes in next to pay the bill for a realignment on a '94 Beretta that his adult daughter drives. He, too, is a regular at F & S.

"My name must be on the title to six or seven cars," he explains. "My own and my kids' and grandkids'. Two Berettas, a Honda, '93 Chevy, '94 Cadillac, and a van. Joe's been my mechanic since 1957, when he was still at Firestone."

Since the bill for the realignment is less than he expected, he gives Sheela enough cash both to pay it in full and to apply $200 to his oldest bill, a repair four months earlier to another car. This customer is one of the few Sheela allows to run a tab. "It started when there was a teachers' strike, and we'd known him a long time so we gave him a break," Sheela explains. "I don't do that with many people."

"Are you still in school, Sheela?" the man asks as she finishes the paperwork.

"No, I'm finished for the semester, and I'm going to take the summer off," she says.

"Those credits must be piling up," he observes.

"Yes, they are," she says. "In fact, I need to put in for graduation, because I've got too many credits, though maybe not enough in either of my fields for a degree."

"Hey, Sheela, would you be on the lookout for a new engine for my Lumina? I want to get me a new one. I need the van for carrying lawn mowers from one daughter's house to another."

"Oh, Mr. Richards, you want to rethink that," she tells him. "We just replaced one in a '90 Lumina, and we had to charge $1,600 in labor alone. It's a difficult job, because you got to go in through the bottom. Is it still running for you?"

"It goes eight or nine miles and then it cuts off," he tells her.

"What it probably needs is a new module," she says. "Before it starts getting really warm and you really need it, bring it up and we'll take a look at it."

"Will do," he says, tipping his hat as he leaves the shop.

Another customer comes in. "I just need some cheap oil," he tells Sheela as he steps up to the counter.

"I don't have cheap oil," she responds. "The best I can do for you is this Wolf's Head, at $1.59 a quart. Is it just running through?"

"Well, I know I've got a leak somewhere, but I can't fix it right now, so I just want to add some oil," the customer says. "I was hoping for ninety-nine cents a quart."

"The service station on the corner will sell you that kind, but it'll be recycled oil," Sheela says.

"Okay, then, I guess I'll take two quarts."

In the distance, Sheela spots a car being pushed down the street. "Here comes that girl who was afraid to leave her car with us," she tells her mother. "Keith's pushing it in."

After he pushes the car into the service bay, Keith comes into the waiting room to confer. "Okay, she's back," he announces. "I told her to call me if it stopped on her, and it did. I took a look at it, and it looks to me like her problem is the distributor module. The thing is, all she's got is $50.

"Here's the problem. The girl's stranded with her kids. I want to let her put that $50 towards the part, and then she says she'll pay the labor off when she gets paid at her job. I'm going to do it on the strength of her word because she's got all her kids with her. I can't stand to leave them stranded. If she pays, she pays. If she doesn't, I'm out a few bucks."

Since Keith feels so strongly about giving this young woman a break, Sheela doesn't overrule him. "You're going to be blessed," Sheela tells him. "God will put you in the big house."

### *"I Like the Vibes I Get Here"*

Over the next few hours, about a dozen more customers come in to buy parts or leave their cars for repairs. A tow truck delivers a '94 Mustang whose owner has called in an authorization for its repair. "The young man who owns it used to live in the neighborhood, and now he lives eight miles from here," Lucille says. "That tow truck passed a dozen repair shops on its way here. That makes me feel real good that he would still bring it here."

Toward closing time, a woman in her early thirties comes in for an estimate on a major repair on her '89 Pontiac Sunbird.

The day before, Mike, the mechanic's assistant, had stopped by the woman's home to look at her car, which hasn't been running for a while.

This woman was referred to F & S by a caseworker at the Michigan Family Independence Agency, which runs Michigan's welfare and welfare-to-work programs. She's currently in drug rehab, but will soon graduate and start looking for work, so the agency will pay up to $900 to repair her car.

For the last few months, F & S has been repairing about one car a week for welfare recipients who are making the transition to work. Sheela found out about the reimbursement program through the old girls' network: Her son, Jordan, goes to school with the son of an agency caseworker.

Sheela and her mother like getting referrals from the agency. Lucille remembers how limited her own prospects were as a young woman when she didn't have a car. "It's such a blessing that the state is providing these young mothers with the money for auto repairs, because with a working car they can get out to the suburbs, where the better jobs are," she says. Because Sheela was once a welfare recipient herself, she empathizes with the young mothers who bring her their beat-up old cars and makes a point to treat them with respect. She knows that most of them don't have much experience with car repair shops and are ripe candidates for swindles.

The customer tells Sheela that she's had the car for a year and that it hasn't worked for a few months. She believes the problem started when it fell off the track at a car wash, causing the oil pan to leak. She had the oil pan welded back on to the engine, but says that it hasn't run right ever since. Her brother thinks it needs a thermostat.

Sheela calls Mike in from the shop to ask him what he found when he looked at it. He confirms that the car lacks a thermostat, but points out that it also has a blown head gasket, a far more serious problem.

Sheela explains to the customer just what that means. She tells her that the absence of the thermostat probably meant that the car's previous owner was having problems with pressure building up, which, in turn, led to the blown head gasket. "Usually people take a thermostat out to let the antifreeze run freely so the engine won't build up pressure, which is what shows signs of a problem with the head gasket," she explains. "If you don't have a thermostat, it doesn't build up pressure.

"The problem is it's a really hard engine to find a head for. It might make sense to just find you another used engine, because it's a very small aluminum engine. Let me see what a used engine would run you, if we can even get one."

Sheela calls around in search of a used Sunbird engine.

"Okay, we've found one for $550, plus $550 for labor," she tells the customer as she hangs up from the final call. "It won't be a rebuilt engine. It will be a used engine, hopefully with lower miles that will give you better service. And then after we put a new engine in, we're going to have to find out why it ran hot. It could be that it was because it had a bad thermostat, or it could be something else."

Mike joins the conversation. "It could be the radiator clogging up," he observes. "Or it could be that the fan wasn't coming on. Maybe the relay or the sensor was knocked loose when it fell off the car wash tracks."

Sheela tells the customer, "I don't think the problem started just from the car wash incident. What I really think is that it started running hot, and you just kept running it. It does not take driving a long time for an aluminum engine to crack a head. Unfortunately, people drive until they get to a safe place, instead of stopping the car immediately and having it towed. Driving it another five or ten miles can do fatal damage."

Sheela pulls out an estimate form and lists $1,100 for the purchase and installation of a used engine, $200 for diagnosis and repair of the overheating problem, and $45 for taxes. The total comes to $1,345.

"If we go this route, minus the $900 the state would give you, we're still looking at another $445 out of your pocket," she tells the customer. She hands her a copy of the estimate.

"So what do I do now?" the customer asks. "Just take it to my worker and then call you back?"

"You need to get two more estimates," Sheela tells her.

The customer looks crestfallen. "What if I just want to deal with you?"

"I'm sorry, but the state requires you to get three estimates, and then they make you go with the lowest estimate," Sheela tells her. "It's only if we're the lowest one that you can use us."

"I really want to bring my business here, because I like the vibes I get here," the woman says. "I go by my first thoughts."

Sheela gives her the names of a few other repair shops she can try and then adds, "If I were you, I'd get into the Work First program and work for a while, because then they'll give you a $1,200 check towards a new car. This car you have now would be okay for a secondary car, but it's not going to be a car for you over the long term because the engine is obsolete and hard to find."

"How do you know so much about cars?" the woman asks.

"From my mother," Sheela tells her. "She got started in the business when she went into a parts shop one day, saw a spot of oil on the floor, and wiped it up. The owner was so impressed with her that he offered her a job."

"It's funny how one little act can change your whole life," the customer muses as she turns to leave.

### *Pay Day*

By now, it's closing time. Three last-minute customers come in virtually simultaneously, and each buys a few dollars' worth of parts. Sheela follows the last one to the door and locks it. It's 5:30 P.M., the end of another workday and, since it's Friday, the end of the shop's fiscal week.

This week, the shop has grossed $1,823, not bad for mid-May. Spring and fall months historically bring the lowest revenues, and winter and summer the highest, because extreme weather causes cars to develop problems. In 2000, the shop's best month was January, when it grossed $15,486; its worst month was October, when it grossed $4,793. It's difficult for Sheela to quantify profitability on a week-by-week basis, since the business uses a cash in/cash out accounting method.

Each of the mechanics is paid half of the labor cost billed for each repair he completes, which works out to an average of $350 a week each, before deductions for taxes. Sheela pays herself a salary of $425 every two weeks. The amount bears no relationship to the number of hours she works. "If I paid myself by the hour, the business couldn't afford me," Sheela jokes. "I just figured out what I needed to live on, and that became my salary."

Sheela and her children live rent-free in a house her mother owns, with Sheela taking care of the property taxes ($1,000 a year) and any necessary repairs. Her salary is supplemented with Amber's $700-a-month survivor's benefits check from the Social Security Administration, which Sheela's entitled to because her father died in a car crash when she was two. In addition, she receives a small stipend from the state for taking care of a cousin's child, D'Rose, whom she's come to regard as her own daughter.

Lucille also has outside income—primarily her late husband's Social Security check—which takes care of most of her living expenses. (He died in 1993.) From the business, she takes an owner's draw of 10 percent of the week's gross. Any cash that's left from the week's receipts after payroll is met goes into the business checking account to pay bills.

### Dealing with a Catch-22

It's just after noon on another weekday in May 2001. Keith Gatewood, a DEI business consultant, has stopped by F & S for his regular weekly session with Sheela.

Gatewood, thirty, is one of seven part-time consultants who work with DEI clients through the FIELD program. Gatewood operates a small business of his own, so he has firsthand experience with some of the challenges facing F & S. Lucille takes over the counter as he and Sheela recess to F & S's windowless upstairs office so they won't be interrupted.

At the moment, Gatewood is helping Sheela get the business's affairs in order so that F & S can apply for a $75,000 loan from the Bishop H. Coleman McGehee Economic Justice Fund, a project of the Episcopal Diocese of Michigan. The fund makes below-market-rate loans of up to $100,000 to businesses in disadvantaged areas.

F & S's most pressing need is for $35,000 for roof repairs. Already, Sheela and Lucille have had to block off a section of the building because the roof is sagging ominously. Every time it rains or snows, more damage occurs. "The roof is caving in," Sheela says bluntly. "There are some sections where we've had to put in posts to hold it up. We need a new roof. There's no way around it."

In the past, F & S has applied for conventional repair loans, but has been turned down. "The issue is that we don't make enough right now to be able to pay back a loan," Sheela says.

But now, she has come up with a plan to increase revenues enough so that the business can afford loan repayments. She wants to install two oil-changing bays and begin offering while-you-wait oil changes. A prospectus that Sheela developed assumes a demand for ten oil changes a day at $21.95 each. At that level of demand, the F & S gross would be $219.50 a day, $1,317 a week, or $68,474 a year (about two-thirds of F & S's total annual revenues in 2000). According to Sheela's calculations, as much as one-third of the revenue from the oil-changing operation would be profit.

However, it would cost almost $20,000 to convert an unused corner of the building to accommodate the bays. So, Sheela is seeking an additional $20,000 to use as operating capital, which, along with the $35,000 for the roof, adds up to a total loan request of $75,000.

Week by week, Keith and Sheela have been tackling some of the problems that Sheela needs to solve before she can apply for the loan. For the most part, Gatewood tells Sheela what she already knows she has to do. However, hearing it from him—and knowing she has to report back about her progress—somehow makes it easier to get done. "This is my baby and my responsibility," she says. "But when the counselor comes, it makes me really think about things and put my ideas in words. He helps me be accountable."

"I'm a consultant, but I'm also a coach," Gatewood explains. "I'm here to help her figure out how to maximize her strengths and minimize her weaknesses."

He and Sheela get down to business. "So, how was last week?" he asks. "Did you do everything that we agreed you should do?"

One of her assignments for the last week was to meet with a certified public accountant to start developing a plan for keeping the business's books in a more professional way. At the moment, Sheela keeps track of revenues and expenses on a computer and then turns the paperwork over to the bookkeeper who has prepared her mother's tax returns for twenty years.

"The meeting went very well," she tells him. "He told me that I should use a payroll service, which would keep track of all my taxes and do it more quickly than I do."

But Sheela isn't sure she wants to turn over her books to this accountant. "I told him I want to make QuickBooks [software] work for me, because I paid all this money for it and I want to get my investment out of it," she explains. "But he doesn't work with QuickBooks, so he told me my choice was to find someone to work with me on that or go to a class or just not use it."

Gatewood wants Sheela to turn the books over to an accountant. "You don't have the time to be tied up doing QuickBooks," he tells her. "Your job is to be the point person for this company. The time you spend doing data entry is a cost center, not a profit center. It takes up too much of your time. The main thing is to get your business under control.

"You're going to have to make some hard choices. Are they going to be painful? Yes. But you'll be better off in the long run."

Sheela acknowledges Gatewood's point. "The accountant said the same thing, that I'd be wasting too much time trying to work on QuickBooks," she says. "But I want to see it up and running. I want to see all my parts on the computer. This has been two years in the making. Then when I go to the CPA, I'll have more information for him to use." Whether or not Sheela hires this particular CPA, she knows she needs a CPA instead of a bookkeeper.

The conversation turns to one of the business's biggest problems, the lack of documentation of its inventory. "The inventory's all out of whack," Gatewood explains. "F & S doesn't know what it has. You can't even quantify from a dollars-and-cents standpoint what's in the store. If you don't know what you have, how do you know what to order? It's all that dollars and cents tied up there, plus the shelf space, and the time spent looking for it. And besides, there is probably some inventory that's rotted and not any good anymore. We need to work on getting those things out of here, even if someone is only going to pay us a quarter on the dollar."

Sheela tells Gatewood that she's planning to take inventory over Memorial Day weekend, two weeks from now. "That's a good move," he tells her.

The next item for discussion is the status of the pre-application for the McGehee Fund loan that Sheela was supposed to have filled out last week. She hasn't finished it yet. Gatewood suggests that she complete it while he's there.

Perhaps the biggest problem F & S has to overcome if it's going to qualify for the loan is its lack of insurance. Lenders require insurance on any property that's being used as collateral. Sheela's mother stopped her insurance coverage years ago because she couldn't afford the premium. Now, with the roof falling in, she probably couldn't even get insurance. "It's a catch-22," Sheela explains. "Without insurance, we can't get a loan for a new roof. Without a new roof, we can't get insurance."

Gatewood is hopeful that the McGehee Fund managers will understand the dilemma and make allowances. "The idea behind this fund is to make loans to businesses in lower-income communities," he says. "We have a building here that's owned free and clear. There's equity in it. Once she gets the roof fixed, she can put in two new bays for oil changes, bring two new people on board from the local vocational school to do the oil changes, and generate enough new revenue to repay the loan, pay the insurance premiums, and invest in inventory.

"This fund is a good fit because this is a business that's been around for thirty-plus years in an area that fits the loan. She meets all the criteria if she can support the loan financially. I know they're going to take a really hard look at it, because loan loss is very expensive. They've had some businesses that haven't repaid. But there's a lot of selling that goes into getting a loan, and I'm going to be there for her."

Gatewood supports Sheela's plan to install oil-changing bays. "AutoZone is going to move in within two miles of here," he notes. "You can't beat them on price. So you're going to have to find a niche, because if a part is a dollar less down the street, people are going to go there unless you can offer something else.

"In the future, I see F & S doing more auto repair and maintenance rather than selling more parts. AutoZone only sells parts. But everybody needs their oil changed. F & S can emphasize other services at the point of sale. It's important that the customer understand that it's a lot easier to shell out $50 for maintenance now than $200 for a repair later."

Sheela nods in agreement. "Preventive maintenance, that's what I like to sell my customers on," she says. "I like to let my customers know, 'These are the things you're going to need. Don't wait until you hear a noise.'"

Gatewood shifts to the next item on the agenda. "Shall we talk about marketing now?" he asks.

"It's going to be short and sweet," Sheela responds.

"Why? What's going on?" he asks.

"Because I have not done any marketing," she says sheepishly.

"We're going to have to set some deadlines for you," Gatewood warns in a mock stern voice.

"We can set some deadlines, because they're workable now that I'm out of school," Sheela responds.

The two agree that in the next two weeks, Sheela will come up with a plan to mail out a promotional postcard for a summer air-conditioning special. Because of a change in the environmental protection laws, the servicing of automobile air-conditioners now requires a special machine and a certified technician. One of the mechanics is already certified, and Sheela recently took the course required for certification as well. She also bought the necessary freon-exchange machine for $425 at a bankruptcy auction of Montgomery Ward's inventory. Sheela believes that the expense involved in complying with the new law means that F & S will be one of the few repair shops in the neighborhood that will be able to offer air-conditioning service this summer.

At Gatewood's urging, Sheela also agrees to put together some promotional literature about her business to take to the Michigan Family Independence Agency. Right now, only one caseworker, the mother from Jordan's school, is making referrals to her. "If you expand that relationship, instead of having them send you two or three people a month, it could grow to twenty or thirty," Gatewood points out.

"Ask if you can make a presentation," Gatewood continues. "I'll help you put it together. You can tell them a little about your history. Include the articles that have been written about the business. Be sure to mention that you were once on aid yourself."

Gatewood concludes the meeting by laying out what he expects of Sheela in the next week—progress on the loan application, the summer promotion, and a presentation to the agency—and what she can expect of him: help with all three.

Gatewood thinks that the business has good prospects for success if Sheela can get the loan. "The business has great customer relations," he says. "Their repeat customer rate is good. But it's going to take some time to get this business to the next level. When you have a company that someone built from the ground up and they're getting older, turning the reins over is hard—even if it's to your own child.

"Sheela has incredible foresight," he continues. "She's very knowledgeable about her trade. And she's very, very personable. She's a warm, friendly woman, but she's also a straight shooter.

"Sheela just needs to get the people in place—an accountant, an insurance agent, an attorney—to help her where she needs it. She can't be the jack-of-all-trades. I'd like her to get away from the counter and attend to other aspects of the business. Her priority needs to be to market and manage and grow her company."

Sheela doesn't quarrel with his assessment. "The biggest part of the puzzle is management," she says. "That's where our weakness is. Until everything internally is organized better, the business can't really grow."

## "The Car Business Is in My Genes"

As the business heads into its thirty-second year, Sheela, thirty-six, is taking increasing responsibility for both day-to-day operations and long-term planning. She and her mother have never formalized their business relationship, but Lucille treats Sheela as a de facto partner and defers to her on most business decisions.

Her one condition is that Sheela keep the business focused on quality customer service. "You've got to do what the customer wants," Lucille says. "That's why we've been able to be in business for thirty-one years."

Even though her mother has given her carte blanche, Sheela is proceeding cautiously for fear of jeopardizing their mother-daughter relationship, which is close. "I'm trying to do it her way as much as I can, because she's still my mother," Sheela says. "She's been running the business her way for thirty years. But sometimes, I'll have to say to her, 'Lucille, we're not mother and daughter between 9 A.M. and 5 P.M. This is business. We've got to do things this way.' Over the long term, I'm going to run it like it's supposed to be run."

Sheela knows that the business faces many challenges if it is to survive, let alone flourish, and that the odds against F & S are long. Of eight black-owned parts stores in Detroit that used to buy as a group as recently as a decade ago, only two remain in business, Lucille says.

That's mostly because the auto parts business is increasingly dominated by corporate players, which can offer better retail prices because they're getting volume discounts on parts. Indeed, fewer and fewer wholesalers are even willing to sell to small stores like F & S. "If you don't spend at least $1,500 a month, you can't even buy from them," Lucille says. "As for delivery, forget about it. They figure the little man is not important, and yet we were the shops that helped get them where they are."

The regulatory climate of the twenty-first century is also more difficult than it was when F & S began servicing cars in 1975, just a few years after the modern environmental movement was born. There were very few environmental regulations then for Lucille to worry about. Now, just the *summary* of the federal and state environmental regulations that affect the auto service industry fills a whole one-inch binder.

Already, F & S has gotten out of the tire-selling business, partly because of the cost of disposing of old tires. "We'll do family and friends, but not walk-ins," Sheela says. Under Michigan law, businesses that generate waste tires must contract with a registered scrap tire hauler to get rid of them or face fines of up to $10,000 and up to ninety days imprisonment. Each used tire costs F & S $1.50 to get rid of.

The disposal of potentially hazardous substances such as motor oil, used oil filters, spent antifreeze, and dead batteries is also highly regulated. Antifreeze can usually be recycled in-house, and battery manufacturers accept used batteries for recycling. But it's up to each individual auto repair shop to arrange for proper disposal of its waste oil and filters. "It used to be that someone paid us for waste oil, and now I need to pay someone to take it away," Sheela says. "I believe in what they're doing, but OSHA and EPA and all those other wonderful government people are a pain in the butt."

With two years of junior college behind her and an aptitude for business, it's clear that Sheela could easily move into a career that requires fewer hours, pays better, and carries less financial risk. But she doesn't want to.

"God didn't bring us this far to drop us," she says. "If we just give it up, everything my mother's done will have been in vain. We have to keep our vision and focus.

"The car business is in my genes," she continues. "I don't care what I do or where I go. I will always want to be up under someone's car, figuring out a problem."

*Life has presented huge obstacles for artisan Roselyn Spotted Eagle, but her Indian crafts business provides her family with enough extra income to meet her family's needs.*

chapter 4

# "I'm Lucky to Be Alive"
# Roselyn Spotted Eagle
# Spotted Eagle Enterprises
# Kyle, South Dakota

When President Bill Clinton blazed across the country on his whirlwind "poverty tour" in the summer of 1999, he stopped at the Pine Ridge Indian Reservation in southwestern South Dakota.

There were plenty of good reasons why the president chose Pine Ridge as a backdrop for his attempt to draw attention to areas left behind in the economic boom of the 1990s.

Shannon County, which includes most of Pine Ridge, is the poorest county in the United States, with two-thirds of its residents living below the poverty line. In good times or bad, the unemployment rate hovers around 73 percent. Almost 30 percent of reservation residents lack homes of their own (they're doubled or tripled up with relatives), and 59 percent live in what the Indian Health Service classifies as substandard housing. Almost a fifth live in homes without running water. A majority lack telephones.

A few years ago, reservation resident Roselyn Spotted Eagle, in her mid-60s, would have fallen into most of these categories. Crippled by rheumatoid arthritis, she was trying to support herself, a physically disabled adult daughter, and a mentally disabled grandson on federal disability payments that barely covered their basic needs.

For sixteen years, the family lived in a two-room cabin without running water. Her daughter sometimes had to crawl to the outhouse in the backyard.

But in fall 1997, Roselyn was able to move her family into a three-bedroom trailer, complete with indoor plumbing and even a washer and dryer. What made that possible was income from an Indian crafts business she started with training, technical support, and loans from the Lakota Fund, a reservation-based economic development organization.

Since 1986, when it began as a project of the First Nations Development Institute of Fredericksburg, Virginia, the Lakota Fund has been assisting small Indian-owned businesses on the reservation, home to 28,000 members of the Oglala Sioux tribe. With the help of the Lakota Fund, Roselyn was able to parlay the traditional beadworking, quiltmaking, and cooking skills she learned from her mother into income that supplements her family's disability payments. While her business income amounts to less than $10,000 a year, it has meant a world of difference to her family's quality of life.

Roselyn's story shows the importance of microenterprise as a "patching" strategy for low-wage workers and people who are dependent on insufficient government benefits for their income.

"I had a difficult life when I was growing up," she says. "I remember my mother telling me to learn how to bead and make quilts so I could earn my own money. She told me, 'One of these days, you can earn money doing this for people.' I'm working so hard now to make sure my family's life is better than mine was."

## "Sometimes, There Was No Food"

Roselyn's life began in circumstances that most Americans can't even imagine—even those born, as she was, in the years just after the Great Depression. She was born in 1938 in a log house near the village of Kyle, which is situated in the north-central part of the reservation, about two hours east of Rapid City. The house had no electricity and no running water; to pick up supplies, family members had to ride an hour in a horse-drawn wagon along dirt roads. Two older brothers died before Roselyn was old enough to form memories of them. After her birth, four other sisters were born in quick succession.

Roselyn's father died during the blizzard of 1949, a series of storms that paralyzed the Upper Midwest for seven weeks and produced drifts thirty-five feet high. He had come home from World War II in ill health and had never really recovered. During the blizzard, he ran out of medication for his epilepsy and suffered one uncontrollable and damaging seizure after another. "We couldn't get help because the snow was too high to get to the road," Roselyn recalls. "Finally, a plane dropped some medication near the house, but it was too late for him. He couldn't even swallow."

Because Roselyn's father had worked before the war, the family received Social Security survivors' benefits—about $35 a month for each child, according to Roselyn's memory, enough to meet the basic needs of his widow and five daughters. "At that time, everything was cheaper," Roselyn explains. "It was easier to live."

Two years after her husband's death, Roselyn's mother married another man and quickly gave birth to two more daughters. Roselyn's stepfather was a traditional dancer, and an adopted brother was a hoop dancer. Their dances required them to wear intricately beaded costumes, and Roselyn helped her mother craft them out of deerskin and elk hide. She also learned to make the traditional Star quilts for which the Sioux are famous. (Around the turn of the century, Mennonite missionaries had taught quilting to the Sioux, who felt a special affinity for the Star design because they viewed it as symbolizing the unity of the Lakota nation.)

When Roselyn's stepfather died just a few years into the marriage, her mother began a downward slide. She drank and neglected her children. Since Roselyn was the oldest, it fell to her to take care of her little sisters. "Sometimes, there was no food around, and I wouldn't know what to cook for them," Roselyn says. "I'd have to go out and dig up some wild turnips and boil them with a little lard for flavoring. Sometimes, I'd take them all down to the creek to gather chokecherries, and we'd grind them and make Indian pudding."

To pay for her drinking, Roselyn's mother sold off the family's sixty horses, one by one. Then she sold the property's windmill and water tank. Finally, she even sold the land her first husband had inherited from his family. "We used to have 360 acres," Roselyn says. "I don't know what she sold it for or what she got for it or where the money went besides drink."

With the family's home gone, Roselyn's formal education ended shortly after she had started eighth grade at Little Wound School in Kyle. "People said I was really smart," she remembers. "I always got all A's. But my mother made me get married."

## "I Feel Lucky to Be Alive"

For the first few years of marriage at the age of seventeen, Roselyn and her husband got along fine, although there's no question their lives were hard. "We lived with his grandparents, who were very old, and I had to do all the work around their house," she recalls. "There was no running water, so I hauled water from the creek in buckets. And it was my job, too, to chop all the wood for the stove."

Over six years, Roselyn gave birth to three children: Daniel, in 1957; Noah, in 1959, and Ramona, in 1961. Her last child, Bruce, was born in 1969. In between Daniel's and Bruce's births, Roselyn suffered five miscarriages or stillbirths, as well as the death of a day-old infant.

She almost lost Ramona, too. When Ramona was seven months old, she began showing signs of cerebral palsy following a bout of what may have been spinal meningitis. (Roselyn never received a firm diagnosis since there was no doctor on the reservation then.) All Roselyn knew was that Ramona had once been a healthy, active baby, but for months after her illness she couldn't move at all.

Soon after Ramona became sick, Roselyn's husband started drinking heavily. "After he started, he couldn't stop," Roselyn says. He spent most of what he earned from his job as a gravel truck driver on alcohol. "Because he was the only one earning money, all his friends would come over to our place, and they'd drink all the money up," she remembers. "He'd go out with them and come home with nothing. He never bought the kids clothes or anything."

During this period, Roselyn sometimes took in piecework from a moccasin factory so she'd have some money to buy her children school clothes. "I laced so many that I got calluses on my hands," she says. Yet the most she ever made was $40 a week.

Besides being a drunk, Roselyn's husband was abusive. Years later, her body still bears scars from the wounds he inflicted. She shows a visitor long, jagged scars on her neck and back from the time he stabbed her—the loss of blood nearly killed her—as well as a scar above her upper lip from the time he kicked her in the face. Once he even pushed her into a reservoir in an attempt to drown her. Roselyn still has flashbacks and nightmares about it. "I fell headfirst into the water," she says. "I can still remember seeing little Ramona, who was only four or five, crying and trying to crawl towards me."

Though she couldn't swim, Roselyn somehow managed to get to shore by herself, and her husband, by then contrite, helped her out.

"I tried to leave a couple of times," she says. "Whenever I'd do that, he'd apologize and say, 'I won't drink no more.' So I'd go back, and then he'd do the same thing. Over and over it would happen.

"I feel lucky to be alive."

## No Place to Hide

One of the reasons Roselyn had difficulty leaving her husband was that there was nowhere for her to go. In that era—the 1960s and early 1970s—the tribal police didn't regard domestic violence as a crime. In addition, there were no shelters for battered women, either on the reservation or in any cities nearby (even in 2002, spaces were still very limited). For a long time, Roselyn's family was reluctant to get involved. "He was really mean, and everybody was scared of him," she says. "I couldn't go back to my relatives, because he'd threaten the whole family."

Finally, after a particularly bad beating sometime in the early 1970s, Roselyn left her husband for good. "I left everything behind and just took our clothes and some blankets and the kids," she says. She and the children began receiving public assistance, "just enough to pay the rent and buy groceries and clothes for the kids to go to school."

To spite her, Roselyn's husband sold the family's furniture and the children's toys, and then began selling off the family's land. "He sold one parcel and drank it up, and then another parcel and drank it up," she says.

For most of the next few years, Roselyn moved from one relative's home to another, trying to stay one step ahead of her husband. She could hardly sleep because of the worry that she might wake up and find him standing over her. "Good thing we were usually living way up the road, because I could see him coming and take off," she says, with humor that belies the terror she felt at the time. "We'd hide in the bushes, and he'd go away." Eventually, Roselyn and the children moved into public housing in Kyle.

In 1977, two years after their divorce was finalized, Roselyn's ex-husband killed himself. The children inherited a little parcel of land along the road leading from Kyle to Wanblee. Roselyn managed to scrape together enough money to buy an old one-bedroom trailer and move it to the land.

With her youngest child, Bruce, finally in school all day, Roselyn was able to go out and get her first full-time job, as an ambulance driver, for which she earned minimum wage. "It was good money," she says. "It kept us going." Working out of the jail in Kyle, she drove an emergency medical technician to the scenes of car wrecks, heart attacks, and illnesses and, when warranted, transported the victims fifty miles to the hospital in Pine Ridge.

It was a tough job for a single mother living in an area where child care generally meant self-care. When Bruce came home from school, he was in the care of Ramona, then sixteen, who still couldn't walk. One day while Roselyn was at work, Bruce, then six, fell off a roof at the home of an aunt and fractured both a hip and a knee. He was confined to a body cast for six months, so Roselyn now had both a sixteen-year-old and a six-year-old who couldn't walk. Roselyn's older sons built a lean-to out of pine logs and pine branches, and Ramona and Bruce spent their days there.

After learning of the family's circumstances, the tribe's Home Improvement Program built the family a two-room cabin next to the dilapidated trailer. Even though it had no indoor plumbing, it was a big improvement over the trailer.

## Another Mouth to Feed

Just when it seemed the family's luck was improving, the grant that financed the ambulance service ran out, and Roselyn was laid off. She went back on welfare while she looked for another job. In 1982 she found one as a bus driver for the Head Start programs on the reservation. "I drove all over the place to pick up little children to bring them to the center in Kyle," she says. "I made $4 and something an hour. It meant a lot to me."

Four and a half years into the job, Roselyn developed health problems. She went to a doctor and found out that she had suffered two dislocated disks in a car wreck a few years before. Untreated at the time, the disks were now too heavily scarred to be repaired, and her spine was riddled with arthritis as well. She also had rheumatoid arthritis in her knees, and her circulation was so bad that she had chronic ulcers on her ankles, which wouldn't heal. "I would hurt so bad that I couldn't stand up," she says. In 1987 she went on Social Security disability.

A few years later, Roselyn learned that a grandson, Chico, was about to be placed in a foster home. Roselyn's son, Bruce, who had fathered Chico, was still in high school and in no position to rear him himself. So Roselyn agreed to take him in and raise him as her own son, even though it meant another mouth to feed on an income, at the time, of less than $900 a month.

To make her own and Ramona's disability checks stretch to cover her new expenses, Roselyn began making beaded moccasins for Indian dancers. But she didn't, at this point, regard what she was doing as a business. It was more like a hobby that provided pocket change.

## The First Lakota Entrepreneurs

Though Roselyn didn't know it when she started making moccasins, in 1986 the First Nations Development Institute of Fredericksburg, Virginia, had begun working with a reservation-based economic development project called the Lakota Fund. There was no source of capital for small business owners—or aspiring owners—on the reservation, and, with technical assistance from First Nations, the Lakota Fund set out to fill that void.

Its founders knew that more than money was going to be needed. There was virtually no tradition of free enterprise on the reservation, a result of both the Sioux culture of sharing and decades of neglect by lenders, so the Lakota Fund organizers knew they needed to offer training and technical assistance along with loans.

"We're the first generation of Lakota entrepreneurs," explains Monica Terkildsen, chief of operations for the Lakota Fund and a staff member almost since the beginning. "There's a lot of interest in starting a business, but not many people have the knowledge to do what it takes. We're coming out of a society that has no history of mom-and-pop businesses, so there's no one to go to, to ask how it's done."

When the Lakota Fund started, there were fewer than forty businesses on the sprawling 2-million-acre reservation, the nation's second largest, and most were owned by non-Indians. Each year, reservation residents were spending about $75 million in personal income outside the reservation's borders, simply because there were few places to buy anything on the reservation.

By this time, the Grameen Bank in Bangladesh had been receiving a lot of attention around the world for helping poor Bangladeshi women become entrepreneurs by lending them tiny amounts of money. The Lakota Fund thought that approach could also work on the reservation, which has much in common with a developing country like Bangladesh. The fund came up with the idea of forming "banking circles" of reservation residents who were interested in making money from self-employment or small business enterprises (similar to the peer lending circles that the Good Faith Fund was running in Arkansas).

When the Lakota Fund began organizing its first banking circle in Kyle early in 1990, Terkildsen went door to door, explaining the concept and looking for recruits. At first, Roselyn was skeptical. "I didn't pay them much attention," she recalls, smiling as she thinks about what her life might have been like if she had never overcome her lack of interest. "I was scared that by joining it would cut down on my disability income. But they gave me a bunch of papers, and after some time I got interested. It seemed like a good opportunity for me. It seemed like it would be interesting to do something like that instead of just staying at home."

Roselyn quickly grasped how beneficial it would be to have a ready source of funds to buy supplies, instead of waiting for her disability check and using whatever was left over after paying her household expenses. "At this time, I was having trouble buying supplies," she explains. "Sometimes I'd run out of supplies and have to wait until my next check came to buy more.

So I had a couple meetings with them about forming a circle, and then I went out and asked people that I knew were making quilts and key chains, 'Do you want to join a circle?' Some of them agreed to come over and meet with us. We finally got enough people together to form a circle, and we started our orientation in August."

## Borrowing Money for Materials

Getting Roselyn on board was important to the project's credibility, Terkildsen says, because the community respects her. "Her beadwork is so well known in the powwow circles," Terkildsen explains. "But the biggest strength Roselyn brought to us was her integrity. And she was very good at helping us recruit others. She had in her mind who she wanted to recruit, so she and I just jumped in our little company car and went and talked to them."

Under the Lakota Fund's circle banking model, members of a new circle undergo five weeks of training in record keeping, cost control, pricing, and other business practices. Roselyn found the training sessions very useful.

"The budgeting and decision-making workshops started me to thinking about how important it was to budget," she says. They also helped her move from thinking of her work as a hobby to regarding it as a real business.

In a Personal and Business Vision Worksheet filled out early on, she expressed her goals for the year: to expand her business and receive more orders; to take on different projects besides moccasins, such as a beaded buckskin dress; and to be able to buy furniture for her cabin.

Somewhat later, in a questionnaire she filled out about her business concept, she elaborated on her vision. She described her key competitive advantages as "personal service, detail, easy to get hold of, reliable, already have a customer market," indicating that she already had a good idea of her strengths. She also wrote about her desire to expand into other products, such as silk baby and full-size Star quilts, cradle boards, and beaded vests.

There were six members of Roselyn's circle, which they named *Pejuta Haka O*, meaning Medicine Root Circle. The four other female members were also interested in developing crafts businesses, and the sole male member, David "Shorty" Janis, was interested in starting a tire repair shop. (Because Shorty is illiterate, the Lakota Fund staff had to develop pictographs to teach him business concepts—for instance, a bag with a dollar sign on it signified "money in," while a truck with a dollar sign on it signified "money out.")

After the training ended, the circle met twice a month in what was then the Lakota Fund's headquarters, a small geodesic dome across from Little Wound School, which Roselyn had been forced to drop out of decades earlier. Each member of the circle contributed fifty cents a meeting to the Inner Circle Fund, which, under the fund's rules, could be tapped for emergencies such as funerals, medical expenses, or an unpaid heating bill. They would talk about ideas for their businesses and, through brainstorming, arrive at a solution to a particularly thorny problem that one of them had encountered (such as how to deal with a customer who hadn't paid).

When one of the circle members was ready to borrow money from the Lakota Fund, the others would vote on the request. Roselyn and Shorty took out the first loans—for about $400 each—in September 1991. The capital came from loans from investors. The interest on the loans was put into the Inner Circle Fund. The collateral was, in essence, the agreement by members of the circle to repay any loans on which a borrower reneged.

Roselyn used the proceeds from her first loan to buy material and thread for quilts and leather and beads for her beadwork. She had never before been able to buy everything she needed all at once. "The loan helped me to expand my business, because it helped me to get my products done on time," she says. "Before, it would take me longer to get the work done because I'd have to wait to get money to buy supplies."

Roselyn took a year to pay off her first loan, in twice-monthly installments of $17.44 each, which included interest calculated at a rate of 15 percent (somewhat less than she would have been charged by a conventional lender in Rapid City, had there been a lender willing to go to the trouble of making such a small loan). In the meantime, she was also putting $5 per meeting into savings, the first time she'd ever been able to set aside money for a rainy day. "It felt really good to know I had money there if I needed it," she says.

In March 1993 she took out a second loan, this time for $840. "That time I bought materials and a sewing machine, too, because my other one gave out," she recalls. The payments on that loan were $35 every two weeks, which Roselyn had no trouble making with the growing income from her business. She paid off that loan in August 1994.

Then in late January 1995, she borrowed $619.50 to purchase leather soles, sinew, beads, and needles. Her loan payments were $25.73 twice a month. She paid off the loan, on schedule, in April 1996. "Roselyn is always really good about paying back her loans," says Lia Whirlwind Horse, the Lakota Fund's loan collection assistant. "I've never had to go after her."

Roselyn's access to capital came just as interest in Native American traditions and rituals was exploding both on and off the reservation. "Long time ago, there was just one powwow and one sun dance every year," Roselyn points out. "Now, there are sun dances all over the district, one in every community." Powwows and sun dances mean ceremonial dancing, and that requires beaded moccasins, leggings, and armbands, which in turn mean more orders for Roselyn.

"In the old days, the family did their own beadwork," she notes. "Now, a lot of them hire people like me. And when the people at the powwows see their costumes, they ask them where they got them, and then they come to me and say, 'I'd like something like that next year.' That's how I get my orders."

At times, Roselyn has found herself with more beadwork and quilt orders than she can handle. When that happens, she farms out some of the beadwork to her sister Delores. "I do the designs, and she does the finishing, but only on things like cuffs, armbands, and leggings," Roselyn explains. "She can't do the moccasins, because they're too hard. It takes special skill to do those."

If a client wants a Star quilt done by hand, Roselyn sometimes gets another sister, Delissia, to do it for her. "I lend her gas money, and she does my hand-quilting to pay me back," Roselyn explains. "That's how I do business with her."

## Growing Responsibilities

From Roselyn's point of view, the Lakota Fund's circle banking project got under way just in time. Taking custody of her three-month-old grandson, Chico, in 1989 meant buying more groceries, clothes, and diapers, so the income from her beadwork business became essential to maintaining the family's stability.

Rearing Chico turned out to be more challenging than Roselyn expected. Although he seemed normal in infancy, his development did not progress. At the age at which other children begin babbling, Chico knew just a few words. At the age at which other children begin to speak in full sentences, Chico gave one-word answers. Although Roselyn suspected there was something wrong with him, she didn't know what, nor did she know whom to ask. "It was only after he started school, when he was about six, that they told me he had serious problems," she says. "He couldn't talk much, and he had epileptic seizures."

No one knows whether Chico's problems are due to a genetic disorder, prenatal exposure to alcohol, or something that happened to him as a baby. Whatever the cause, he's unlikely ever to be able to live independently. In 1995, with the help of school officials, Roselyn got Chico qualified for Supplemental Security Income of about $500 a month, which, in effect, increased the household's monthly income by about 50 percent, since Roselyn and her daughter each received about $500 as well. Chico also began attending special education classes, where he eventually learned to talk. But at age eleven, he still has not learned to read. "He once said to me, 'Mom, I need a new brain so I can read,'" Roselyn says.

In the summer of 2000, while school was out, Roselyn worked hard to teach him numbers. Although he seemed able to memorize the words for numbers, Roselyn wasn't sure how well he comprehended the concepts behind them. "They say a baby born with a pierced ear, like Chico has, they're like an old man," Roselyn says. "That's what he's like."

## Pricing for Profit

Although the heart of the circle banking model was peer-to-peer lending, with circle members deciding which of their individual enterprises to invest in, the support services provided by Lakota Fund staff members have been key to the success of the businesses. As circle members encounter issues involving their growing businesses, Terkildsen and other staff members offer training to help tackle those issues. "I took all of their classes—budgeting, pricing, record keeping, time management," Roselyn says. "I took them all, because I just love them. I listen and write down everything. I like to think of new ways to earn money."

Pricing has been a problem for every member of Roselyn's circle. "Entrepreneurs always struggle with this, but especially around here," Terkildsen explains. "Customers want to pay the same price they've always paid. And our artists feel bad about asking too much for the cost of their labor.

"Another problem is that craftspeople who haven't been trained are hurting the market. If Roselyn decided she needed to charge $100 for a pair of children's moccasins to make it worth her while and someone else was charging $50, she couldn't compete, even if her quality was much better."

Roselyn remembers the first time Terkildsen chided her for charging too little for a pair of moccasins. "One time a man wanted to pay me $65 for a pair of plain moccasins," Roselyn recalls. "Monica told me, 'I think they're worth more than that.' She told me to keep track of my time and the stuff I used. The next time I made a pair that size, I kept track of my time and the cost of supplies, and it came to $75, so that's what I charge now."

Roselyn tries to price her labor at $5 an hour, but she can't always charge that amount, for fear of losing business to a cheaper competitor. For instance, right now she's hard at work on an order for thirty full-size Star quilt tops, placed by a family in nearby Porcupine for a "giveaway" ceremony at a powwow in August. (To mark special events, such as a college graduation or a child's departure for the Army, many Sioux families give away Star quilts as a way of expressing thanks to the cycle of life.) She'll be paid $45 for each for these tops.

However, each of the star's eight points takes her thirty minutes to stitch together, for a total of four hours of work. Then she has to join the points, attach the corners, add a border, and sew on a back. Not counting the time she's put in shopping for the fabric and cutting it into little pieces, she'll have at least seven hours invested in each quilt top, plus $15 worth of materials. After paying for the materials, that means she'll be making $30 from each quilt, or about $4 an hour, well below her goal.

Roselyn prefers not to think of it that way. Instead, she thinks of it as a $1,200 order. After she pays back the $292 loan she took out to buy some of the materials, she'll have a $900 profit, enough to pay some of her outstanding bills.

## A "Duffel-Bag Approach" to Marketing

Almost from the beginning, marketing has been one of the most important services Lakota Fund staff members provide to their lenders, most of whom are arts and crafts producers. "We had two enterprise agents, me on the west side of the reservation and someone else on the east side, and we were always looking for places to sell artwork," Terkildsen recalls. "When we first started, it was just a duffel-bag approach, hauling it here and there. I'd carry art with me wherever I went, and we'd set up a booth at all the powwows. I was always hustling markets."

As the number of active banking circles grew to five, it became clear to the Lakota Fund's board that it would make sense to open a retail center committed to both stocking the raw materials the craftsmen needed and selling their goods. In 1995, when the Lakota Fund moved into its new 13,000-square-foot headquarters in the Lakota Trade Center, just across the parking area from the old geodesic dome, it dedicated part of the space to the Spirit Horse Gallery. For the first time, local artists had a local, Indian-owned outlet for their products, as well as an on-reservation source of beadwork materials reasonably priced. By 2000 annual sales at the gallery had reached $72,537, much of which went right back into the pockets of the local artists and artisans whose wares were available there.

Nanette Kills-in-Water is the manager of the Spirit Horse Gallery. Under her leadership, the gallery in 1999 began selling arts and crafts to the world through the internet, exposing the reservation-based artists and craftspeople to markets they could not otherwise have hoped to access on their own. One of the gallery's first on-line customers was President Clinton, making his first-ever on-line purchases.

"President Bill Clinton went shopping on-line for the first time on Monday, buying horsehair bracelets and children's books as holiday gifts," a news bulletin from Reuters reported on December 21, 1999. "The self-professed 'technologically challenged' president got on the Internet from the White House Oval Office, using a Compaq laptop computer emblazoned with the presidential seal and a mouse set on his antique wooden desk. Clinton bought the bracelets at www.lakotafund.org, a Web site run by a private nonprofit group set up to help South Dakota's Lakota Native Americans."

Among the items that are usually listed for sale on the gallery's website are baby moccasins made by Roselyn. "Cute doesn't say enough about these little mocs," reads the description on the website. "Hand-beaded on durable comfortable leather. The design will be the same, but the three colors can be specified. There is a leather fringe around the back and leather ties. Crafted by Roselyn Spotted Eagle, and others. Draw an outline of your baby's feet. We will add some for growth."

Kills-in-Water describes Roselyn as her "best beader" and one of her most dependable producers. "She does really top-quality work," she says. "I go to her all the time with orders and with repairs on moccasins I've bought from other artists."

Although her beadwork was already widely known across the reservation, Roselyn is appreciative of the referrals from the Spirit Horse Gallery, since off-reservation customers are usually willing to pay more than locals. For instance, there's a shop owner in Switzerland who orders about a dozen pairs of baby moccasins every year from Roselyn. Roselyn charges him $30 a pair. "He says if I could make more, he'd buy more of them, but that's all I can do for him without hurting my other customers," Roselyn says.

Another order she got through the gallery was for ten pairs of size-two children's moccasins. She charged $45 a pair because of the intricacy of the beaded turtle design the buyer wanted. The previous year, the buyer, a gift shop owner from New Mexico, had ordered only four pairs, so Roselyn regarded the increased order as a vote of confidence in her work. She expected to make $360 from the order.

The Spirit Horse Gallery was also the source of the order for the most expensive single item Roselyn has ever made: a beaded buckskin wedding dress, for which she was paid $1,000. "It was for a white lady in Pine Ridge who was marrying an Indian guy," Roselyn recalls. "She put the design on it, and I had to bead it. I sat in my little house working on it day and night. It took me four or five months. The bride looked real pretty in it."

Periodically, Roselyn places items she's made on consignment at the gallery, "generally when I need some money for something special or to make my loan payment," she explains. The shop charges a 15 percent consignment fee. Roselyn's items usually sell quickly. "Her color choices are really good, and she sets the price right for a quick sale," Kills-in-Water says.

## The Paperwork Problem

If Roselyn has a weakness as a businesswoman, it's that she doesn't like to keep records. She keeps seven years' worth of receipts for business-related purchases in a zippered green vinyl bank bag. An old day planner contains some notations about orders and payments, but it's by no means complete. "I've got all of my expenses written down somewhere, but they're all over, in little notepads," she admits. "And sometimes when I get paid, I do forget to write it down."

The trainers at the Lakota Fund have tried for years, without success, to persuade her to keep better records. One big reason she doesn't is her fear of jeopardizing her Social Security benefits, which is a common concern among all of the Lakota Fund's borrowers who receive disability payments. Roselyn already has experience with the loss of public benefits because of a rise in income: She and her family became ineligible for food stamps and food commodities when Chico began receiving disability payments, which pushed the household income above the poverty level.

Although the Lakota Fund disbanded the lending circles in 1998 when interest began waning, it still provides entrepreneurs with microloans, training, and technical assistance whenever they require it. The fund's staff members continue to help entrepreneurs who have outstanding loans in ways that go way beyond their job descriptions.

For instance, Monica regularly drives Roselyn to off-reservation communities like Gordon or Rapid City to buy fabric for her quilts, saving her the $60 she would otherwise have to pay a neighbor to drive her, since no public transportation serves the reservation. "We don't mind doing it, because she's an inspiration to us," Terkildsen says. "She's gone through so much in her life, and she still keeps going. She's really incredible."

Also, the trainers continue trying to help Roselyn impose some order on her paperwork. On a summer day in 2000, Roselyn brings her receipts into the organization's conference room, and Annie Means, the enterprise agent, and Lia Whirlwind Horse, the loan enforcement officer, help her sort through them. Terkildsen stops in to say hello, and when a question is raised about how much Roselyn can make without losing her disability income, she provides the answer. "Last I heard, you can earn up to $700 a month," she says. Roselyn is somewhat reassured. "I don't make that most months," she says.

Annie and Roselyn look through check stubs that Roselyn has kept from 1999 and 2000. Many are for meals she catered for the Lakota Fund—for instance, $37.50 for a January 1999 meeting of the fund's board; $50 for an April 1999 luncheon for visiting program officers from the Ford Foundation; $375 for a May 1999 meal for 75 people attending a business opportunities conference; and $100 for a June 2000 meal for the marketing committee meeting. Others are for articles sold on consignment through the gallery—for example, $67.50 for beaded picture frames in the summer of 2000 and $150 for a Star quilt in February 1999.

Annie has prepared a ledger book for Roselyn and sits down next to her to explain it. "You can list the cash you take in under different categories, like moccasins, Star quilts, baby quilts, and so on, so you can keep track of what's selling," says Annie, who's nursing her year-old baby as she talks. "This will help you when customers come and ask you, 'When was the last time I bought moccasins from you?' And at the end of the month, you can add up how much you've taken in. On the other pages you can list the money going out, like for fabric and leather and beads. Then at the end of each month you can add up how much you spent on each material. When you subtract your costs from the money you've taken in, you'll know what your profit is."

Roselyn nods in agreement, but appears somewhat exasperated. "I've taken a class on this already," she says. "I learned how to write it down, but then when people come and pay me, I'll forget to write it down. I'm not really organized that way."

Sensing that Roselyn's receipts are likely to remain in the green vinyl bank bag for the foreseeable future, Annie closes the ledger and assures Roselyn that her feelings about paperwork aren't unusual. "A lot of our entrepreneurs don't like doing the paperwork," she says. "They just want to get their products done and start making money."

## "Things Are So Much Better"

Roselyn doesn't judge the success of her business by what shape her paperwork's in. Instead, she thinks about what her family's life is like now compared to what it was like before she began putting so much time into her business—and what Ramona's and Chico's lives are like compared to what hers was like at their ages.

The most visible evidence of the difference the business income has made is the cozy three-bedroom trailer that the family moved into in 1997. Roselyn used the deposit she'd gotten for the beaded wedding gown, along with a bank loan of $1,000, to make the down payment on a $28,000 ten-year mortgage on a used mobile home. It cost another $400 to have it transported to the land her children inherited from their father, right next to the little two-room cabin that the Tribal Assistance Project had built for the family years before and just across a creek from her son Daniel and his family. The reservation's vocational rehabilitation department constructed a wheelchair ramp so that Ramona could get in and out of the trailer in a wheelchair, and a tribal improvement program put in water lines and a septic tank.

For the first time in twenty-four years, Roselyn and her family had indoor plumbing.

Roselyn is proud of her home, which, besides having a modern bathroom, also has a washer and a dryer, an all-electric kitchen, and an electric furnace, amenities that her old cabin lacked. "Things are so much better for us now," Roselyn says.

But these comforts come with a price—a $424 monthly payment and an electric bill that averages about $200 a month—whereas the cabin cost her virtually nothing to live in. She could have reduced her monthly payments by forgoing mortgage life insurance, but she wanted to make sure that Ramona and Chico would continue to have a roof over their heads should something happen to her. "Someday, I'm going to be gone," she says. "I keep thinking about that. What are they going to do? If I pass away, the insurance will take care of the payments, and they'll have a home. I had to think about them."

Not surprisingly, given the high rate of homelessness on the reservation, Roselyn lives in fear of missing a payment. "No matter what, I make my trailer payment each month," she says. "That's the first bill I pay. It takes two of our disability checks to pay all of our bills, which leaves me one check for food and gas. It's with what I make through my quilts and beadwork that I buy all the other things we need."

Roselyn found out how dependent her family had become on her business income when, in 1999, she was unable to work for several months. She underwent knee replacement surgery in June, which laid her up for a few months. Then, just when she should have been becoming mobile, she developed a serious infection in the new knee. It had to be removed and replaced with a temporary prosthesis, and she spent six weeks in the hospital hooked up to IV antibiotics. After the infection cleared up, Roselyn underwent yet another knee replacement in March 2000—her third in nine months.

"I had some orders before I went to surgery, and then I got some when I was in the hospital, and they've all stacked up on me," she says. "A couple months of the last year, I couldn't do any of my orders. When I'm in pain, I can't concentrate. So I really got behind in my bills. I had to borrow money to keep the electricity on, and I'm still overdue on the phone."

For a while, Roselyn considered selling the trailer and moving back into the cabin to cut her living expenses. But she felt she couldn't do that to Ramona, who no longer uses a wheelchair but has chronic problems with her legs. "Even though she's walking now, it's so hard for her to get around," she says. "I didn't want her to have to use the outhouse again."

## Back in Business

Four months after her third knee surgery, Roselyn was once again working hard at her business, although she required a walker to move from one end of her trailer to the other. One night, for instance, she was up until 2:30 A.M. working on both a new moccasin order—for Monica Terkildsen's three-year-old daughter—and an emergency repair job. A reservation resident had come by around 9 P.M. to ask if she could repair a pair of moccasins she'd made him a few years ago. The soles were worn through. The catch was he needed them in two days because he was going to take part in a powwow. She figured it would probably take her four hours to do, and she was really too busy to do it, "but I don't like to say no," she says.

She does most of her quilting during the day, but waits until late at night for beadwork so she can do it while lying in bed, propped up on pillows. "I do quilting when my feet hurt and the beading when my back hurts," she says. "Nighttime, when everybody else is sleeping, is a good time to do my beadwork."

Without the assistance of the Lakota Fund over the past decade, Roselyn believes, her business would have been much smaller and her ability to fill orders in a timely fashion would still be compromised by cash-flow problems. "If the Lakota Fund wasn't there, I would really be struggling," she says. "I know that for a fact, because before I got hooked up with the fund, I couldn't pay for the supplies I needed. Now I can borrow money, get what I need, and make orders for my business."

The support she gets from the fund isn't only technical and financial. It's emotional as well. The hardships Roselyn experienced during her childhood, the abuse she suffered during her marriage, and the daily challenges of caring for a disabled daughter and grandson have left her exhausted and world-weary. In addition, because of the loss of many loved ones over the years through tragic circumstances, she has lived in a state of near-constant grief. There were her five children lost to miscarriages or stillbirths, and one death of a newborn. She lost two grandchildren and a daughter-in-law in a car accident in 1980. Her mother died from a heart attack and exposure in 1983. And her companion, Luther, her son, Noah, and a nephew died in car accidents in 1995.

"Sometimes, with all the problems my family has, I feel ready to give up," Roselyn says, her voice cracking. "But at the Lakota Fund, they're always there for me, encouraging me on, telling me I'm doing good. I don't know what I'd do without them."

Whenever Roselyn begins to dwell on how hard her life has been, she shifts her thoughts to what her family has now that it didn't have just a few years ago. All three of them used to sleep in a single room in the old cabin; now each has a separate bedroom. Roselyn no longer needs to spend endless hours chopping wood, since their furnace is fueled by electricity. A satellite dish permits them to watch reruns of the Andy Griffith and Lucille Ball shows, their favorites, and Chico spends hours each day playing video games. They've got a telephone, which fewer than half of the households on the reservation have.

And their old outhouse, once the bane of their existence, stands unused in their backyard, a daily reminder of how far they've come.

*America Ducasse finds joy in caring for children in her home-based day care.*

chapter 5

# Chasing the American Dream
# America Ducasse
# America's Family Day Care
# Lowell, Massachusetts

Since the early 1800s, Lowell, Massachusetts, has been a magnet for immigrants chasing the American dream.

At first, the immigrants were mainly English and Irish. Then came French Canadians, Greeks, Italians, Swedes, Portuguese, Polish, Armenians, Lithuanians, and Syrians. Through the nineteenth century, Lowell's appeal was the promise of plentiful jobs in its red brick textile mills. But by the Great Depression, most of the mills had closed and immigration all but stopped.

However, as the area's economy revitalized over the last two decades of the twentieth century, new immigrants began streaming into Lowell once again. This time, they were mostly Cambodian, Laotian, and Latin American, and the lure was no longer the textile mills, but affordable housing, a welcoming social climate, and the prospect of employment in either electronics manufacturing jobs or the service sector.

One of these recent immigrants was America Ducasse, a native of the Dominican Republic. America came to Lowell in

1996, when she was pregnant with her second child. After a year on welfare, she found her future in Lowell: in home-based self-employment, taking care of the children of other immigrants whose dreams brought them here. With the help of Acre Family Day Care Corporation, a unique community-based organization whose mission is to help low-income women become licensed child care providers, America moved her family from the welfare rolls into self-sufficiency. Just as important to her, she found a way to do that while staying home with her own children.

## Factory Worker and Avon Lady

America Ducasse arrived in the United States in November 1991 with her two-year-old son, Ivan. Her reason for coming was the same as that of most immigrants from Latin America: a better life.

"Many Dominicans want to come to the United States," she says. "In my country, the economy was so bad that I earned not much money, maybe just 1,337 Dominican pesos [$83] a month. Besides, most of my family was already living here—my mother, my father, and many brothers and sisters—and I wanted to be near them. I always knew that sometime in the future I will go to live in the U.S."

When America landed at Kennedy Airport in New York City, she already had a prized permanent resident card—the so-called green card—because her father, a naturalized American citizen, had sponsored her as an immigrant. She had prepared herself well for life in the United States, studying English in adult school and poring over handouts from the U.S. Information Agency on what life is like in the United States. "I like to know about places before I go there," she explains. "I like to research about everything."

America and Ivan had a home waiting for them with her mother and stepfather in the Washington Heights area of Manhattan. Also living there were three of America's half-sisters, two half-brothers, and a niece.

Unlike most immigrants from her country, America was well educated. She had earned a bachelor's degree in psychology from the University of Santo Domingo, the oldest university in the Americas. She had worked as a clinical psychologist for a few years and hoped to find work in her field in the United States.

However, she soon found that working as a psychologist was not an option for her here, because she wasn't fluent in English and because becoming licensed as a clinical psychologist here usually requires an advanced degree. So she took a job at a factory in Englewood, New Jersey, for $5.25 an hour, which produced a paycheck of $171 a week. She supplemented her wages by selling Avon and Shaklee products to other Dominican immigrants.

"My check from the factory was so little money," she says. "I had to help my mother with rent and electricity and pay my friend $50 a week to take care of Ivan, so I had to do something to make more money."

America hated the rote aspect of the factory work—attaching department store labels to designer sunglasses. After two months, she was promoted to a job that required slightly more skill—sorting the labels in cabinets—but still she was bored.

For lack of a better prospect, she stuck with the job for eight more months. Then one day she saw an advertisement in a Spanish-language newspaper that read something to the effect of, "If you like sales, we have an opportunity for you."

"I call and have an interview with the man," America recalls. "We talked, and I like what he offer." America became a partner with a man named Juan in the business of selling advertising signs to small stores.

America learned quickly that her merchandise wouldn't move by phone, that a personal visit was essential to make a sale. So for nine hours a day, six days a week, she walked the streets of Brooklyn, Queens, the Bronx, Manhattan, Jersey City, West New York, Union City, and any other nearby community with a neighborhood business district that seemed ripe for her product.

She took subways, buses, and trains, but mostly she walked. "Much walking," she laughs. "Good thing I like to walk."

She made cold calls to hairdressers, barbers, green grocers, variety stores, tailor shops, and confectioneries. In a good week, she could clear $300 or $400. She kept at it for four years. In her spare time, she volunteered at Ivan's Head Start Center, serving as a parent representative to the board, and took classes in English and leadership skills.

In the fall of 1996, America became pregnant by her steady boyfriend, also a Dominican immigrant. America felt marriage wasn't an option. She didn't want to worry her mother, who suffers from several chronic illnesses, but she discussed her plight with a younger half-sister, Librada, who lived near Lowell.

"My sister said, 'Come to Lowell,'" America recalls. "'Lowell is a good town to live in. It's quiet, and it's much cheaper than New York. You can get your own apartment.'"

America decided to move to Lowell.

### Eight Months in a Shelter

America and Ivan moved to Massachusetts just before Thanksgiving 1996. They stayed with relatives for two weeks before moving into their own two-bedroom apartment, for which America paid $450 a month. The apartment was barely livable, with no heat and an erratic water supply, but it was the first home of her own in the United States, and she was happy to have it.

America enrolled Ivan in elementary school and then began trying to sell her signs in Lowell and other cities nearby. "I brought my business with me," she says. "That's how I was planning to support us."

However, after only a month, it became apparent that she wasn't going to be able to continue with door-to-door sales much longer. "My sister kept saying to me, 'Soon you are going to have a big belly. You can't keep doing this. What are you going to do? If you can't sell your signs, you can't pay your rent. You need to plan for the future.'

"I was not married, and I had nobody to help me," America continues. "In a few months, I was going to have to take care of a new baby. I knew that if I went back to my mother's house and explain things to her, maybe she want to help me. But I have to take responsibility for myself and Ivan and my newborn. It was a difficult time."

With reluctance, America applied for cash assistance from the Massachusetts Department of Transitional Assistance, which administers the state's welfare program. Because the monthly benefit for a family of two was under $500, she had to give up her apartment. With so little income, her housing options were limited. She felt her best hope was to obtain a housing subsidy, but was discouraged by the long waiting list. She and Ivan camped out for a few days with a cousin, and then, at her sister's urging, they moved into Merrimack House Family Shelter, a shelter for homeless families in Lowell.

Merrimack House provides more than just a bed and a roof. Operated by Community Teamwork, Inc., the community action agency for the greater Lowell area, the shelter helps homeless families achieve long-term self-sufficiency.

The social workers there helped America get her name on the waiting lists for both public housing and the Section 8 program, which provides subsidies that can be used to rent privately owned housing. They talked with her about her goals in life and helped her work out a plan for achieving them. A host of educational, financial, emotional, and legal resources were made available to her. "The shelter was nice," America says. "The people there provided information and support."

America's second child, Francisco, was born on March 31, 1997, in a local hospital. She brought him home to the shelter, where the family had its own two-room apartment. Five months later, the family received a Section 8 certificate, which enabled them to move into a two-bedroom apartment that rented for $689 a month, with Section 8 paying all but $90. America had little furniture (only a television and a bed), so a social worker at the shelter arranged for her to receive two hand-me-down loveseats, a kitchen table, a bed for Ivan, and a bookcase.

With her welfare benefit of $539 a month, America knew it was going to be tough taking care of her family's needs, even with food stamps and housing assistance. But with an infant to care for, she also knew that it was going to be difficult to work full-time or even to go to school to perfect her English and get the American credentials she needed to use her psychology degree. She spent hours and hours thinking about what she could do.

## "Always, I Thank God"

Soon after she'd moved to Lowell, America had noticed a fleet of eight-passenger vans transporting young children around town. The lettering on the side of the vans identified them as belonging to the Acre Family Day Care Corporation.

"I asked people, 'What's that mean?'" she recalls, "and one lady finally explained it to me."

America learned that Acre operated a training program to prepare low-income women to become home-based child care providers. As soon as she heard about it, America knew that Acre's program was the answer to her dilemma.

"Always I had the idea in my mind to have a day care business," America says. "When I was living in New York, I took some training and got the paperwork to apply for a license and even went to a doctor and got a medical exam. But the rents in New York were too expensive for me to afford my own place, and I couldn't do it in my mother's."

Acre's annual training course was about to begin, and America was offered one of the twenty slots. There's usually a long waiting list of women who want to take the course, but one of Acre's priorities since 1996 has been to train welfare recipients, and one more was needed to round out this particular class. "I think God helped me get in the course," America says. "Things come to me when I need them, and always, I thank God."

Acre's program is the brainchild of Anita Moeller. In 1987 Moeller had been a college student assigned to Coalition for a Better Acre (CBA), a community development corporation, as an intern when the group's resident-run board asked her to undertake a needs assessment in Lowell's low-income Acre neighborhood.

Going door-to-door in what was then a neighborhood of mostly Spanish-speaking immigrants, Moeller and a group of CBA staff and volunteers found both jobs and child care options in short supply. There wasn't a single licensed child care provider in the whole neighborhood, and as far as Moeller could tell, there were no licensed Spanish-speaking providers anywhere else in Lowell either.

For a while, Anita explored the possibility of starting up a day care center in the neighborhood, under the coalition's auspices, but found the costs and the licensing requirements prohibitive. Then she began to think about how the CBA might help residents become licensed home-based providers. At the time, Massachusetts required no special training of its licensed home-based providers, only a year of child care experience, a requirement that anyone who had a child of her own could easily meet.

"That presented us with an opportunity," she recalls. "We said, 'Let's encourage women to go into the family day care business, but let's also develop a training program to help them succeed in it.'"

After talking further with Acre residents, Moeller developed a detailed proposal for a training program. The coalition spun the project off as a separate legal entity, and Moeller was hired to run it. She convened the first class in 1988. Each of the ten students spoke only Spanish, so that became the lingua franca for the classes, with Moeller, who is bilingual, teaching some of them herself and CBA staff and volunteers with specialized knowledge teaching the others. "I was taking child development courses at the university and then going over to Acre and teaching them myself," she says, laughing now at the audacity of youth.

When the course concluded, Moeller helped the students obtain state licenses to provide child care in their homes. Since the state's licensing materials were published only in English, Moeller encouraged the Massachusetts Office of Child Care Services to translate them into Spanish. She also pressed the agency to hire a bilingual licensing worker, which was going to be essential if her mostly non-English-speaking graduates were to succeed in their new businesses.

Over the next three years, Acre offered several more training classes in Spanish. In between the classes, Moeller served as a resource and sounding board for the graduates as they established themselves in business.

Then, in 1991, the fledgling organization received a $150,000 three-year grant from the Ms. Foundation's Collaborative Fund for Women's Economic Development, a funding consortium that supports innovative organizations that promote economic self-sufficiency for low-income women. The grant enabled the Acre Family Day Care Corporation to become a full-fledged organization with its own office and staff.

Acre used part of its grant to expand into the Cambodian community, which was growing because of an influx of refugees. (Lowell now has the second largest population of Cambodians in the United States, after Long Beach, California.) Like the Spanish-speaking immigrants before them, the Cambodian immigrants' prospects were limited by a lack of child care options; there were no Khmer-speaking child care providers in town.

Acre offered the first Khmer-language training program for day care providers anywhere in the country. With grants from other funders (plus an additional three-year grant from the Collaborative Fund), Acre was later able to begin offering training in English as well. Since the federal welfare reform bill passed in 1996, forcing millions of welfare recipients into the job market, Acre has made training welfare recipients one of its

Because many low-income women entrepreneurs live in isolated areas, the marketing services they receive through organizations such as Appalachian By Design and the Lakota Fund are key to enabling them to sell their goods to customers around the world. Above, Ollie Barkley empties her mailbox in front of the rural mobile home park where she and her family live. Below, a road sign on the Pine Ridge Indian Reservation symbolizes the distances residents must travel to access basic amenities. Roselyn Spotted Eagle travels forty miles to purchase quilting supplies.

Family involvement is the rule for many small businesses. Above, Sheela Drummer (left) and her mother, Lucille Barnett Washington, check the store's computer for the price of an oil filter. Below, Caleb Barkley (left) and his older brother, Joshua, help their parents ready knitted baby blankets for delivery to Appalachian By Design.

Above, Jackson Clark prepares a bed of seedlings using a propagation technique he learned in college, as his mother, Jackie Clark, watches. Jackson majored in horticulture so he could help his mother build her business. Below, Sharon Garza (foreground) and her daughter, Michelle, hitch their hot dog cart to the family car after a long day of work. Michelle's brother, Nikko, often helps out.

Teaching others is an explicit part of the work of some entrepreneurs. Left, Jeanette Bradshaw shows a part-time employee, Carolyn Jackson, a new cake-decorating technique. Below, America Ducasse reads to the children in her care. Her youngest son, Francisco, is on the left.

The desire to spend more time with their children motivates many women entrepreneurs. Above, Ollie Barkley helps her oldest son, Joshua, with an assignment, while her other son, Caleb, works on his own. Below, both Danielle Franklin (standing) and her mother, Jacqueline Wilson, help Danielle's daughter, Samyiah, with her homework.

A good relationship with each customer is the secret to the success of many small businesses. In her inviting showroom, Yasmina Cadiz (opposite page) is able to show customers the quality of her upscale goods, including the $510 furrowed silk velvet shawl she's holding and the $3,950 Fortuny lamp that hangs from the ceiling. Above, Lucille Barnett Washington explains to a customer exactly what repairs his car needs. Below, Michelle Garza chats with some of her regular customers outside a skate park in Denver.

Computer technology has helped many small business owners become more productive and, in some cases, sell to customers thousands of miles away. Above, Yasmina Cadiz checks her e-mail for inquiries from customers. Most of her sales result from a website she designed. Below, America Ducasse uses a computer she bought with savings from her Individual Development Account to keep track of her business expenses and as a teaching tool for the children.

priorities: At least half of the trainees in each class are welfare recipients.

Besides providing training to aspiring providers, Acre has developed an extensive support system for any provider who agrees to take part in its network. It currently administers state contracts for subsidized day care for more than 250 children of parents who are transitioning from welfare to work or working in low-wage jobs. It provides technical assistance, personal support, and professional development classes to the forty-six caregivers in its network. In addition, it runs a transportation service that delivers 100 children each day to their providers' homes.

## Back to School

America started the Acre course in January 1998, one of ten welfare recipients in a class of twenty women. There was no cost to her beyond a supply fee of $75, for which a loan would have been available had she been unable to pay.

For the next three months, she attended eight hours of classes a week (a total of ninety-six hours altogether) on topics such as infant-child CPR, child development, nutrition, and the detection of child abuse. "I learned a lot," America says. "Because I had studied psychology, I already understand a lot about child development. But the other things they taught me—about taxes and state regulations and the food program—I didn't know anything about these things. It was all new to me."

The state only requires fifteen hours of classroom training to qualify for a home day care license; Acre's program goes much further. There's no state requirement for an internship, but Acre believes that's an essential component of its training, since it enables women to get a firsthand view of the realities of providing care to other people's children. The students' mentors are expected to give them a realistic view of the job, not a sugar-coated one.

America spent twelve hours a week over three months (144 hours altogether) in internships—at a Head Start center in Lowell and in a family day care home operated by Maribel Aviles, a Spanish-speaking provider in Acre's network. Helping Maribel care for six children from before dawn until after dark, America got a hands-on preview of the career she was about to move into.

"She taught me many things," America says of her mentor. "She helped me develop a schedule. She teach me how to put children down for sleeping time, at which times you give the snack, when you read, when you play. She said to me, 'It's hard work. But all jobs are hard work.'"

America graduated from Acre's course in April 1998 and signed a contract with Acre to join its provider network. A state licensing worker inspected her apartment and approved it for use for child care. America arranged to take out a loan from Acre for $300 to pay the annual premium for liability insurance, which Acre requires all its providers to carry.

Then came an unexpected blow. "I told the landlord I was going to put a day care in, and she said, 'Oh, sorry, you can't do that,'" America says. "'If the child have some problem here, we have the liability. This apartment is only for people to live in, not for a business.'"

## Deferring Her Dream

America was forced to put off starting a day care business while she looked for another place to live, one that would allow a home-based business. She applied for apartments all over town. A lot of other landlords didn't like the idea of a home day care business any more than her current landlady did. Months passed, and America continued to support her sons with welfare and food stamps.

The year before, while still in the homeless shelter, America had put in an application for an apartment in Massachusetts Mills, an attractive apartment complex that was created in the late 1980s inside the skeleton of a long-abandoned textile mill. America knew that other Acre providers worked out of their homes there, so she kept her fingers crossed that an apartment would become available.

Finally, a two-bedroom apartment opened up in the summer of 1998 at a rent of $800 a month. Based on America's income from welfare, her contribution to the rent was set at $90; the Section 8 program was to pay the rest.

A bureaucratic snafu over transferring America's Section 8 certificate to the new apartment delayed her move—and her prospects for starting her business—until November 1. By the end of the second week of November, America had obtained her state day care license. Acre lent her some toys, and she used some of her savings to purchase others. Her apartment passed muster with a state licensing worker, as did her paperwork and her plan for daily activities.

Two days after she got her license, America welcomed her first child, Naomi, just shy of one year old. "I was so excited to start the business," America recalls. Four others, all age three or younger, started over the next few weeks, which brought America to her licensed capacity of six children, including Francisco. Starting with just one other child and then building to capacity one child at a time enabled America to get used to being home all day with six infants and toddlers. "They had warned me at Acre that it might take a long time to get full," America says. "But almost right away, my business started growing."

As soon as she received her first check from Acre, America notified the welfare office that she no longer needed state support. "That first check from Acre was less than my welfare had been, but it was so good to get it," she says. "We had had a long time, more than a year, on welfare, without much money."

## Up Before Dawn

It's a typical workday for America in early spring 2000. She gets out of bed at 5:45 A.M. and immediately kneels for prayer. She reads her Bible for ten minutes and then further fortifies herself for the day with a cup of strong *café con leche*, made with Dominican coffee beans. It's the first of several cups she'll drink during the day.

The first child, Tomas, four, arrives at about 6:20 A.M. He is still sleepy, so America makes him comfortable on the couch, and he goes back to sleep for an hour. At 7 A.M., José, one, arrives, just as Ivan gets up to prepare for school. America turns on the television so that José can watch cartoons.

At 7:30 A.M., Ivan, José, and Tomas sit down to a breakfast of cornflakes, raisins, and milk. Within minutes, Francisco wakes up and bounds into the living room, ready for the day.

Breakfast takes almost an hour, during which the children babble with each other in Spanish. They then watch cartoons while America cleans up the breakfast dishes.

At 8:30 A.M., Ivan leaves for his elementary school, a magnet school about a block from home. Shayla arrives about the same time, and America puts her in the high chair to eat breakfast. Shayla rushes through her cereal so she can join Francisco in the toy car he's driving around the living room.

While the children are occupied, America heads into the bathroom to ready it for the heavy use it will get through the day. She leaves the door open so she can listen for any changes in mood. Soon, Tomas decides that he wants a turn in the toy car. Francisco cheerfully vacates it and mounts a plastic horse. Shayla remains in the car, and because Tomas is so big, she has to hang out the side door to maintain her claim.

At 9:50 A.M., America summons the group, now four strong, for a snack of tortilla chips and grapes. Naomi arrives fifteen minutes later, much later than usual. Her mother, a recent college graduate, hasn't yet found a full-time job and so sometimes allows Naomi to sleep late. Shayla rushes over to hug Naomi and then helps her take her coat off, as she's seen America do countless times before.

Because Naomi hasn't had breakfast yet, America gets her a bowl of cornflakes with raisins and milk, instead of the tortilla chip snack. America lifts Naomi into the high chair and washes her hands with a washcloth. Then Naomi digs in.

Naomi's late arrival has interfered with America's schedule, which calls for arts and crafts activities at 10 A.M. So while Naomi is dawdling over breakfast, America puts a video of *The Fox and the Hound* into the VCR. Nobody pays attention except for Naomi.

Instead, Shayla stands by America's computer, switching it off and on, and the other children zoom around on riding toys. When Naomi finishes breakfast, America washes her hands again and then wipes down the high chair tray. "Now, it's coloring time," she announces as she gets some coloring sheets and crayons out of a drawer.

Francisco is the first to sit down at the child-sized table in the living room where the art activities always take place. Tomas and Shayla join him. America hands Francisco a pink crayon, Tomas a green one, and Shayla a brown one.

"I color too," Naomi announces, as she runs over to the table and sits down in a chair with an expectant look on her face. America gives her a purple crayon and then passes around sheets torn from a coloring book.

All this time, America has been kneeling by the tiny table; noticing that she's the only one without a chair, Francisco suddenly jumps up and gets her a miniature chair. "Mommy sit here," he says considerately.

By now, nobody's watching the video, so America switches it off. Each of the children is coloring earnestly. Even though Tomas is the oldest of the children at the table, he has to be shown how to color. America takes his hand in hers and moves it back and forth across the paper, careful to stay within the lines.

After America withdraws her hand, Tomas watches all the other children carefully. Then he tentatively moves the crayon across the paper by himself and looks up at America for approval. America claps. "*Muy bueno, Tomas*," she says.

## A Welcome Visitor

At 10:30 A.M., Maria "Zuly" Montoya, one of Acre's trained home visitors, arrives for an unannounced visit, as she does once a month. Though not required by the state, the monthly visits to providers are a cornerstone of Acre's services, helping to ensure that the providers are offering a quality child care experience.

"When a provider first starts, she calls the office every day for two months," Zuly explains. "She's taken the training, but the daily practice is different. She's got one-year-olds, three-year-olds, and four-year-olds. What can she do with them all at once? Maybe it takes six months until she feels fully comfortable. Some providers don't last more than a year or two. The ones who are always learning, like America, are the ones who are happiest."

The children are excited about having a visitor, especially since it's Zuly, who gathers each of them into her lap, one by one, for a snuggle. The children abandon their coloring books and find some balls in a corner of the room, which they start throwing at each other and, soon, at America and Zuly too.

Zuly can't help but notice that Tomas is afraid of the ball and cringes when it's thrown to him. She asks America how he's been doing, and they exchange concerns about his very apparent developmental delays.

Tomas had moved to the United States with his family from Columbia only a month or so before he started coming to America's. He's four years old, but looks a year or two older, which makes him seem even more developmentally delayed than he is.

"He has many problems," America says. "When he first came, his father told me, 'He doesn't speak.' It was true. At first, too, he was crying, crying all the time for his daddy."

After a month of virtually nonstop crying, America called the social worker at Acre for advice. "They gave me the address of a specialist who could do some tests, and I gave it to his father, and he took him there," America says. "They still have more tests to do, but they say his intelligence is normal."

Recently, America has noticed some improvement in his behavior. "Now, after four months, he can talk a little," she says. "Now, too, he plays with the other children."

Zuly was a provider for six years, so she knows firsthand the stresses that come with the job and offers providers tips on how to cope. "Providing is a difficult job," she says. "It's a very long day, and you have to constantly set a good example for the children. The provider's tone of voice when she greets the children can set the tone for the entire day."

Zuly says that America is an excellent child care provider. "She is very pleasant, both with the parents and the children," Zuly says. "She is always saying positive things, never complaining about either the parents or the children. And the parents never call us with complaints about her. She always calls us when she has a problem with a child or with a parent, like when a parent brings in a child who is sick, or a parent is bringing a child at a different hour than their contract says they will, or a child has behavior problems. If there's a problem, she looks for a solution." America beams as she hears Zuly compliment her.

Zuly wanders through America's apartment, casually double-checking that the outlets still have protective covers on them, that the kitchen cabinets have safety latches, and that there are screens on the windows. She asks America if she needs any special help with anything, and again America mentions her concerns about Tomas. Zuly promises to schedule Acre's social worker for a visit and says good-bye. By now, it's time for lunch.

## Shrimp Stew and Rice

Lunch today is shrimp stew with rice and salad. Like all of Acre's providers, America receives money from the U.S. Department of Agriculture's Child Care Food Program to ensure that the meals she serves the children in her care are nutritionally balanced. The federal program is designed to improve both the quality of day care for low-income children and their nutrition. Every day, about 2.6 million children around the United States receive meals and snacks paid for by the program.

While America cleans up the lunch dishes, Francisco and Tomas ride wheeled toys around the living room. Shayla, who's still eating, watches from the high chair. "For me, it's good to have this opening," America says, nodding toward the pass-through between the living room and the kitchen, which enables her to watch the children in the living room as she's tidying up the kitchen. "I can see everything."

After she puts away the lunch dishes, she calls the children back into the kitchen for milk. "*La leche, Tomas*," she sings out. "*La leche, Francisco. La leche, Naomi.*" America sits down in one of the kitchen chairs, and Naomi climbs onto her lap to drink her milk.

Francisco and Tomas are still too busy playing to take time out for a drink. But after Naomi finishes, America coaxes Tomas onto her lap and holds him while he downs his glass of milk.

By the time they finish, they all look like they belong in a milk advertisement. America wipes their faces. "Okay, sleeping time now," she says.

Francisco races into his bedroom and obediently stretches out on the bed he shares with his brother at night, a Transformer clutched tightly in his hand. Tomas follows and pulls a sleeping mat for himself out of the closet. America carries Shayla into her bedroom and puts her down in the crib, patting her head and murmuring "sleeping time" as Shayla finds her thumb and closes her eyes. Naomi, meanwhile, is running back and forth between the boys' bedroom and the living room, whimpering. "No sleeping," she cries.

After Shayla has settled in, America catches Naomi and carries her into the boys' bedroom and puts her down on her own sleeping mat. She kneels on the floor between Francisco and Naomi, one hand on each back, gently rubbing while she repeats over and over, "Sleeping time."

When it's clear that Francisco isn't going to sleep as long as he has the Transformer in his hand, she takes it away from him. Fifteen minutes pass before all the children are asleep.

### "This Is My Day"

By now, it's 2 P.M., and while the children sleep, America sits down at her kitchen table to fill out her daily paperwork.

Providers must keep meticulous records of the foods they serve to receive compensation: ninety-two cents for each breakfast served, $1.69 for each lunch, and fifty cents for one snack a day (America serves two and absorbs the cost of the second). Providers must also keep detailed attendance records for each child for whom they receive state subsidies (in America's case, all of them but her own child, Francisco).

After only fifteen minutes of nap time, Tomas comes into the living room. He tells America in Spanish that he can't sleep, so she makes a bed for him on one of the couches.

At 3:35 P.M., Ivan arrives home from school and enters quietly. He and his mother have a few minutes to talk over his day before the other children start to awaken.

As America is readying the post-nap snack of ramen noodles, the door buzzer sounds. "Mommy, mommy!" Naomi squeals. But it's not her mommy. It's Tomas's twelve-year-old cousin, who's been sent up in the elevator to pick him up. Tomas's face lights up when he sees him, but America tells him he can't leave until he's had his snack. She also tells the cousin that she can't let the two of them leave alone, that his mother must come and pick them up.

A few minutes later, Tomas's aunt comes up from the parking lot to find out why her son and Tomas have been delayed. At first, she looks a little peeved, but America explains to her that she can't release Tomas to a twelve-year-old, and the aunt seems to understand.

America gets down on one knee to put Tomas's jacket on him. "Tomasito, can you give me a kiss?" she asks him, first in Spanish and then in English. He reaches up and kisses her cheek. "See you *mañana*," she tells him as he leaves with his cousin and aunt.

At 4:15, America's seven-year-old niece, Francheska, arrives. (America's license allows her to care for Francheska part-time before and after school.) A school bus has dropped her at the front door. She sits down at the table with the other children and starts eating her snack.

At 4:40, Ivan announces, "It's story time." Ivan, now ten and a star in his fifth-grade class, loves to help his mother with the children. He looks through a pile of books while Francisco pulls up a chair, picks up one of the books, and pretends to read.

With Shayla and Naomi each occupying one of America's knees, Ivan begins to read from a children's book called *The Trip*. Unfortunately, the book doesn't capture their interest. Francheska looks through her backpack and brings out another book that she thinks the children might like better, *Bringing the Rain to the Plain*. Ivan approves. "That's good," he says. "It's a rhyme book. They'll like that."

Just as he starts reading, the doorbell buzzes again. "My mommy, my mommy!" Naomi shrieks as she jumps from America's lap and runs to the door. To her obvious disappointment, it turns out to be Shayla's father. He comes into the living room, and Francisco runs over to him, indicating he wants a hug. Naomi follows and begs for a hug too.

When Shayla and her father head out the front door, Francisco escapes with them. Holding Naomi, America stands in the doorway and summons him back.

At 5:05 P.M., the buzzer rings again. "My mommy, my mommy!" Naomi cries. Finally, she's right. Naomi runs into her arms and nuzzles, while her mother and America discuss how Naomi's day has gone.

Naomi's mother tells America, "I had a job interview today. Keep your fingers crossed for me." She's been receiving welfare benefits and child care subsidies while finishing a college degree in computer science. She and America spend a few minutes talking about how difficult it is to be a single mom.

At 5:15 P.M., when the door closes behind Naomi and her mom, America's workday is officially over, almost twelve hours after it began.

Not once, all day, has America ever raised her voice. Not even when she found her couch all wet from a child's accident. Not when Shayla's foot crushed a grape into the beige carpet. Not when Naomi smashed a strawberry onto the table, making a mess. Not when Francisco threw a tantrum, disrupting story hour.

"This is my day," America says as she sits down on the couch and puts her feet up, finally getting a minute to herself for the first time since Tomas arrived eleven hours ago. "Same thing, every day. Good thing I love my work."

By 8:30 P.M., she'll be in bed with a book, resting up for the next day.

## Saving for the Future

Although providing home-based child care pays poorly in many parts of the United States, that's not the case in Massachusetts for those providers who take care of children who are eligible for state subsidies. In 1998 the state's provider networks lobbied the legislature to raise daily compensation rates for state-subsidized children, arguing that it was both a matter of equity and a necessity to ensure sufficient capacity as hundreds of thousands of Massachusetts's welfare recipients were moving into the workforce because of welfare reform.

The legislature responded by approving an additional $25 million to boost rates. Rates now range from about $20 to $24 per day per child, depending largely upon age—a few dollars more per child than in most other states.

That means that for watching four children full-time and one child part-time, America receives about $2,050 a month in state child care payments, or a total of $24,428 in 1999. With deductions for the self-employment tax and business expenses such as insurance, supplies, and food, the net profit she reported on her 1999 tax return came to $18,783. That put her family firmly above the federal poverty threshold ($13,700 for a family of three in 1999) and well above the average income of child care workers nationally ($14,820 in 1999, according to the U.S. Department of Labor).

Since she also qualified for an Earned Income Tax Credit of $2,760, her effective income came to $21,543.

The average gross income for the providers in Acre's network was $33,000 in 1999. America's income is lower than Acre's average partly because Francisco occupies one of her six licensed slots, and she receives no compensation for caring for him. Another reason her income is lower is that Acre's network includes several day care homes that are licensed to care for up to ten children and hence receive more compensation from the state.

All in all, America is quite pleased with her income and her work. She's been managing to save between $800 and $1,000 a month, an extraordinary amount, given her income. One reason for her high rate of savings is that she doesn't have the clothes and transportation costs that she'd have if she worked in an office, or the child care expenses she'd have to pay for Francisco if she weren't able to care for him herself.

After seven months as a child care provider, she felt secure enough to use some of her savings to buy a '90 Toyota Camry to replace the '85 Honda Accord that she'd had when she moved to Lowell from New York. "I paid the whole cost at once," she says proudly. "No loans. I know how to take care of my money. I know how to make the most of it. I don't buy anything on credit. I buy all of our clothes at sales. And I only buy what I need."

Right now, she's saving up for some new furniture—bunk beds for Ivan and Francisco. Eventually, she'd like to buy new living room furniture to replace the hand-me-downs she received from the homeless shelter, but realizes that a purchase like that doesn't make much sense at the moment, given the hard use it would get from the children she cares for.

Sometime down the road, her goal is to buy a house in the Dominican Republic, a dream, she points out, of many Dominican immigrants. "Most of us immigrants come here with the idea of someday going back to our country," she says. "Maybe in a few years I'll have enough for a house."

In addition to her personal savings account, America established a special savings account called an Individual Development Account (IDA), with the help of Acre, in 1999. The IDA provides her with a $3 match for every $1 she saves, up to a maximum of $25 a month. The match money comes from a combination of public and private sources.

Acre's IDA program was Massachusetts's first subsidized savings and financial education program. Its goal is to increase the financial stability of welfare recipients and low-income workers by giving them an incentive to accumulate assets. Under the program's rules, the savings can only be used to buy or repair a house, pursue higher education, or build a business. America plans to use her IDA savings to buy a new computer to replace the old computer that Acre lent her. "We only use that one for the children to play on," she says. "I want one more modern and with a printer, so that I can keep my records on it."

The one weak spot in the family's financial picture is health insurance for America. Both boys receive health coverage through Massachusetts's subsidized MassHealth plan, which costs America just $20 a month. But America has no coverage for herself, a common problem among self-employed day care providers. A 1999 study commissioned by the Massachusetts Office of Child Care Services (OCCS) found that nearly 40 percent of licensed child care providers identify health insurance as an "extreme need." Acre and other provider networks have been advocating before the state legislature for a pilot health insurance program to cover family day care providers, but so far have not prevailed.

## From Welfare to Self-Sufficiency

As a member of the vanguard of former welfare recipients who have sought financial self-sufficiency through self-employment, America is clearly a success story. A year and a half after leaving welfare, she was supporting her family without any income assistance or food stamps, and with only a modest housing subsidy (she's paying $611 in rent, up from $90 when she first moved in).

In fact, America and the other former welfare recipients who have graduated from Acre's training program are doing much better, as a group, than the typical former welfare recipient in Massachusetts. According to a study by the Massachusetts Department of Transitional Assistance, just over one in ten respondents to a survey of former welfare recipients had participated in a training program. Only half of all respondents had a job a year after leaving welfare, despite the fact that Massachusetts was experiencing the lowest unemployment rate in a decade. Of these, only half were earning more than $250 a week.

Elsewhere in the United States, many other organizations have had difficulty helping welfare recipients become self-supporting through microenterprise alone. The Self-Employment Learning Project (SELP), the definitive study of the impact over five years of microenterprise programs on low-income people, concluded in a 1999 report that for former welfare recipients, microenterprise serves mainly as a crucial supplemental income, "possibly being the 'patch' that brings a household out of poverty."

In that context, Acre's record is exemplary. Of the fifty-nine providers Acre trained between 1996 and 1999, forty-one (or 70 percent) had been welfare recipients. Of these, twenty-one are still running child-care businesses full-time through the Acre network and two are employed at Head Start centers. More than half have been at their jobs for three or more years. Acre's record in assisting low-income women to succeed as entrepreneurs earned it one of sixty-five Vision 2000 Model of Excellence awards from the U.S. Small Business Administration in November 1999.

Anita Moeller thinks that the Acre providers who were once welfare recipients have been able to succeed in self-employment partly because of the extensive support that Acre provides. "One year, the state put a lot of money into training welfare recipients to be child care providers and it was a huge flop, except for our program and one other in Springfield," she says. "In my opinion, it's because they didn't focus on hooking providers into a system. The providers got no support after they finished the training."

In contrast, she notes, Acre's providers "can call us at any time with concerns or questions. They get one-on-one technical assistance during the monthly visits by our staff. We have a bilingual social worker on retainer who can come out and observe a specific child. And we have monthly meetings of all the providers on topics that they want information on—taxes, record keeping, marketing, curriculum development. Once you've finished our training, that's really only the beginning."

## "They Need Love"

What does America see in her future?

Ultimately, America would like to work again as a psychologist and specialize in counseling women. First, though, she has to improve her English, which she's trying to do by taking English lessons at Middlesex Community College at night.

For now, she's content to continue with her family day care business. Besides good money, among its main benefits is that Francisco, who's nearly three, spends every waking minute with her, and Ivan has the satisfaction of knowing that she's going to be there every day when he comes home from school.

"They are my children, and as long as I can, I want to be the one taking care of them," she says. "I am happy when I am with my children."

Although some might view America's work as tedious, she doesn't regard it that way. Every day brings something different—a new skill mastered by an infant, new words spoken by a toddler, previously unseen evidence of cooperation between two strong-willed two-year-olds, a good-bye kiss from Tomas, who used to do little besides cry.

Then, too, there's the power of personal attachment. Three of her charges—Naomi, Shayla, and Sabrina—have been with her almost from the start, and America is very fond of them.

"I get very attached to the children," she says. "They need love, and that's what I give them."

*With some trepidation, Jackie Clark bought a nursery, only to be nearly forced out of business by freakish weather two years in a row.*

chapter 6

# "Making the Planet a Better Place" Jackie Clark Moon River Nursery Albion, California

For the first time in her life, Jackie Clark had a job she loved. A divorced mother of four, Jackie had spent ten years on welfare and six years in unsatisfying retail jobs before she found the work of her dreams at a wholesale plant nursery in rural Albion, California, in 1993. Within two years, she had worked her way up to assistant manager.

"It was love from the first minute," Jackie recalls. "Anything the owners wanted done, I would do—mix the soil, drive the Bobcat, spray the plants, do the fertilizing. I was completely into it."

In July 1997, a new owner decided he didn't really want to be in the nursery business. He put the nursery back on the market, but got no takers. Jackie was faced with a choice. "It was either buy it or lose a job I loved, because they were going to close it if I didn't buy it," she says.

Jackie negotiated a reasonable purchase price and very favorable terms for a five-year owner-financed loan. The West Company, a nonprofit organization in Fort Bragg, twenty miles away, provided Jackie with business consulting services, and a community bank and nonprofit lender offered $20,000 in loans for operating capital. Although nervous about taking on debt, Jackie signed on the dotted line.

Today, Moon River Nursery employs all four of Jackie's children, one full-time and three part-time. In 2000 the business grossed $61,730, about half of which was family income. Just as important to Jackie as the income is the reputation she's earned among high-end retail nurseries in the nearby San Francisco Bay Area as a reliable provider of high-quality, hard-to-find perennials.

Jackie's first few years in business didn't proceed as expected. When she took over, the nursery was suffering from a year of owner disinterest. Within months, Jackie's silent partner—Mother Nature—tested her commitment to the business in a way she had never imagined. El Niño brought more than seventy inches of rain to Mendocino County, twice the normal amount, drowning many of the plants and diminishing demand for those that survived. In Jackie's second year in business, the weather system known as La Niña brought night after night of hard freezes, again reducing her stock. "It's insane to have a business based on the weather if you have to make money," Jackie observes.

But compensation comes in other forms besides cash.

"To make a business like this successful, you have to love what you're selling, and I do," Jackie says. "It's not Fuller brushes I'm talking about or videos. It's something truly beautiful, and that makes a difference."

### Gorgeous Scenery, Few Jobs

Mendocino County, where Jackie lives and does business, is known for its gorgeous scenery and quaint oceanside villages. Every Friday night from early spring through late fall, job-stressed Bay Area residents drive four hours over serpentine roads to jam the county's high-priced restaurants and fill up romantic country inns. Then on Sunday nights, they drive back home again, leaving

Mendocino County to its 84,085 year-round residents. The week-enders who think of the area as a luxurious escape are largely mindless of the fact that it's among the poorest counties in California. Per capita income is $12,000 lower than the statewide average and the unemployment rate typically runs five percentage points higher, except during the summer tourist season, when service jobs as maids and waiters are easy to find.

Jackie and Howard Clark and their three young children moved to Mendocino in 1979 from Alabama. They were attracted both to the spectacular scenery and the counterculture lifestyle that flourishes along the county's back roads. A friend had told them that he could use their help with his solar panel business. "We were going to manage the business," Jackie recalls. "Only it turned out there was no business for us to manage."

For a while, the couple supported the family on Howard's disability checks from the Veterans Administration and his meager wages as a dishwasher. Within a year, the marriage fell apart. The couple divorced in 1981. Jackie got involved in a new relationship, and in 1982 she gave birth to a fourth child, Bohdanya, who's called Bohdy.

For the next five years, Jackie supported her four children with welfare benefits. "I could have gone to work, but I opted to stay home with my kids," she says. "I was very active in the school and the community. I ran the school lunch program at the school my three older children attended. I was never not busy."

Late in 1986, Jackie took the first step back into the world of work. She took a job at a surf and skateboard shop in the town of Mendocino, about thirteen miles from her house. "My boys were skateboarders, and I wanted to be able to give them Christmas presents that year, so I worked for trade," she says. "I love being around teenage boys, so going to work was fun."

After Christmas, the owner, about to leave on a surfing trip to Indonesia, offered to sell her the business for the cost of the inventory. She thought it sounded like a good deal and scraped together the purchase price. During the day, while the children were in school, she ran the shop. Several evenings a week, she worked at a video store nearby for extra income. But welfare remained the family's main source of support.

Within months of buying the surf shop, it became clear to Jackie that she'd made a bad investment. "The rent was high, and there was very little foot traffic," Jackie explains.

She stuck with the business for almost two years, but closed it in 1988 and sold her inventory for pennies on the dollar. "I paid off all the bills I could and later worked off the rest," she says. "Bankruptcy is not in my vocabulary. I would sell my redwoods before I would declare bankruptcy, and I consider them sacred, so you know I'd never do that. I feel like there's always options."

## A Fortuitous Run-In

After she closed the surf shop, Jackie began supplementing her earnings from her part-time job at the video shop with an additional part-time job at the Albion post office. (Because of the shortage of full-time, year-round jobs, many Mendocino County residents work two or three part-time jobs.) She made about $6 an hour at each job.

A few years later, the owner of the Albion Grocery Store decided to put in a video shop so that the 300 or so residents of Albion would no longer have to drive the ten miles to Mendocino to rent videos. He asked Jackie to set it up and manage it. "So I did," she says. "I was real good at it, but I hated it. I am not a sit still–type person, and I was stuck in the shop all day."

Though the job paid less than $10 an hour, it was full-time, and Jackie felt secure enough financially to buy the house she had been renting since 1979. The landlord gave her credit for all the rent she'd paid over the years—$50,000—and she took out a mortgage for another $50,000.

One Friday afternoon in 1993, Jackie found herself in line at the bank behind Tom Wodetzki, one of the owners of the Moon River Nursery, a wholesale plant nursery about a mile from her house. They got to talking, and Jackie asked if the nursery was hiring. Wodetzki said he didn't think so, but when he got home he mentioned the conversation to his wife, Sharon Hansen. Sharon knew Jackie from their children's school and told her husband, "Hire her right now."

Jackie started at the nursery the following Monday.

## "The Work of My Dreams"

Jackie had no formal training in horticulture and hadn't even begun gardening until just a few months before the fateful conversation in the bank line. "I always had geese, so I never had much of a garden, because they eat everything you plant," Jackie laughs.

However, she took to the nursery job immediately. "It was the work of my dreams," she says. "It was all physical work, no dealing with the public. I loved my job so much that I was the first person there in the morning and the last to leave at night. The owners would tell me, 'We love your energy.' But I felt like I should be paying them for the privilege of working. I'd go home in a good mood every day, thinking about what I was going to do at work the next day. It was wonderful."

Hansen, who had previously managed the nursery at Coast Botanical Gardens in nearby Fort Bragg, knew a lot about plants and shared her knowledge with Jackie. Jackie was a quick study, and soon knew all the botanical names for the plants in the nursery's inventory. One of five part-time employees, she made $6.50 an hour.

In 1995 the owners made Jackie the assistant manager and left her in charge whenever they went out of town. Over time, her wages rose to $9.50 an hour.

Then, to Jackie's dismay, the owners put the nursery up for sale early in the summer of 1996. "I was totally depressed," she recalls. "I was really, really happy working for them. They were excellent employers. I really didn't know what the prospects for a sale were."

### "It's Yours If You Want It"

In October 1996 a retired couple bought the nursery and asked Jackie to stay on as manager, since they lived in Santa Rosa, about ninety miles away. "They gave me a raise, to $10 an hour, and a lot of responsibility," Jackie recalls.

Within a few months of taking possession of the nursery, however, one of the new owners took a job in Napa. There was no way he could give the nursery the attention it needed and work a full-time job, so he put it back on the market in July 1997. No buyers came forward, and in December 1997 he walked away from his investment. The nursery reverted to the original owners.

"They turned around and said to me, 'It's yours if you want it, for $10,000,'" Jackie says. The owners offered to finance the purchase price over five years and to allow Jackie to make payments only during the six months when most of the business income came in.

From her yearlong stint as manager and her two years as assistant manager, Jackie knew enough about the economics of the business to think that she could make a living from it. However, she had thought that about the surf shop too. She sought advice from others.

Jackie knew that the previous owners had always borrowed operating capital to purchase inventory every spring, so she went to the Savings Bank in Fort Bragg to find out whether she could qualify for a loan. A loan officer there referred her to the Economic Development and Funding Corporation in Ukiah, which specializes in small businesses. A loan officer there sent her to yet a third place, the West Company, which would help Jackie perfect her business plan.

The West Company was founded in 1988 to promote microenterprise as a strategy for increasing economic self-sufficiency and social well-being for Mendocino County women with limited access to economic resources. Since its founding, it has assisted about 800 small businesses in one way or another, including the provision of technical assistance and loans. Over thirteen years, it has issued about $300,000 in loans ranging from $150 to $10,000; its loan portfolio in 2001 amounted to about $35,000. In 1992 it began assisting men as well as women, though women still make up about 75 percent of its clientele.

Jackie called the West Company and explained that she needed help figuring out whether the nursery business could support her family. The West Company's Fort Bragg office, which is about twenty-five miles from Jackie's home, offered her the services of Rick Moon, a consultant who works with West Company clients under a contract with the Small Business Administration.

Moon was ideally suited to advise Jackie on the acquisition of Moon River, since he had consulted with the nursery's founders on accounting practices a few years before. Moon helped Jackie put together a business plan. "We went over the financials," Moon recalls. "We did some historical analysis of the business, then some marketing and operations planning and cash-flow projections so she could figure out what she wanted to do with the business to make it grow. She was very concerned about the finances. But she finally decided to do it, with some trepidation. It was either do it or the nursery would close and she wouldn't have a job."

Business plan in hand, Jackie went back to both the Economic Development and Funding Corporation and the Savings Bank. "Between the two of them, I borrowed $20,000," she says. "I was really nervous about taking on debt, but I didn't believe that I could walk away from the opportunity. I thought there was definitely a lot of potential there. For the previous few years, not much energy had gone into building the business. The owners weren't aggressively trying to find new retail nurseries or stock new plants. They were moving at a pace that was comfortable for them, and they didn't really need the nursery to make more money.

"I thought it could grow. But the main reason why I bought it was to save my job."

## From Employee to Boss

Jackie took ownership of Moon River Nursery on January 1, 1998. The $10,000 purchase price included a small inventory of plants, an office and a few sheds, a Bobcat, use of an irrigation system, and the customer list.

At first, the biggest difference between managing the nursery and owning it was that instead of drawing a biweekly paycheck, Jackie was writing checks to other people. A lot of checks. In addition to the loan repayment of $400 that she had to make to the previous owners six months of the year, she also had to pay them $250 a month year-round in rent for the one-acre property. On top of that came the costs of buying dirt, fertilizer, pots, and root stock. When it came time to deliver to retail nurseries in the Bay Area, she had to pay a driver 15 percent of the wholesale value of the delivery.

That first winter in business brought something else she hadn't counted on—rain. Lots and lots of it. The weather system known as El Niño dropped 73.33 inches of rain on the Mendocino Coast during the 1997–98 rainy season, which caused many of her plants to rot. With rain falling daily for months, home gardeners couldn't get outside to work in their gardens, so sales languished at retail nurseries all over northern California. As a result, those nurseries cut their purchases from wholesale suppliers like Moon River.

At the same time Jackie was struggling with the effects of El Niño, she started having problems with her delivery man. Though she couldn't do much about the weather, she decided to solve her delivery problem by delivering the plants herself. One day while shopping in Fort Bragg, she saw a 1972 Ford-350 panel truck in a parking lot with a For Sale sign in the window. "They wanted $5,500 for it, and I talked them down to $4,000," she says proudly.

Although the truck was twenty-six years old, it had only 18,000 miles on it. Jackie got a loan that spread the payments over two years and bought the truck. Then she and her youngest son, Jackson, then 19, began making the weekly deliveries to the Bay Area themselves. Jackson was attending a community college in Ukiah, about fifty miles away from home. He would drive home after classes every Thursday so that he could help his mother deliver her orders every Friday.

The other bright spot in 1998 was the opening of a Moon River retail outlet at the Village Hardware Store in Albion, just off the road to Mendocino. "They had bought a few plants here and there the year that I managed the nursery, but nothing regular," Jackie says. "They already had a little greenhouse set up, and they suggested to me that I stock it and pay them a commission on each sale. It's worked out really well for us, because it's close by and I don't have to pay rent and it doesn't take a lot of work. Plus, it's a lot of fun having a local retail outlet. Every now and then, I'll schedule a sale and take a truckload of plants down there and groom them and stand around talking to people. That social aspect is really nice."

All things considered, though, 1998 was a tough time to be getting into the nursery business. In Jackie's first year, she brought in a total of $51,000, not nearly enough to pay all of her business-related or household expenses. "We got by on credit cards, and I took on extra work—painting houses, light carpentry, whatever people needed," Jackie says. "I was scared. I was thinking the whole time, 'I don't want to lose this business.' I really felt overwhelmed, and I don't think I've felt underwhelmed ever since.

"It's definitely not like selling videos."

## Washington Comes Through

Once again, Jackie went back to the West Company for advice, and, again, the West Company put Rick Moon at her service. Together, they decided that she should refinance her home so that she could discharge some of the high-interest credit card debt she'd amassed while coping with El Niño, pay off her nursery-related loans, and obtain operating capital for the coming year.

(The interest rate on a home loan is typically much lower than that for a business loan.) Moon also helped Jackie begin thinking about how she could build more of a year-round business, with a more specialized product base.

Early in 1999, Jackie learned that because of El Niño, her business would be eligible for a federal disaster grant. "You have no idea how hard I worked to get that and how long it took me," she says. "First, the Department of Agriculture said because I grow in containers, I wouldn't qualify for their assistance, but that the Small Business Administration should help me. So I talked to the SBA, and they told me, 'If your business is growing stuff, then the Department of Agriculture should help you, not us.' So I went back to the Department of Agriculture again. Back and forth, back and forth. In the meantime, President Clinton, bless his heart, told the Department of Agriculture to include nursery businesses in the disaster declaration."

Moon helped Jackie figure out the financial impact of El Niño. "It wasn't so much the plants she lost, but the loss of her customer base," he says. "There was no spring that year. People stopped doing their gardening, so nurseries stopped buying wholesale."

After filing what seemed like reams of paperwork, Jackie received a check from the Department of Agriculture for $23,550—a portion of the losses attributable to El Niño. The disaster relief check enabled her to pay off many bills, including her truck, and buy root stock for the 1999 growing season. She had every reason to expect a better year.

## A Killing Frost

"We went into the next spring with high hopes, thinking, 'Well, it can't happen two years in a row,'" Jackie says.

"And then it did. Only this time it was a killing frost, night after night. I remember getting up early to get ready for a delivery April 15 to Sonoma County and coming down to the nursery at

7:30 A.M. to find everything coated with frost. I said to myself, 'This is it. I can't cope with it anymore. I'm out of here.'"

The killing frosts were attributed to La Niña, another unusual weather system that hit North America in the spring of 1999. Jackie lost a lot of plants and ended up with many more that were bruised and stunted. Although she sold many plants in May because home gardeners were replacing their own lost stock, she had trouble getting replacement plants from her suppliers, and by June she had virtually nothing to sell.

By the end of 1999, the nursery's gross sales had reached only $52,800, about $25,000 less than the last full year of the founders' ownership.

Again, the nursery qualified for disaster assistance—$17,444 this time, based on a complicated compensation rate set by the Department of Agriculture. "I included pictures of ruined plants with my application," Jackie says.

"I know the drill now, but I certainly hope I never have to do it again. I would like to make money by running a profitable business rather than receiving a disaster grant."

## Finally, a Year with Good Weather

Thankfully, Jackie's third year in business, 2000, brought no weather disasters. With no crisis to drain her resources, Jackie was finally able to implement her initial business plan.

Whereas the original owners had operated on a year-to-year basis, selling virtually all of their inventory by the end of each year and starting from scratch the following year, Jackie had always believed that she could increase her profits by increasing the proportion of plants she propagated herself. She had nearly $25,000 worth of purchased inventory on hand when 2000 began (almost all of it ordered the summer before, when she was reeling from the La Niña losses), but she mapped out a strategy for reducing her plant acquisition expenditures to $1,500 a year by increasing propagation.

The business's plan to propagate became a reality when Jackie's youngest son, Jackson, began working at the business full-time in January 1999. When Jackie had bought the business in 1998, Jackson had been taking general education courses at Mendocino Community College in Ukiah, unsure of what he wanted to do with his life. "I didn't have much direction," he acknowledges. The more he worked in the nursery with his mother, the more he realized he liked the work. He took classes in nursery management, plant propagation, and plant identification, and finished community college with a certificate in nursery production.

The propagation techniques Jackson learned in college proved to be much more successful than the ones that he and Jackie had previously used. "I had done propagation before, but I didn't know what I was doing," Jackson explains. "I was just cutting a piece off of a plant and sticking it in the ground and hoping it would root. I didn't know the reason why it would or anything like that. The most valuable thing I learned in school was the importance of cleanliness for propagation. I bleach all the cuttings and try to keep everything clean. It cuts down on the rot. I also learned a lot about plant mixes—what to put in to make it more or less water-retaining. I don't have an exact formula, but I know what works."

At the beginning of 2000, Jackie made Jackson a partner in the business. The decision reflected both his dedication and a desire on Jackie's part to cut her workers' compensation premium. Her first year in business, Jackie hadn't purchased workers' comp for her employees because she didn't know she was supposed to. "Then I took a business accounting class at the College of the Redwoods from a real wizard, a former businessman named Tom Taylor," she says. "I learned a lot of things from him, like the fact that I should be buying workmen's comp. I had operated a whole year without it. I hate to think of how much trouble I could have gotten into if somebody had gotten hurt."

Workers' compensation coverage is required for employees, but not owners. By making Jackson a partner in 2000, the business's premium came to $1,600 instead of $2,400.

By the end of 2000, the gross for the business had grown to $62,000, plus about $75,000 in wholesale sales potential from the stock that was wintering over. That year, Jackie paid herself a total of $17,000 and Jackson a total of $11,000, and each of her other children made a few thousand dollars from the business as well.

Late in 2000, Jackie was chosen as the recipient of the West Company's Entrepreneur of the Year award. As the year turned, prospects for 2001 were looking great.

"Spring's going to happen, and I'm going to have big plants that have over-wintered from last year," Jackie says. "It's the first year that I'm starting off with such a large volume of mature plants. I can't charge more, but the size is going to make people want them more. You don't want to have a reputation for being a nursery that sends out plants that are too small. And in June and July, when everybody else's plants are looking burned out, I'll have fresh ones from our propagation."

## www.moonrivernursery.com

As 2001 began, Jackie's first priority was to complete the redesign of her business website so that she could begin selling plants through the internet. While she expects the bulk of her business to continue to be wholesale sales to retail nurseries, she believes that retail sales through the internet hold the potential for vastly increased profits, since she would not only earn more on each sale but also cut her delivery costs.

"I kind of got the idea from the women at Mountain Maples, a Japanese maple nursery in Laytonville," she explains. "They used to do wholesale, like I do, and now they don't do wholesale at all. One day, they came here and walked around and said to me, 'We don't understand why you're not doing mail order. You could make so much more money. You make twice the wholesale price, plus the buyers pay for the shipping.'

"I thought about mail order, but I think internet sales will work even better for me, because I won't have the cost of the catalog."

Jackie had posted a rudimentary website sometime in 1999, but she'd made no effort to get it listed with search engines, so the only people who ever saw it were those who set out to. "It was designed by the teenage son of one of my best friends, and it was his first website," Jackie says. "He was a bad speller, so all the keywords in the metatags were misspelled, which meant no one could find it." (For instance, horticulture was spelled "hortaculture," so anyone using "horticulture" as a keyword couldn't find her site.)

To move into e-commerce more seriously in 2001, Jackie met several times with Joy Calonico, the West Company's technology manager. Then she asked a friend, Sam Gitchel, to supervise the redesign and relaunching of the Moon River Nursery website.

On a drizzling mid-February day in 2001, Sam brings his laptop to the nursery office to show Jackie the progress he's made. The office is filled with the organic smell of potting soil that's piled on a table waiting for Jackie's next potting session, which is her favorite part of the business.

Sam, a burly, bearded man in his mid-forties, is in the process of reinventing himself as a website designer. "I had never even laid eyes on a computer until two years ago," he admits. "I worked in the woods, and I had a lumber mill and a fishing boat. Both of those industries have gone downhill, so I decided to go into the web design business. Luckily, my place is all paid for, so I don't have any payments."

In fact, Jackie's website reflects the collaboration of three entrepreneurs: Jackie, who's written the copy; Sam, who's photographed the plants on a digital camera and come up with the page design; and a programmer in Siberia. "Isn't that a kick?" Jackie comments about the location of her programmer. He is twenty-four years old and works out of his home in a city that doesn't even have a bank. He and Sam "met" through eBay, the internet auction site. They have a modified barter arrangement. Sam handles all of the programmer's financial transactions in the United States and sets up his eBay ads; in return, the programmer charges Sam only about 20 percent of the going rate for programming.

Sam wires him his compensation via Western Union. (Sam has a similarly unconventional compensation arrangement with Jackie. "I'm going to give him a percentage of whatever I sell through the website," Jackie says. "He told me, 'Whatever you think is fair,' so I'm thinking 5 percent, with maybe a bonus built in, like 7 percent for over $20,000 in sales. We're friends, and I want him to make money too.")

Sam shows Jackie how to check a listing he's posted for her on eBay. As an experiment in e-commerce, she's offering a collection of rare primulas for $19.95, plus shipping. "Let's try sticking in 'primula' and seeing if your item comes up," he tells her.

"It will," she replies. "I already tried it first thing this morning."

Sure enough, when Sam types "primula" in the search box on the eBay site, Jackie's offering pops up. "There it is," he says. "You've had fifteen hits."

"There were only twelve earlier today," Jackie notes. "So at least people are looking at it."

Now they turn their attention to perfecting Jackie's listing on www.freetailer.com, another e-commerce site through which she's hoping to sell plants. "Okay, it says that the description has to be less than 4,000 letters, so I guess I'll just eliminate some plants from my list," she says. Her regular website lists eighty plants for sale, and she had hoped to list forty of them on the freetailer site, but there doesn't appear to be room. "I think I'm going to have to go back to this and edit it later," she says. "That'll give me something to do tonight."

They decide to take one last look at the latest version of Moon River's website (www.moonrivernursery.com) before e-mailing their comments to the Siberian programmer. "This is just the first draft," Sam warns her as they enter the URL for the nursery in the search area. "I've already gone through it and checked everything and marked down what I didn't like. For instance, the order form was going to take two pages, which isn't a good idea. And I want to put your Paypal account information on it too." (Like many small e-tailers, Jackie plans to use Paypal, an on-line credit card payment system, rather than accept Visa or MasterCard, whose fees are higher.)

When Jackie types the name of her website into the search field and presses the "Enter" key, her welcome page pops up. The background is a lovely shade of lavender with green highlights. The message on the page reflects Jackie's folksy nature. "We are a small family owned and operated nursery located in Northern California at the edge of the Redwood Forest on the beautiful Mendocino Coast approximately 150 miles north of San Francisco and five miles south of the town of Mendocino," the message begins. ". . . We endeavor to raise long-living, healthy plants, and lean toward the unusual. . . . Our plants are grown with care and a lot of attention, and they respond with beauty and vigor, bringing you years of enjoyment. While we use the best inorganic time-released fertilizer available, the plants you receive will arrive free of dangerous pesticides or other additives designed to artificially 'pump up' the plant material."

Jackie is pleased with what she sees. "He must have done a lot of work on it while I was sleeping last night because it looks completely different than it did last night," Jackie observes.

"Don't forget, they're fourteen hours ahead in Siberia," Sam says.

## Rolling with the Seasons

The nursery business is by definition seasonal, even in Jackie's part of California, where the growing season is almost year-round. In general, January and February are cleanup, propagation, and paperwork months. It's one of the few times of the year that Jackie can catch up on back issues of *Fine Gardening*, *Horticulture*, *Pacific Horticulture*, and *Garden Design*, her favorite gardening magazines.

March through June are the biggest selling months. "From mid-March through June, hopefully it's insanity around here," Jackie says. Throughout that period, Jackie spends one day each week, usually a Saturday or Sunday, examining her inventory of plants that are ready to sell. "Mostly, I'm looking at size—a plant that's big enough to look good," she explains. "And, of course, it has to be healthy. And I like it to be blooming or ready to bloom."

Then, on Sundays or Mondays, she fills out a plant availability list and faxes it to the twenty retail nurseries that regularly place orders. On Tuesdays, she calls the nurseries she hasn't heard back from and takes additional orders. "When I'm trying to make a sale, I'll take my portable phone out into the nursery and start walking around it describing what's blooming, and I'll end up with a $300 sale," Jackie says. In a typical week, seven or eight nurseries will place orders. Almost always, the largest order comes from Berkeley Horticulture, a high-end retail nursery in Berkeley. Its median weekly order is $400.

When all the orders are in, Jackie and her children pull the sold plants from their holding areas, array them on four tables, and groom them. The grooming takes a total of 24 hours, generally split between two people working two six-hour days to replenish the soil, add a dose of fertilizer, and shape the plants headed for market.

The day before the delivery, they load the truck. To make the trip worthwhile, Jackie likes to deliver at least $1,500 worth of plants, since the delivery process takes both her and Jackson away from the nursery for a full day and costs them about $100 in gasoline. If she has room in the truck, Jackie always carries extra plants. "Very rarely do we bring anything back, because, of course, we're going to take the prettiest, most outrageous stuff," she says. "Taking along extra plants has often doubled our sales at a particular nursery. And if I'm making a trip to Berkeley Hort, and Smith & Hawken in Berkeley hadn't ordered that week, I'll usually stop at Smith & Hawken and let them buy off the truck."

On delivery days, Jackie and Jackson are usually on the road by 8 A.M. The truck's radio is always tuned to a station that features sports talk, a passion of theirs. Jackie loves delivery day. "I love the whole thing," she says. "Just being in that enclosed space with Jackson really cements our relationship. And developing the relationships with the buyers and nurseries, that's something I couldn't do over the phone."

Delivering the plants herself has helped developed loyalty among her customers, Jackie believes. While she's dropping off plants, she spends time cultivating her relationships with the nursery buyers. "I love developing relationships," she says. "I get attached to people really easily, so the delivery days feed my need for that. We always have a good time talking about the Raiders versus the 49ers. Plus, when I'm visiting with them, I invite retailers to tell me what their customers are looking for. Especially at the beginning of the year I tell them, 'If there's anything you're having a hard time getting, let me know, and I'll try to grow it for you.'

"I really think that some of our customers buy from us because it's us, because I've gone and visited them a couple of times and let them buy off the truck and started a rapport. It's not an easy business to get new customers in because there's so much competition.

"And by delivering the plants myself, I have the opportunity to do whatever it takes to make things right. If the buyer tells me, 'Half a dozen of those plants you brought me last week died,' I fix it right then and there," she continues. "One of our mottoes is that nobody should take plants they don't want. If I sent the plants with a paid driver, he's not likely to take time to make sure that the buyer's satisfied."

At every delivery site, Jackie usually takes time to check out her competitors' stock. "There's new plants coming out all the time," she says. "You really have to keep your eyes open if you want to be on the cutting edge. When I go to nurseries, I'll ask them, 'Do you have anything really cool?' They'll show me, and I'll buy one of them to use as a mother plant, and the next year I'll have them to sell myself."

A typical delivery day ends when Jackson steers the truck into the driveway at home at 11 P.M., fifteen hours after they set out. Between early March and late June, the peak planting season, Jackie and her son will make probably two dozen delivery trips, most of them to the Bay Area, but also to Napa Valley, plus a few up to far northern California, where few other wholesalers will deliver.

When June comes to an end, so does most of Jackie's wholesale business. "It's like a big Halt sign goes up," she explains. "Nobody buys in July. The business just dies. So July and August are big cleanup months for us. And then we start propagating again in late August, not as actively as in the winter, but especially for winter bloomers like *pulmonarias* and hellebores, which we want to be big enough to bloom."

Late summer is also when Jackie begins to draw up a list of plants that she wants to purchase for the following selling season. For seedlings, she goes through a plant broker based in southern California. "They broker plants from companies we used to buy directly from—all of the really high-quality producers of wholesale plants," she says. "They go to the nurseries and check things out. If I get a group of plants in that are turned upside down and broken, they'll take care of it."

Jackie buys most of her bare root stock from a supplier in Holland. "Once or twice a year their rep comes and visits," she explains. "If I'm looking for something special, he's really good about finding it. I get things from him like *sidalceas* and *liguilaria*, which are really hard to come by." The bare root stock is flown in crates to the San Francisco airport, where it's scrutinized by customs and agricultural inspectors before being released for delivery to Moon River.

"The advantage of bare root is that you can plant them and in two weeks to a month they're fully grown," Jackie explains. "It's the best way to do it, but it's also the most expensive way—75 cents to $1.25 per plant."

## 60,000 Potential Customers

Today is the opening day of the annual San Francisco Garden Show at the Cow Palace, which sprawls across six acres in Daly City, a close-in suburb of San Francisco. If you're a serious gardener and live within 100 miles of San Francisco, you're likely to make a pilgrimage to the nation's fourth largest garden show sometime over the next five days. Sixty thousand gardeners are expected to pass by the 400 vendors' booths set up in the exhibition halls. With any luck, several hundred of them will stop and buy Jackie's special offerings: bleeding hearts, primulas, and a few other unusual perennials.

Jackie set up shop here for the first time the year before, in 2000, and went home four days later with almost $2,500 in her pocket, about half of it profit. This year, she's cut her expenses by subletting space in another exhibitor's booth for $350, half of what she paid last year for a booth of her own; by staying with a friend in nearby Mill Valley; and by driving her pickup truck down from Mendocino, rather than her big delivery truck, which will save about $125 in gasoline costs. She's hoping to gross $2,500 to $3,000 for five days' work, about the same amount that her wholesale business has grossed in the previous three weeks.

Two hours into the show's first day, sales are slow, but Jackie's mood is upbeat. "I think most people spend the morning looking around, and then they make their purchases in the afternoon," she says.

Jackie and Jackson drove down from Mendocino the day before with 140 gallon-size *dicentras* (commonly known as bleeding hearts) and a few flats of primulas and unusual perennials, such as corydalis (her biggest-selling plant) and *omphalodes cappadocica.* The year before, Jackie had sold out of the bleeding hearts early, so she brought more this year. She also raised her price to $12, up from $10, but she admits that her bleeding hearts don't look quite as good as last year.

"This is the thing about the plant business," she says, pointing to a bleeding heart that's just barely in bloom. "These guys got planted ten days earlier than last year, and they're ten days behind where they were last year. They're healthy, but they don't have as many blooms as last year. It has definitely been colder up in Mendocino this winter."

A woman stops to ask Jackie a question about how to care for bleeding hearts. "I bought bleeding hearts here last year, and they've died back to nothing," she says.

"That's what they're supposed to do in the winter," Jackie explains.

"But there's nothing visible yet above the soil," the woman continues.

"Everybody's are late this year," Jackie assures her. "The ones I have that overwintered in the ground are just starting to come up. Be patient."

The woman moves on without buying, but Jackie doesn't mind. Jackie does the garden show as much for the social interaction as for the profit. "Interacting with people is one reason I like coming here," she says. "One of the really fun things is that you get together with people from other nurseries and develop relationships."

At 12:30 P.M., two and a half hours after the doors opened, Jackie lowers the price on her bleeding hearts to $10 each. On one of her scouting jaunts around the plant market, she'd found that another vendor was selling bleeding hearts for $6.75. She doesn't think his are quite as nice as hers, so she won't even consider pricing hers that low. She's hoping that he only brought a few and that he'll sell out early.

As she's talking, she's ringing up a sale for $50 worth of primulas. "That sale was really fun," Jackie says afterward. "The lady knew exactly what she wanted. She went right for the primulas and picked out the nicest ones."

Two friends laden with shopping bags each pick out a four-inch corydalis, one of Jackie's favorite perennials. "We were one of the first nurseries in the country to carry that plant," Jackie says proudly. "The nursery's previous owners carried them back from England. They're still hard to find."

By 1 P.M., Jackie has sold about $100 worth of plants. "I'm a third of my way towards making my rent," she says after counting her money. As she's putting her money back in her pocket, a customer comments on a gallon-size corydalis. "I love the color of that blue," she says. "It's so pretty." Sensing the potential for a sale, Jackie jumps in. "And it blooms all winter long," she points out. "Plus, when they get warm, the scent is so nice. It's really sweet."

The woman doesn't buy, but two other customers come by and ask Jackie for help picking out a collection of primulas. "These are wonderful," one of them exclaims as she picks up a four-inch pot to examine it more closely. The women leave the booth carrying $40 worth of primulas.

The afternoon passes quickly, although for every customer who buys a plant, it seems as though two or three ask about how they can get the bleeding hearts they have at home to put out more blooms. "As long as you keep cutting the flower off after it's done, new ones will shoot out," Jackie advises over and over again. But there are enough buying customers to make the day worthwhile. When the show closes at 6 P.M., Jackie has about $400 in her pocket. And Jackson has arrived from Mendocino with more plants in his car.

By the end of the five-day show, Jackie will have sold about $2,000 in plants, less than she had hoped, but enough to make participation worthwhile. "For the energy we put into it, it was okay," she says a week later. "I'd always like it to be more, but we really didn't take that much plant stock down there. We sold 120 *dicentras* and brought about twenty home with us. I felt really good about what I sold. The guy who'd been selling them for $6.75 never did sell all of his either, even though he reduced them to $5 on Saturday."

## Carving Out a Niche

Jackie hopes to be in the nursery business for the rest of her working life. Despite the weather-related problems she experienced in her first two years, her experience in 2000, a relatively normal weather year, has confirmed her belief that her initial business plan is solid.

"There was a lot of learning done my first two years, but it wasn't the kind of learning I did last year," Jackie says. "It was basically learning to survive. Now, we're starting to do the fine-tuning. I feel we get more and more efficient every year, in lots of different areas. We're more efficient with our deliveries, and our production is way up. If 2000 had been my first year in business, I would be cruising now. But I had accumulated debt from the two years before, and I had to pay that off."

In 2001, she'd already taken several steps to put her business on a firmer footing. For one thing, she made all four of her children partners, which has saved at least $1,600 a year in workers' compensation insurance costs. "My insurance agent told me, 'For God's sake, make 'em all partners,'" Jackie says. "He couldn't believe how much they were going to charge us to treat them all as employees." So far, Jackson, twenty-three, a partner since 2000, is the only one of her children who works at the nursery full-time virtually year-round. During the selling season, Sky, twenty-two, works about twenty hours a week to augment her night job as a waitress, and Bohdy, eighteen, works about twenty hours a week. In the summer, when Jackie's oldest child, Donovan, twenty-seven, would be home from college, he would probably work there too—"By then, everybody else will be burned out, and he'll pick up the slack," Jackie says.

One day early in 2001, the three children (minus Donovan, who was away at college) sat down with Jackie to draw up a partnership agreement. Each now owns a portion of the business commensurate with the amount of time spent working in it. Jackie owns the largest share, at 35 percent, and Jackson the second largest, at 25 percent. Sky and Bohdy each own 15 percent, and Donovan 10 percent.

"If there's a profit at the end of year, most will have to go into the business, but everybody would get a bonus based on the hours they've worked," Jackie explains.

To cover the family's household expenses, Jackie periodically takes out an owner's draw. Each of the children gets paid an hourly wage based on experience. Jackson makes the most, at $9.25 an hour for nursery work and $10 an hour for driving, and the others each make a few dollars an hour less.

Being given ownership in the business has made her children feel more vested in its success, Jackie says. "Everybody fights to be able to be the one to check the mail for the checks from the retail nurseries," she laughs.

## "Success Is a Process"

Over the last six months, Jackie has spent a lot of time thinking about just how big she wants her business to grow. While she hopes to increase her gross revenues annually, she doesn't really want to preside over the helm of a truly big business.

"I am so much of a hands-on person that I would rather it be smaller than bigger," she says. "Everybody I know who is in this business is constantly struggling with this. When I go to the garden shows and talk to people, it's something they all say. That's one reason I like to go to the shows, because sitting here I feel like I'm the only one having this struggle."

To reach $100,000 in gross wholesale sales would require sacrifices that Jackie is unwilling to make. "It would take two trips a week to the Bay Area, which is another day away from the nursery for both Jackson and me, plus more gasoline costs," she says. "I don't want to put myself through that."

Jackie wants to relocate the nursery to the two-acre property on which her house sits, both for convenience and economy. "I want to develop my property into a wonderland of shade gardens," she says. "There'll be more space, and at two o'clock in the morning, if I want to go out and pot something, I can do it. You don't know how many times it's been midnight and I've been thinking, 'I didn't cover this or that, and it's going to freeze tonight.' It would be a lot different if I could just walk out the door and do it. And that $250 a month I now spend on rent could go into my property, not to a landlord."

There's some urgency to Jackie's plan, because a disease is killing many of the trees that provide shade at her nursery, which could spell disaster for her desire to specialize in shade plants.

"More and more, I want to specialize," she says. "I've found I really like specializing in primulas. They're expensive to acquire, but once you get them, they're dividable. Eventually, I'll have enough mother plants that I won't have to order any in.

"The most beautiful plants I have are shade plants, like corydalis, *omphalodes*, and *pulmonarias*—and not many wholesale nurseries carry them. It's a niche that really isn't being filled, and when you're a little guy, you've got to carve out a niche. The competition is unbelievable, so you can't really go head-to-head on common plants and beat the big guys."

Jackie's approach to her business has changed over the last few years. "I think the secret to succeeding in business is true of succeeding at just about anything: In order to succeed, you can't quit," she says. "One thing that I have discovered this past year, talking with Rick Moon and other people, is that success is a process. It's not a destination. In my mind, it always used to be a destination. You work, and you know you're successful when you have lots of money in the bank. But my whole concept has changed. I think I'm a success now. I really do feel successful. But it took a lot of consulting to get to that point."

"About two months ago, my mother told me that she was really proud of me because I was running a business that was making the planet a better place, and I was doing it for my family," Jackie continues. "It was one of the biggest compliments I've ever gotten from her. And, come to think of it, it sums it all up."

*Yasmina Cadiz was never the same after she set her eyes on Fortuny lamps—and started a business to sell them.*

chapter 7

# Lighting the World

## Yasmina Cadiz

## Punctilio, Inc.

## Chicago, Illinois

Oak Street is one of the most prestigious retail addresses in Chicago. Just around the corner from the famed Magnificent Mile, the tree-lined street is known for exclusive boutiques like Kate Spade and Ultimo and Prada.

Since May 2000, Oak Street has also been the home of the showroom for Punctilio Inc., a home accessory boutique business operated by Yasmina Cadiz.

Punctilio's space is like no other on the street. Incense perfumes the air, French café music creates a soothing atmosphere, and soft, silk-filtered lighting casts a golden glow. Not a week goes by without a customer telling Yasmina, "I feel like I'm in another world" when in her store. A comment like that makes her day.

Only a few years ago, Yasmina was unemployed and unsure about her future prospects. Headstrong, opinionated, and certain of her eye for good design, Yasmina had often tangled with her bosses, never staying in a job for more than two years. After a series of frustrating job experiences, she vowed to never put herself at the mercy of another employer again.

"In my last job, I worked nine months without a single day off," she says. "I had no life outside my job, and even though I did it very well, my employer didn't appreciate me. I never wanted to work for anyone else again."

A close friend suggested she start an internet business. So in the fall of 1998, Yasmina parlayed a loan of $15,000 and a flair for marketing into her own business: selling exquisite hand-painted Fortuny lamps from Italy through well-placed advertisements in home decor magazines and a website she designed mostly by herself. In 2000 she began selling lamps and furniture of her own design.

For Yasmina, the motivation behind starting her own business was an overriding desire to be her own boss. But the business had to be one that allowed her to use her talents to best advantage. "I just want to make a living being creative," she says. "It's about being creative and designing things that people want and making a mark."

Getting a business likes hers up and running has been complicated. She's had to cope with international currency fluctuations and master the complexities of the internet. Sometimes, cash-flow problems have sent her into a state of panic. So far, she has conquered every one of the challenges.

In 1999, her first full year of operation, she grossed $110,721. In 2000 she grossed $136,212.

## An Eye for Detail

Yasmina was born in Chicago in 1969 to parents who had moved there from Puerto Rico. Her father is Spanish by birth; her mother can trace her ancestry both to the Taino Indians, the original inhabitants of Puerto Rico, and to Africans brought there as slaves.

Both her parents are hairdressers. They separated when she was nine, and her mother struggled while raising Yasmina and an older sister on her own. "She was really strict," Yasmina says of her mother, her voice tinged with both affection and respect. "She was hard on us. But I'm glad she was the way she was, because it made me who I am. My mother raised two really strong women."

Yasmina grew up in Chicago's largely Latino Logan Square neighborhood and attended Carl Schurz High, which was designed by a famous architect, Dwight H. Perkins, and designated a historical landmark. Even as a high school student, Yasmina had an appreciation for good design, and she felt privileged to attend the historically significant school.

After high school, Yasmina enrolled in Columbia College, a downtown Chicago institution that specializes in visual, performing, and communication arts. "It's a fabulous college for studying the arts," she says. "The instructors come from all over the world, and they're people with real experience as artists."

Yasmina spent two years taking classes in photography, interior design, architectural history, and art. "I once sat down with a counselor there who said, 'You're all over the board. You need to focus,'" she recalls. "I said, 'No, you don't understand. I photograph. I paint. I make furniture. Why should I have to put myself in a box? I like being all over the place.

"So I would sign up for classes that interested me. I didn't have the goal to get a degree."

During college, Yasmina supported herself by working in the fine arts department of an art supply store. Although the job paid little more than minimum wage, it had other perks. "I got a good discount, and because I had to understand the products, I learned a lot about different mediums," she says. "That's when my painting started to really evolve. I wouldn't trade that experience for anything." She was eventually promoted to assistant manager, which meant more money and considerable responsibility, even though she was still a teenager.

While there, Yasmina began her first business under the name Punctilio: designing business cards for a fee of $25. She chose the name after much deliberation. "I looked in a thesaurus for words that describe me, like *detail*," she recalls. "I was also looking for a word that I could extract the letters *inc* out of. Under *detail*, I came across the word *punctilious*. It was like, 'Oh, my God, that's it.' But I wasn't totally happy with it. Then I found *punctilio*, and I knew that was it."

According to a dictionary, punctilio means "careful observance of forms and minute detail or observance of code." On her business card, Yasmina used one of the vertical legs of the letter *u* to stand in for the *I* in Inc.

Yasmina left Columbia before earning a degree and, in 1991, took a drafting job with an interior architecture and design firm. A few months into the job, she decided to look for a full-time job in the fashion industry.

"It was really just a whim," she says. "I've always loved looking through fashion magazines, and I have a talent for putting clothes together in a stylish way, even if I don't have a penny in my pocket."

Because the owner liked her look, she was hired as a sales associate at the Giorgio Armani store, even though she had no previous experience selling high-end apparel. The salary was good, and the owner let her try her hand at decorating windows and coordinating local fashion shows, so Yasmina learned other skills that would come in handy later.

Yasmina stayed at Armani for about two years and then began to get bored, a pattern that was to repeat itself five times over the next seven years.

## Moving On

In the fall of 1992, she moved to Miami Beach for four months. She stayed with a friend and supported herself by painting trompe l'oeil wall murals, the second incarnation of Punctilio. She charged by the square foot and earned as much as $4,000 per mural.

The Chicago she returned to early in 1993 didn't seem to be interested in someone with her skills. "I couldn't find a job to save my life," she recalls. "I knew I didn't want to work for another designer. Two creative people—it's really tough to work together. So I was looking in retail, mainly home furnishings. About this time, a lot of the big furniture stores were starting to employ in-house designers, and I thought that was something I'd be good at. I was sending out résumés all the time, but not getting any offers."

It took almost a year for Yasmina to find a job, during which she lived with friends and depleted her savings. Finally, she was offered a job selling low-end Italian leather furniture. "I showed up, and as soon as I saw what they carried, I said to myself, 'I can't work here.' It was tack-y," she says with exaggerated emphasis. "It was for people who couldn't afford Roche Bobois, but wanted that look. But then I told myself, 'I've got to have a job.'"

As at many furniture stores, the sales associates at this store worked entirely on commission. Despite her disdain for the furniture, Yasmina threw herself into the job, learning arcane details about the furniture so that she could impress customers. In a good month, she could earn as much as $2,000, but most months, her commissions were barely enough to live on.

After about eight months, Yasmina began looking for a job at a higher-quality store. "Now I had this furniture selling under my belt," she says. "I thought I was more marketable." Within a few weeks, she got a job with a new, more upscale furniture store. But the store never developed a clientele, and Yasmina never made over $250 a week. (She had to work part-time as a painter to make ends meet.) After eight months, she was let go. The store closed soon afterward.

For a few months, Yasmina was again unemployed. Then she got a job at Roche Bobois, the upscale furniture chain. She spent a year there, drawing a salary of $350 a week against sales of $25,000 a month, and from the start sold enough furniture to cover the draw. For sales above $45,000 a month, she earned a commission of 5 percent.

Again, Yasmina got restless. Serendipitously, a friend gave her name to a headhunter for a furniture store that needed a manager. A major selling point was the compensation: $12 an hour, plus a 5 percent commission on storewide sales over $50,000 and a 6 percent commission on sales over $60,000. "That was real enticing," she says. "They were selling anywhere from $50,000 to $100,000 a month, which meant I'd be making more money than I was at Roche."

Yasmina was somewhat apprehensive about whether she possessed the managerial skills required for the job. "I hadn't ever been exposed to having to keep books before," she says. Plus, she had reservations about whether the type of furniture the store sold would be popular with Chicagoans. Still, she took the job. "I will try anything if someone gives me the opportunity," she says. "I will totally dig in." It was July 1996.

## Falling in Love with a Lamp

At first, Yasmina was clearly in over her head administratively. "I kind of felt lost a little bit," she admits. "But that was okay, because as a friend of mine always says, I'm a Julie." She's referring to the cruise director on the old television sitcom *Love Boat*, who took on whatever task presented itself and did it well.

"I had to create what worked for me," Yasmina elaborates. "I actually revamped the way they did a lot of things and implemented things that were easier."

At this store, Yasmina was exposed for the first time to the Fortuny lighting collection. "When I walked in and saw these lamps, I thought, 'Oh, my God, I could sell these all day long,'" she recalls. "They're all Islamic-inspired designs, and the design just spoke to me. I swear I must have had a past life in the Middle East."

The Fortuny lights, which range in price from $600 to $8,000, were designed by Mariano Fortuny, a Venetian who was one of the premier stage, lighting, and costume designers in Europe for the first half of the twentieth century. Best known for his collection of pleated silk tunics, Fortuny also designed opalescent, silk-shaded ceiling and wall lamps that are widely admired for how they radiate and diffuse light, as well as for their intricate hand-painted designs.

The store's home office had promised Yasmina a fair amount of freedom, and almost right away she began thinking about how to increase the Chicago store's sales. Gradually, Yasmina persuaded the out-of-state owners to let her change the store's whole look.

She says she told them, "You really have to understand something about the Chicago market. Our summer here is like a month long, and Chicago people like chenilles and velvets and dark colors. Most of what we have in stock here is pastel-colored linen furniture. Why don't we feature some really opulent slipcovered furniture in dark colors?" The owners gave her the go-ahead.

Selling more Fortuny lighting was another obvious sales strategy. When Yasmina took over the store, the lamps were just a sideline. "They only had like four, and they weren't being displayed well," Yasmina recalls. "They had little to no literature about them.

"So I got the Fortuny catalog and saw that they had a lot more lamp designs than we had in stock. I decided to call Italy directly to find out more about them. The representative there explained Mario Fortuny's background to me, and I got even more excited about them. I went out and found any books I could about the man and his work."

Yasmina persuaded the owners to let her stock the store with Fortuny lamps, rather than just take orders for them. "I told them, 'Everybody wants the floor lamp, so let me buy six,'" she says, noting that it was a hefty investment in inventory, given that the floor lamp retailed for almost $1,700. "They invested a lot of money in letting me redo the store. We changed it all over. It was fabulous. I created an atmosphere. We were pulling people in from the street with our window displays, and they were buying." Largely because of increased sales of Fortuny lights, Yasmina raised the store's gross to as much as $130,000 a month, 30 percent higher than her predecessor's record. "The owners were real happy with me, because the store was doing so well," she says. "And I was really happy working there. My visions were coming to life."

Yasmina ran the store for almost two years. But over time, she and the owners began to disagree about what look the store should feature. And then the company lost the right to sell Fortuny lamps in any of its stores. "When I heard that, I got upset, because losing the right to sell Fortunys was going to take away half of my income," Yasmina says.

Yasmina confronted the home office about what she felt were management problems there. The next thing she knew, she received a letter informing her that her services "were no longer required." It was the eve of her annual two-week vacation.

"I cried, not because I couldn't believe it, but because I felt it was my business," she says. "I was proud of myself. It felt like a well-oiled business to me. I felt like it was being taken away from me."

## "What Am I Going to Do?"

Even though she was facing unemployment, Yasmina decided to go on vacation anyway.

"I was lying around a pool in Palm Beach with my friend, Dee Dee Falon, and all I could think about was, 'What am I going to do with my life?'" she remembers. "I wanted the same level of control and responsibility that I'd had before, which is very rare. I didn't know where I could find that, and I was also feeling that I never wanted to work for another employer ever again."

Dee Dee asked Yasmina why she didn't start her own business. "Doing what?" Yasmina says she responded. "I don't have any money to start a business. I spent everything I earned."

"You could start an internet business," Dee Dee suggested.

Yasmina laughed. She later explained, "I had only taught myself to use a computer two years before. I still didn't surf the net at this point. I wasn't even using e-mail."

Yasmina and Dee Dee were staying with a friend in Florida who was internet-savvy, and Yasmina consulted with her about the fledgling idea.

"She told me there was a lot of potential for internet business," Yasmina recalls. "I asked her, 'How much do you think it would cost to set up?' She said, 'You can probably get a website for $1,000.'"

That sounded manageable to Yasmina. But she still needed a product to peddle. "I said to Dee Dee, 'What could I sell?'" she continues.

"And Dee Dee said, 'Why don't you sell Fortuny lamps?'

"I jumped out of the pool, and I said, 'Get me to a computer. I've got to send the Fortuny manufacturer an e-mail.'"

Yasmina dashed off an e-mail to Matteo Lando, her contact at Venetia Studium, the Venice company that makes the Fortuny lamps. She told him that she was starting a new business, reminded him of her success selling the lamps for her previous employer, and asked to be designated as one of Fortuny's Midwest representatives.

Within days, Lando wrote back: "I will be pleased to start a business relationship with you. I think you are a very smart person and appreciate the way you work. I look forward to hearing from you soon."

## Starting Up

It's one thing to daydream about starting a business while lounging around a swimming pool in Palm Beach. It's another to actually launch it.

Most small-business experts would advise someone who wants to start a business to begin by writing a comprehensive business plan. That's not how Yasmina operates. Her style is to act first and think later. She thought that her previous jobs had prepared her to run her own business. "Every person I've ever worked for taught me what *not* to do," she says.

Yasmina had learned a lot about how to sell Fortuny lamps while she was working at the furniture store. Among the lessons she'd learned was that she would need to always have enough in stock to give her a competitive advantage over the other retailers who handled the lamps, since they could only promise delivery in four months. So her first priority was to place an order for lamps.

"I put together an ideal first order and realized I was going to need to spend $25,000 on inventory," she says. She had no hope of raising $25,000 to buy inventory, so she sent her contact at the Fortuny laboratory an e-mail asking if the factory would ship her first order on consignment. The answer, predictably, was a firm no.

However, the Fortuny rep informed her that she wouldn't have to pay for the lamps until they were shipped. That gave her four months of breathing space. She took a hard look at her order, pared it to about $4,500, and placed it.

With the lamps on order, the next thing Yasmina needed to do was to advertise. Magazines have a long lead time, so she had to get moving to make sure the ads began running at about the same time the lamps were arriving from Italy. "I knew from my last job where it made sense to advertise," she says. "*Metropolitan Home* and *Elle Décor* worked. When we ran ads in those magazines, we'd had to put in a separate phone line to handle all the calls."

Yasmina designed her first ad herself, a practice she continues to this day. Then she called an ad rep for *Metropolitan Home* whom she knew from having placed ads for the furniture store. "I said, 'I'm starting my own business, and I have no money, so I want to make a deal,'" she says, smiling now at her naivete. "She laughed, and then she told me about remnants—ad space available only at the last minute, but at a substantial discount. I got a quarter page that would ordinarily go for $3,200 for $1,200."

Even better, the magazine agreed to defer payment until thirty days after the ad ran. Since there was a three-month lead time for publication, that gave Yasmina basically four months to come up with the money.

Yasmina also committed to a $900 ad in *Elle Décor*. To reach the upscale Chicago market, she placed a quarter-page ad for $1,000 in *Chicago Social*, and a $1,450 ad in the *Chicago Home Book*. "It's a resource book with the best of the best in the Chicago area," she explains. "I called them after they had closed the space, and they had two pages left, which normally would have cost $4,200, but I got for $1,450."

Again, Yasmina was not required to pay up front. "But here I was committed to thousands of dollars even before I received a single lamp," she notes.

Yasmina still had no idea how she was going to raise the $4,500 she needed to buy lamps, plus the $4,550 she needed to pay for ads that would be running over the next several months. Nor did she have any idea how to pay for her other start-up costs or even what they might amount to.

"No phone lines, no business cards, no fax, no office space, no website costs—I wasn't counting any of that yet," she says. "I was just thinking of what I needed to spend on inventory and advertising."

## www.punctilio.com

One of the first things Yasmina did after her epiphany by the pool was to begin searching for a website developer. It was the summer of 1998, just before e-commerce became a household word, and it wasn't easy finding that kind of assistance.

"I went through the Yellow Pages to try to find out how much it would cost me to put together a website, and I was getting quotes in the $40,000 range," she says. Spending that kind of money was clearly out of the question, so she looked for a bargain-basement alternative. She decided to write the content herself and hire an acquaintance of an acquaintance to do the programming.

"He told me the first thing I needed to do was secure a domain name, and I was like, 'What's a domain name?'" she recalls. "Well, I found out that the domain name is like gold. I knew my domain name needed to be punctilio.com, and he told me, 'Fine, but you've got to find out if it's available.' So he searched, and, luckily, it was available. I borrowed Dee Dee's credit card and secured it."

Just in time, as it turned out. The very next week she got an e-mail from a merchant in Maine who wanted the punctilio.com domain name for his store, which was coincidentally named Punctilio. She refused and told her lawyer to start the process of establishing it as a trademark.

With her domain name secured, the next thing Yasmina needed for her website was a design. "I sat down with the web designer for maybe an hour and a half and told him I needed a home page with a contact list page and a couple of other things," she says. "From the start, the point of the website was really to make it feel like a real brick-and-mortar business, since I wasn't going to have a showroom or anything. I wanted a profile page about me, so people could see who was behind the business. He was excited about doing something creative, and he said, 'Let's give you a splash page, something that splashes up there for 10 seconds before you go to your home page.'

"I still wasn't even surfing the net myself, so I didn't know the terminology. He'd use a term, and I'd have to ask him what he meant, and he'd say, 'Here, let me show you.'"

If Yasmina was a technological neophyte when she first sat down with her webmaster, she was an enthusiastic convert to the promise of the internet by the time she got up. "I went to Kinko's after I left there, and I spent like $70 on computer time," she says. "I went in and opened up PhotoShop and started to scan in my different pictures. I taught myself what I could and then printed out a page, because I needed to see a mock-up. I put everything where I wanted it and wrote down the type fonts—every piece of information so that when he ultimately scripted, it would all be there for him. I laid out all my pages just the way you see them now on the website. I did all ten pages and went back to him and gave them to him. All he had to do was HTML it."

Yasmina uploaded the website, www.punctilio.com, in September 1998. She was immensely proud. "I basically created my website for $1,000," she says. "When I tell people how much I invested in my website, they can't believe it."

## "Honey, You Need a Microloan"

With most of the groundwork laid for the launch of the business, Yasmina now had to figure out how to pay for it. At the time, she didn't even have a major credit card. "I was about a month away from having to start paying for stuff, and I started getting really nervous," she says. "I realized that I needed to borrow some money."

She got in touch with the Small Business Administration, which sent her a pamphlet about local resources. Among them was the Service Corps of Retired Executives (SCORE), which provides free mentoring and computer-based tutoring to owners of small businesses.

Yasmina went to SCORE's Chicago office to see what kind of help she might get. "They have programs set up in a computer on how to put together a business plan," Yasmina explains. "When they told me that, I was like, 'What is in a business plan?'"

Yasmina spent a few days at SCORE reading up on business plans. "Then I sat down and outlined what I thought my business plan was going to be, and after that I went and talked to one of their counselors," she says.

"My first business plan was very loose. It was not typewritten or anything. The counselor thought I was crazy. But he also thought I was interesting. He said to me, 'I'm going to tell you right now, honey, you're not going to get any money from any bank. You have no collateral. You own nothing.'

"He was right. I wouldn't have loaned me money either. But I was thinking that because I was so passionate about my business concept and because it was such a good idea, someone would give me money."

Yasmina then went to her personal bank to ask about getting a business loan. Because of the small amount of money involved, the bank discouraged her from applying. She went back to SCORE for more advice.

"The counselor said, 'Honey, you need a microloan,'" Yasmina recalls. "I said, 'What's that?' And he explained that a small business loan is $100,000, and a microloan is $1,000 to maybe $20,000. I said to myself, 'Yeah, I need one of those.'"

The counselor also told her about several nonprofit organizations in Chicago that provide microloans to businesses.

"At the first one, they totally didn't even give me the time of day," Yasmina says. "They wouldn't even let me finish my pitch. They just said, 'Well, maybe we can give you $2,000.' I said, 'You're not hearing me. I need $10,000.' And they said, 'No, we'll lend you $2,000, and then when you pay back that $2,000, we'll lend you more.'

"That was their business model. They didn't individualize. They just processed people."

Yasmina was so demoralized by that experience that she didn't even want to approach the second microloan provider, the Women's Self-Employment Project (WSEP). For one thing, she knew that WSEP charged for its services. "They have a sliding scale, but I didn't have *any* income, so I couldn't really pay anything," she explains.

She called the attorney friend who had incorporated her business and filed for trademark protection. He told her about WSEP too.

Still wary from her experience with the other microlender, she was reluctant to call. Her friend, a longtime contributor to WSEP, made the call for her.

## "I Was *No* Income"

WSEP is a pioneer in microenterprise development in the United States. Since its founding in 1986, it has disbursed more than $1.9 million in more than 700 loans to just over 600 low-income female borrowers—entrepreneurs whom conventional lenders would likely have rejected as either uncreditworthy or too small to bother with. In 1999 WSEP was certified as a community development financial institution, enabling it to begin operating an Individual Development Account (IDA) savings program along with its lending and entrepreneur training programs.

WSEP's overarching goal is to help low-income women become economically self-sufficient through self-employment and asset development. WSEP's customers range in age from nineteen to seventy-five, with a median age of thirty-nine. More than 80 percent are African American; 10 percent are Caucasian, and 4 percent Latina. In 1997, the latest year for which figures are available, 91 percent of WSEP's customers had incomes of less than $25,000 a year, and 78 percent were the primary providers for their families.

"We get a lot of customers with credit problems, a lot who have gone through messy divorces," says Eden Hurd, WSEP's director of loans and assets. "They're unconventional businesses, microbusinesses, ma-and-pa shops that are hoping to make maybe a $10,000 profit in their first year. Banks can't work with that."

There was no doubt that Yasmina qualified for WSEP's assistance on the basis of her income. "I wasn't just low-income," she says. "I was *no* income." Normally, prospective business owners who want to borrow money through WSEP must first complete a twelve-week course in small business management. Because Yasmina had already committed to $4,500 in inventory and more than $6,000 in business start-up costs (mostly advertising), WSEP agreed to waive the training requirement and put her request for a $15,000 loan on a fast track.

"Someone from WSEP called me and said, 'I need to see your business plan,'" Yasmina says. "I worked day and night on it, and put together a killer booklet. I didn't know what reaction to expect, because I'd never done a business plan before, but I sent it to them. The next thing I knew they set up a date for me to appear before their loan committee. They knew that time was of the essence, that I needed the money right away."

## "Why Wouldn't It Work for Me?"

Yasmina approached her presentation as she approaches everything in life—with passion and intelligence. Figuring that no one on the loan committee was likely to have seen a Fortuny lamp before, Yasmina had taken one with her to the meeting. "I told them Mario Fortuny's whole story," she says. "I had to make them understand that these are products that people want. I kept saying, 'People search for months to find these lamps, and I'll have them in stock. They won't have to wait four months for them to come from Italy. It worked at my old furniture store, and they never even put them in an ad. Why wouldn't it work for me? I need you to believe in me.'"

It takes only a few moments in Yasmina's presence to understand that her passion for these lamps is genuine. She believes that they are among the most beautiful manmade things on Earth and that anyone who can afford one would naturally want to own one.

Laverne Hall, WSEP's acting lending officer at the time, says the loan committee was initially skeptical about Yasmina's application. "When the committee first heard that I was recommending a loan for someone who wanted to sell $4,000 lamps, they were like, 'Oh, come on. Who would buy them at that price?'" she recalls. "But when they saw it, everybody oohed and aahed. The lamps are so unusual that they sell themselves."

The committee members were impressed by Yasmina's belief in her business concept. Still, they needed to make sure that WSEP's money—which, in this case, was actually the Small Business Administration's money—was going to be invested in a business with good prospects for success. They interrogated her about the details.

"They were trying to find a place where I didn't have it together," Yasmina says. "One thing that made them nervous was my lack of collateral. But once I helped them understand the value of the lamps, they started to look at them as collateral.

"They were also apprehensive about my plans to sell over the internet, since they hadn't funded any other businesses that were doing that yet. I tried to make them see that from the experience I'd had in retail, I had the skills to run the day-to-day business and that I would somehow figure out how to cope with challenges I hadn't come across before. Remember, I'm a Julie."

Yasmina impressed WSEP's loan committee, Hall says. "She had a very well put together business plan," she says. "She had quite a bit of experience in the industry. She had a great relationship with the supplier. And she had a wonderful website, which looked pretty sophisticated to us, given the other kinds of businesses we were used to seeing. Basically it was clear that all she needed was money."

In August 1998, less than a week after she appeared before the loan committee, Yasmina learned that she had been approved for an SBA loan. The money would be enough to cover the lamps already on order and four ads, plus a little bit of operating capital. The terms called for monthly payments of $745 for two years, at a 13¼ percent rate of interest.

"The bottom line was that I was going to have lamps, and people were going to see the ads and know what Punctilio was," Yasmina says.

The money arrived just in time. Two days after she received WSEP's check, "all the bills started to roll in—the phone line, the website, the business cards," Yasmina laughs. (Business cards might not sound like a big expense, but a business card designed by Yasmina is like nothing you've ever seen before. "If you're going to sell the Mercedes Benz of lighting, you've got to have a double-sided full-color card to assure people that you mean business—and that costs," she says.)

Yasmina's first order of eleven lamps arrived from Italy late in October 1998. Since they were imports, they first had to go to the Customs House in Chicago, where they were assessed 3.9 percent customs duty.

With the lamps came a bill for 8,335,000 lire. By Yasmina's calculations, based on the exchange rate for lire at the time she placed the order, that came to $4,525. Unschooled in international finance, Yasmina simply wrote Fortuny a check on her Chicago bank account for $4,525.

## Undercutting the Competition

About the same time the lamps arrived, Punctilio's ads were appearing in *Metropolitan Home* and *Elle Décor*, and Yasmina began getting calls. The callers often asked to be sent a brochure, something Yasmina hadn't anticipated in her business plan, since she intended for the website to serve as the catalog. She didn't want to go to the expense of creating a professionally printed brochure, so she designed one on a computer and photocopied it in color at Kinko's as the requests came in.

She also began getting calls from people who were already familiar with the Fortuny collection, ready to buy, and simply comparing prices. "They'd ask, 'How much is the Cesendello a Stello (Fortuny's floor lamp)?' And then they'd say, 'Oh, you're cheaper than (another store). How do we activate the order?' They were people who were already shopping for the lamps and had seen my ad."

Yasmina had initially priced the Fortuny lamps the same as her previous employer had. As she heard from prospective customers, she began to realize that to be competitive, she would have to undercut other retailers.

"I started calling around to find out what other people were charging," she remembers. "For some styles, some of the other retailers had better pricing than me, so I had to come down. On others, I could go up, as long as I priced myself $5 cheaper than the next cheapest one available."

Yasmina knew from her previous retail experience that the standard markup on most retail items was two to two and one-half times the wholesale cost. Given the high costs of shipping the lights from Italy—almost $500 for the largest light, the Scheherezade model, which retails for almost $4,000—she should have been marking the products up two and one-half times.

"But I had to do better than that to stay competitive," she says. "I know that's not the smartest thing to do, to price your product without taking into account your costs, but I have to do that in order to sell. My only angles were that I had the lights in stock and had better pricing than the established retailers."

## "We Had Words"

Once Yasmina started getting phone calls from people who had seen her ads, she found out what the $1,000 she had paid for her website had *not* bought her.

"I'd get these calls from people saying, 'I'm at your website and nothing is showing up. Can you tell me what's wrong?'" she says. "I'd tell them, 'Maybe you don't have tables enabled or Java enabled,' and then I'd hang up and go back to what I was doing, because I could get to my website just fine on my computer.

"Then one day I went to a friend's house and tried to get to my website on her computer. She had an old version of AOL (America Online) loaded onto her computer, and using that, I couldn't get to my website either. I went back to my webmaster and asked him, 'Why can't anyone using AOL 3.0 get to my website?'"

It turned out that the website developer had designed the site so that only people using the latest web browsers could access it, a problem for prospective customers who had older versions loaded into their computers. "If you had AOL 3.0, you'd just see Punctilio and a line," Yasmina explains.

The webmaster told Yasmina it would cost her another $1,000 for him to rescript her website to make it accessible to users of older browsers. "We had words," she says, in what sounds like an understatement. "I said, 'You're the one who made the decision to script for 4.0, not 3.0.'"

In the end, he rescripted the site for free. "And I decided I needed a new web developer," she says wryly.

Within two months of her rescripted website's relaunch, it received Netscape's Cool Site of the Day designation. That produced more than 4,000 hits to her site in one day and a couple of orders that she probably wouldn't have gotten otherwise.

Yasmina sold $12,616 worth of lights in the two months she was in business in 1998—enough, in her mind, to validate her business concept. Capping 1998 was an e-mail from *Hispanic Business*, a national magazine with a circulation of 200,000, informing her that she had been selected for one of its Entrepreneurial Spirit

Awards. The awards recognize entrepreneurs who "possess a remarkable business concept, marketing niche, organizational approach, or success story."

An article about the awardees said, "Whether or not these entrepreneurs ever reach the million-dollar revenue milestone, they have entered the game, and until now they have survived. In the risky world of small business, that means they have beaten the odds."

## Caught Up in Currency Fluctuations

Early in 1999 Yasmina found out that buying merchandise from another country was more complicated than she'd thought.

"At the time my shipment arrived, there was a lot of fluctuation in international currency markets, a lot of drama," she explains. "After they got my check, my representative at the Fortuny laboratory got in touch and said I still owed them $1,200, and they wanted to be paid in lire."

Yasmina was faced with a financial crisis. With bills also coming due for her advertisements, she didn't have money to send to Fortuny. Nor did she have enough money to pay for her second order of lamps, which was about to be shipped. In February 1999 she went back to WSEP, hat in hand, and asked for a loan of $6,500.

Worried that Yasmina might be in over her head, the loan committee quizzed her even more closely than previously. "They were worried that I hadn't covered all the details," Yasmina says. In the end, the committee turned down her request, but agreed to refinance her existing loan, at a slightly lower interest rate, and to lend her $3,200, the amount she'd already repaid. It also added an additional year to the term of her loan, which reduced her payments to about $430 a month from $715.

"At first, it really stressed me that they turned me down, because I wanted more of a cushion," Yasmina says. "But it turned out to be a good thing. I really didn't want a bigger loan, because it freaks me out to owe money."

The higher-than-expected cost of inventory that resulted from the lire's fluctuation gave Yasmina a big scare. "It hit me that this kind of thing could happen to me all the time, that I could never be sure when I placed an order what the lamp was ultimately going to cost me in dollars," she says.

## Perfecting the Business Plan

Throughout 1999 it sometimes seemed to Yasmina that every month required a modification to her business plan.

Yasmina spent part of the first half of 1999 investigating ways to protect herself from currency fluctuations. By this time, the lire had stabilized, but she was still fearful of getting caught up in another inflationary spiral. Plus, she was wiring her payments to Fortuny through her bank, which gave her a bad exchange rate. Her advisers at WSEP pressed her to come up with a reliable, low-cost way to transfer her payments to Italy. "The international aspect of her business scared us," recalls Laverne Hall. "There are so many horror stories out there about doing business with other countries. The whole thing was new to us. We didn't know how to technically advise her on it."

Every alternative Yasmina looked into seemed to have disadvantages. "I found one company that was going to give me a little bit better rate than the bank, but was actually going to be trading with my money," she remembers. "It made me kind of uncomfortable."

While running errands one day in her car, Yasmina was listening to National Public Radio, which was broadcasting a story about exchange rates. "I got so totally focused on the program that I pulled over," she remembers. "They were saying that you get the best exchange rate for foreign transactions if you use your credit card, and American Express gives you the best rate of all.

"I thought, 'Why didn't anyone tell me this before?' But I had my answer. I could use a credit card. And that would also give me another month to pay."

The problem was, Yasmina didn't have a bank-issued credit card, only a Marshall Field's card with a credit limit of $200. Coincidentally, Yasmina found a preapproved application for a credit card in her post office box one day. "It was addressed to the business that used to have my P.O. box," she says. "I decided to just enter my own information on this prequalified application and hope that maybe they would just process it. It worked, and I got an America Express card, and a gold card at that. I could charge like up to $10,000." Since July 1999 Yasmina has charged all of her orders on her American Express card, generally paying the full balance every month to avoid interest charges.

A cornerstone of Yasmina's initial marketing strategy was to stock the most popular styles of Fortuny lamps so that they could be delivered to a customer within days of placing an order (as opposed to the other U.S. Fortuny retailers, which didn't keep the lamps in stock and so couldn't guarantee delivery for four months). But Yasmina found a few months into her business that she couldn't stick to her "quick-ship" strategy. "I was placing stock orders, but oftentimes I'd get customer orders for everything in the shipment before it arrived," she says. "I didn't have the operating capital to simply increase my stock orders." So Yasmina had to stop promising delivery within a week. Yasmina still believes that being able to promise a quick turn-around on orders is important if she is to grow her business, but she's reluctant to incur more debt to pay for additional inventory. Instead, she contents herself with the knowledge that she can still deliver faster than her competitors by placing regular orders for the most popular designs, like the $1,900 Scudo Saraceno and the $1,690 floor lamp, rather than just ordering when she has a customer in hand, as her competitors do. She's usually able to fill an order for one of the most popular models within a month.

"Most people don't mind waiting four weeks when they'd have to wait two to three months everywhere else," she says. Besides, customers who are used to working with interior designers, as many of hers are, sometimes wait a year for custom-made furniture.

## The Importance of Metatags

Well into 1999, prospective customers were still having trouble finding her website when searching the internet using keywords like *Fortuny* and *lamps*. Punctilio was rarely turning up among the top ten hits, a major drawback for a business that was trying to lure customers from around the country with advantageous pricing as bait. It took Yasmina a few months to figure out the problem.

"My webmaster, being a programmer and not really a professional web developer, knew how to do the scripting, but not marketing," she explains. "It turned out he did not put keywords in my metatags. At the time I learned this, I had no clue what a metatag was."

Putting the right keywords in the metatags is crucial. Yasmina got another programmer to add keywords to her metatags—and to show her how to do it herself. But still, Punctilio wasn't always coming up as a link when she searched.

Yasmina asked everyone she knew with any computer experience how she could make sure her website was listed on the most popular search engines. Finally, someone provided a simple answer. Yasmina has since found that it takes regular maintenance work to keep her site listed with the major search engines. "I have to continually revisit them because I get bumped by other more recent listings," she says.

In the end, it took a year from the time Yasmina launched her website to figure out how to make sure its URL popped up near the top of the list of search results for Fortuny lamps.

## A Trip to Italy

In November 1999, around the anniversary of her first sale, Yasmina rewarded herself with a trip to Italy.

One of the primary reasons for the trip was to cement her relationship with the Fortuny people she had been dealing with only by fax, phone, and e-mail. She had also learned that Fortuny offered more favorable "dealer" prices to some other retailers, and she wanted to persuade the company to give her those same discounts. In addition, she had begun designing lights herself and wanted to look for fabric for the shades.

Yasmina spent her first week in Italy visiting textile companies in Milan, Bologna, Sienna, and Rome before traveling to Venice, the home of the Fortuny workshop, for four days. There she met Matteo Lando and Alessandra Sorato, her main contacts, for the first time.

"When we met, Matteo told me, 'I have a lot of respect for your business skills. I know you've risked a lot,'" she recalls. He took her on a tour of the Fortuny laboratory, a privilege rarely accorded to outsiders.

For Yasmina, in awe of the Fortuny lighting designs since the first time she laid eyes on them, the visit was one of the highlights of her adult life. "It was the most gorgeous building I've ever seen," she says. "There were frescoes all over the ceilings and the walls, and they had workmen working on them constantly to uncover them."

Yasmina studied the manufacturing process with great interest. "Making these lamps is an art," she says. "It's an incredible process. Now I know why it takes four months to make the lamps."

In addition to enhancing Yasmina's appreciation for the workmanship in the lamps, the trip paid off in concrete ways as well. Because she had by now sold more than $50,000 in lamps, Fortuny offered her a better dealer's discount. In addition, the company gave her a box of pleated silk scarves on consignment, making her the first U.S.-based retailer to offer them.

At the end of 1999, when she added up her sales, Yasmina found to her surprise that she had sold $110,721 worth of lamps that year. She can't really say how much of that was profit, since she plowed most of what she made back into the business. But she managed to pay all of her living and business expenses, make a few buying trips to New York, take a vacation, and set aside more than $10,000 for operating capital.

## An Ultimatum from Venice

The year 2000, Punctilio's second year of operation, brought more changes to Yasmina's business practices, some planned and some not.

Even as she was committing to a two-year advertising contract, the owners of Fortuny were becoming finicky about the ad content. They had previously objected to some of the photographs she featured on her website, and she'd had to replace them. Now they objected to her use of pictures of specific lamps in her ads, perhaps, Yasmina thinks, because of complaints from other retailers. So she had to figure out a way to put the Fortuny name in her ads without featuring the lamps, her primary product. She decided to run an ad for Fortuny's decorative tassels, which sell for $75, about half of which is profit, and hope that people who saw them would call to ask if she also carried the lamps. "I wasn't really trying to sell tassels," she says. "I wanted to sell lamps."

The strategy paid off. "The West Coast went crazy for the tassels," she says. "I've probably sold over seventy of them. That helps pay some of my bills. And when clients called to buy the tassels, a few people would ask me, 'Do you have the lamps too?'"

Late in the spring of 2000, Fortuny's executives delivered an ultimatum. They had learned that Yasmina didn't have a showroom, as she had hinted she did, and told her that she would lose her right to sell their lamps unless she opened one.

"The people at Fortuny said that the other distributors complained that I was making out like a bandit because I had lower overhead and it wasn't fair," she says. "What they didn't factor in was the costs of my marketing. I'm the only dealer in the U.S. who places ads, which are really expensive. The other stores have plenty of walk-by traffic because they're in high-traffic spaces, like Soho in New York City."

The Fortuny officials weren't sympathetic to her argument. They gave her two months to open a showroom, which threw her into a panic. "They were willing to kick me to the curb if I didn't get with the program," she says.

In a way, though, the timing of Fortuny's ultimatum was fortuitous. Yasmina knew that she needed a space in which to show off her wares because she was losing local sales to the other Fortuny distributors in Chicago, which had showrooms. "When they're buying a $4,000 lamp, most people want to see it first," Yasmina observes. "So I was losing sales of the $4,000 Scheherazade all the time. I knew I needed to do something."

As Yasmina began looking for a space, her first priority was to keep her overhead as low as possible, since her business was still young. She would have loved to find a space near Chicago's Merchandise Mart, but the rents there were out of sight. "The only places I found were all going to cost $1,000 or $1,200 a month, and they were far out on the west side," she says.

By chance, Yasmina came across a newly vacant space on Oak Street. The rent was reasonable and the location couldn't be beat, but the two-room space definitely needed a makeover. "It was really nasty," Yasmina recalls. "The window looked out on an old brick wall, maybe three feet away. The walls were water-stained, and the stain on the floors was worn off. There was a track light dangling from a conduit, and a drop ceiling made it feel like a cave."

Yasmina set about turning it into not just a showroom, but also a showplace. She decided she wanted the showroom to give the feel of having entered another world. "I wanted it dark and mysterious, like a shop you'd find in Turkey, or Marrakesh, or somewhere else totally exotic," she says.

Yasmina did all of the renovations with the help of her friends Dee Dee and Fabiola. She knocked down some walls, added some others, and carved out a Moroccan keyhole-type door to add to the Middle Eastern look. She sanded the floors and painted the walls.

Yasmina kept her remodeling costs low by improvising and by designing and constructing most of the furniture herself. Whereas the Fortuny factory in Venice has Fortuny fabrics hanging on the walls, which cost $600 a yard, Yasmina hung cotton saris, which cost only $38 each. "And the things I made myself didn't cost me more than $100 each—the mirror, the desk, the display, the table base for the vases," Yasmina says proudly. "For a while, I was at Home Depot every day." All told, Yasmina spent only $1,600 on renovations and furnishings to achieve an upscale, exotic look.

The Punctilio showroom opened on June 23, 2000, just over a month after Yasmina rented the space. Yasmina e-mailed pictures of the showroom to Fortuny. "My rep at Fortuny sent me an e-mail saying, 'The showroom is beautiful, very, very nice and tasteful,'" Yasmina says. "'Matteo is positively impressed!!!!!'"

Having a showroom has enabled Yasmina to display and sell other products—the Fortuny tassels, silk scarves, and purses, which are popular impulse purchases; a line of flower vases made by two artists from Brooklyn; and silver candlesticks made by New York designer Lazaro, who is an acquaintance. To Yasmina's delight, several walk-in customers have even commissioned copies of the furniture she built. By the end of 2000, she had sold four copies of her Indonesian bamboo–framed wall-sized mirror for $800 each, for a $2,800 profit.

"What's so great about having this showroom is that people come in and say, 'That is the most beautiful mirror I've ever seen' or 'Oh, my God, that desk!'" Yasmina says. "That makes me feel so good. I just need to hear it from somebody who doesn't know me personally and isn't saying it just to make me feel good."

## Facing Down a Crisis

In July 2000, just over a month after she moved into the showroom, Yasmina experienced a serious cash-flow problem.

The Fortuny workshop was about to send her bills for a slew of orders, and her American Express card was already almost maxed out. She knew that Fortuny would refuse to ship the order if she couldn't pay.

The cause of the problem was that her receipts for the nearly two months she'd been working on her showroom were lower than expected. "Anything under $10,000 is a bad month," she explains. "If I have a $5,000 month, that means Punctilio makes less than half that amount. Then there is my rent, and my phone is at least $400. Then there's my cell phone, my loan, my car lease, and electricity, and the monthly fee for my website. And that's not even factoring in advertising.

"I had some money, but paying the bills was going to leave me totally broke. I was doubting myself. I was stressing."

In a panic, she asked WSEP for an emergency loan. WSEP turned her down. "They were hard on me," Yasmina recalls. "They wanted to know, 'Why isn't your business working? What are you doing wrong?' I told them that I had been pushed up against the wall by Fortuny telling me to open a showroom or lose the lamps. The point was, I needed to save my business."

Hurd, Yasmina's loan officer at WSEP, offered Yasmina the option of paying only interest for two months, which would temporarily reduce her monthly payment by about $300. The lower loan payment reduced the pressure somewhat. But Yasmina ended up paying her American Express bill forty-five days late, which cost her in interest. Plus, she had to dip into her cash reserves to pay other bills.

The episode made Yasmina keenly aware of the risks of financing a business with high-interest credit cards. "It's really stressful being a one-person business and not knowing if you're going to have the money to pay a $10,000 bill that's coming due," she says. "It took me three or four months to build my reserves back. I'm in a semistable state right now. Ultimately, I'm glad I didn't get another loan, because I'd just have another bill to pay each month."

Although Yasmina's overhead has increased with the opening of her showroom, so have sales. Her total revenues in the first six months of 2000, when she was operating out of her apartment, were $59,319. Her total revenues for the second six months, after she had moved into her showroom, were $76,893. Altogether, in 2000 she sold $136,212 worth of merchandise, $25,490 more than in 1999. When the year ended, she had $16,000 in the bank.

Yasmina also managed to offset some of her new overhead costs by cutting other expenses. For example, by purchasing her own credit card machine, she did away with monthly fees of $75 for leasing. She gave up a leased car, which had cost her $257 a month, plus insurance, since her new location made a car unnecessary. Because she's improved her accounting methods, she's now able to take better advantage of tax deductions available to businesses. "Pretty much everything's a business expense, except for my food," she says.

## Ms. Cadiz Goes to Washington

Besides providing continuing technical assistance to its borrowers as their businesses develop, WSEP also involves them in advocacy work. In June 2000 Queen Rania Al-Abdullah of Jordan visited WSEP to gather information that might help the Jordan River Foundation, a nonprofit organization she'd founded in 1995 to provide microcredit and business development assistance to poor rural women in Jordan. Yasmina was one of several WSEP borrowers who met with the queen.

"She thought I had done well with what I was given," Yasmina says about their conversation. Later, Yasmina and the queen's chief of staff exchanged several e-mails, and Yasmina received some Jordanian fabric samples to consider using in her showroom.

It was the first inkling Yasmina had that she was involved in something larger than her own business. Further evidence of that came later that month when WSEP flew her to Washington, D.C., to take part in a press conference with her congressman, Bobby Rush, about the Prime Act. The act would have provided $10 million to help groups like WSEP provide technical assistance to microbusinesses.

It was Yasmina's first trip to the nation's capital and her first foray into national political issues. "I'm not political," she says. "I don't understand how these things work. I had never even heard about the Prime Act before. But they were trying to put a face on the issue, and they wanted somebody from Bobby Rush's district, since he was the sponsor of the legislation."

At the press conference on the Capitol lawn, Rush first gave a little talk about the importance of the bill. "And then someone said, 'Now we're going to hear from one of the entrepreneurs who has actually received help from WSEP,'" Yasmina recalls. "I got up and told my story.

"I told them I went to WSEP for assistance, and they were interested enough to want to do something for me. Now I'm ready to take my business to the next level, which is where technical assistance could help me. I'm interested in manufacturing and wholesaling my designs to other retailers, and there's a lot of information I need to know about the manufacturing process and how to organize my business to go in that direction. Passing the Prime Act would definitely benefit people like me."

Yasmina found the press conference somewhat disillusioning—only one reporter showed up—but afterward, during discussions with two other entrepreneurs who'd come to Washington to lobby their congressmen, she began to understand the importance of the event.

"I was really impressed with what I heard from the other entrepreneurs," she says. "They'd made a difference. They'd switched someone from a no vote to a yes vote, which is headway. They had done something that was going to end up getting people like me more money for our business.

"I felt like they were really involved in something important. And they convinced me I had done something important, too, because Bobby Rush was not going to do the press conference unless someone like me came to Washington, and it was important to have the press conference to close the process.

"They told me, 'We needed you. Without you, this all would have been for nothing.' In the end, I felt like I made a difference too."

## Hard at Work, Whatever the Weather

It's a mid-December weekday, a day when Yasmina could normally count on walk-in shoppers who have already stopped in at some of her building's other tenants, such as Alfred the Tailor, Mon Ami Coiffeur, or Milani Boutique.

But a blizzard is raging outside that will leave fourteen inches of snow on the ground by the time it stops later tonight. The wind chill is minus thirty degrees. The only people who are on the streets are those who have to be. So Yasmina is spending the day answering e-mail, working on her website, and thinking about the design for her next ad.

Even with sixty-mile-per-hour wind gusts blowing icy air west from Lake Michigan and rattling the building's windows, Yasmina's showroom feels like an oasis. The golden light given off by the silk shades makes it feel warm and cozy. Occasionally, the phone rings with a call from a prospective customer, usually in another state, with questions about price, availability, or styles. E-mail inquiries, unmindful of the weather, keep coming.

Initially, most customers found out about Punctilio through magazine ads, but increasingly, as e-commerce has taken hold, more have been finding it through internet searches.

"More people are using search engines to find what they want to buy, and that is totally changing my business," Yasmina says. "I get e-mail from Australia, Tokyo, Singapore, Puerto Rico. These are prospective customers that I never would have been able to reach without the internet."

Yasmina's website no longer gets the thousands of daily hits it got in the weeks after it received the Netscape award. Now, late in 2000, traffic hovers at around 300 visitors a month. However, these are usually visitors who are getting ready to buy a Fortuny light, so they're quality hits. This morning's e-mail traffic is typical:

> *I am interested in your lamps, as well as your decorative tassels, and any other decorative items or furniture that you may have. Do you have catalogues? Donalee in Soulsbyville, CA*
>
> *I am very interested in learning more details about your gorgeous lamps and the costs, particularly the Scudo Saraceno and Scheherazade. Thank you for your time. Jacquelyn in Laguna Niguel, CA*
>
> *Please send us a catalogue of products. We are a design firm in SF looking for new items for high-end residential use. Thank you. Martha in SF*
>
> *I am a designer and saw the tassels in a magazine. Can I get a catalogue ASAP? Linda in Cornelius, NC*

Yasmina went through two more programmers before she found someone who could help her achieve the look that she wanted on her website. "I'm a perfectionist like you wouldn't believe," she says. Now, with her current programmer's technical advice, she's redesigning her website. This time, she's not only doing the design and content herself, but most of the programming as well. She's gotten so adept at it that recently she started designing websites for other businesses.

### "Remember, I'm a Julie"

With lamp sales fairly steady at the end of her second full year in business, Yasmina turned her attention to the next phase of her business plan: manufacturing and selling furniture and lamps of her own design.

In the fall of 1999, she had test-marketed a forty-two-inch-tall table lamp, which she named the Sussex Lamp, in honor of the country of origin of the fabric's designer (England's Trisha

Guild). Her friend Dee Dee wrote the copy for an evocative ad that she ran in *Metropolitan Home*. "A chromatic kaleidoscope of colored breezes frolicked through a linear existence and burned the room with rhythm and pulse," the ad read. "I once was blind but now I see."

The lamp featured a decorative metal base and rod topped by a long, narrow cloth shade in a choice of brilliant colors. Callers invariably referred to it as "the kaleidoscope lamp."

Yasmina sold a half-dozen of these lamps, at $395 each, plus another half-dozen floor lamps of the same design. "I hadn't even planned to make a floor lamp, but someone called and asked, 'Do you have a floor lamp?' 'Sure,' I said. Remember, I'm a Julie." On the spot, Yasmina figured out how she could transform the table lamp into a floor lamp and came up with a price of $595.

Yasmina's experience with the Sussex lamp proved to her that there's a demand among affluent consumers for distinctive designs. "I'm constantly thinking about the next step," she says. "I've got a whole list of designers who want me to send them information when I start making furniture because they can't get their hands on anything with a fresh look."

After selling the Sussex Lamp for nine months, she stopped in order to rethink the design and find another metal fabricator. She's saved most of the $6,000 she needs to manufacture the new lamp, which she plans to market in three sizes. "The whole process is extremely costly, and I really need an artisan, somebody with a sculpting background, to sculpt the shape out of wood, make a cast, and then pour the metal," she explains. "I found one whose work I like in New York, but he won't offer a quote unless I send him a drawing, and I don't want to do that because I'm afraid of its being knocked off."

After she perfects the design, she'll have five or six of them cast. "Then I'll have to spend another $1,500 to advertise and another $1,000 to print a color pamphlet about it, which I have to do or no one will take me seriously," she says.

She's also working on an improved design vision for the desk she built for her showroom, a striking Oriental-inspired structure made from, of all things, plywood, two-by-fours, and joint compound.

"Everybody who comes in here wants this desk," she says. "I have a list of people who want to know when I'm ready to offer it. Right now, I'm looking for someone who can build it for me. It would probably cost me up to $3,500 to make if I hired a carpenter, and I could sell it for $7,000 to $9,000."

Nine thousand dollars for a desk? she's asked. "That would be cheap," she says. "At the Merchandise Mart, it would cost $13,000 to $15,000 for something like it, and they're mass produced."

## "It's Just Something I Love"

Two and a half years into operating her own business, Yasmina is almost exactly where she wants to be at this point in her life. "If you'd have asked me ten years ago what I'd want to be doing today, it would be designing my own furniture line," she says.

The days of sleeping on friends' couches and borrowing other people's credit cards are long past. She can afford to take a foreign vacation every year. And she is getting an increasing amount of recognition for her business. In 1999, *Today's Chicago Woman*, a 100,000-circulation city magazine, named her one of the 100 women who make a difference in Chicago. WSEP featured her business in a brochure early in 2000. *Crain's Chicago Business* featured her in a July 2000 article about financing options for small businesses.

"My next goal is to get on Oprah," Yasmina says. "She has this segment called 'My Favorite Things.' If Oprah mentions you and you have a product she likes, you're a guaranteed overnight success."

Yasmina has gotten where she is by making the most of every one of her experiences, good and bad. "Nothing I learned in school helped me with my business," she says. "I taught myself almost everything I needed to know. But just about every person

I've ever met has taught me something—a business owner who said, 'Here are the keys, good-bye.' A website developer who said, 'Here's the software, good-bye.' My mom, a disciplined, strong woman, who sent me out on my own at 19.

"I was born with a very good eye, and my experiences in life made it even better," she continues. "There's nothing scientific about it. It's just something I have. And when you have it, that's it. It's all over. When I get my act together and get time to really sit down and create, I'm going to truly blossom.

"My goal is not to get rich. Dee Dee says she thinks I want to be famous. But it's not that either. I just want to be able to be creative and to have people like what I create."

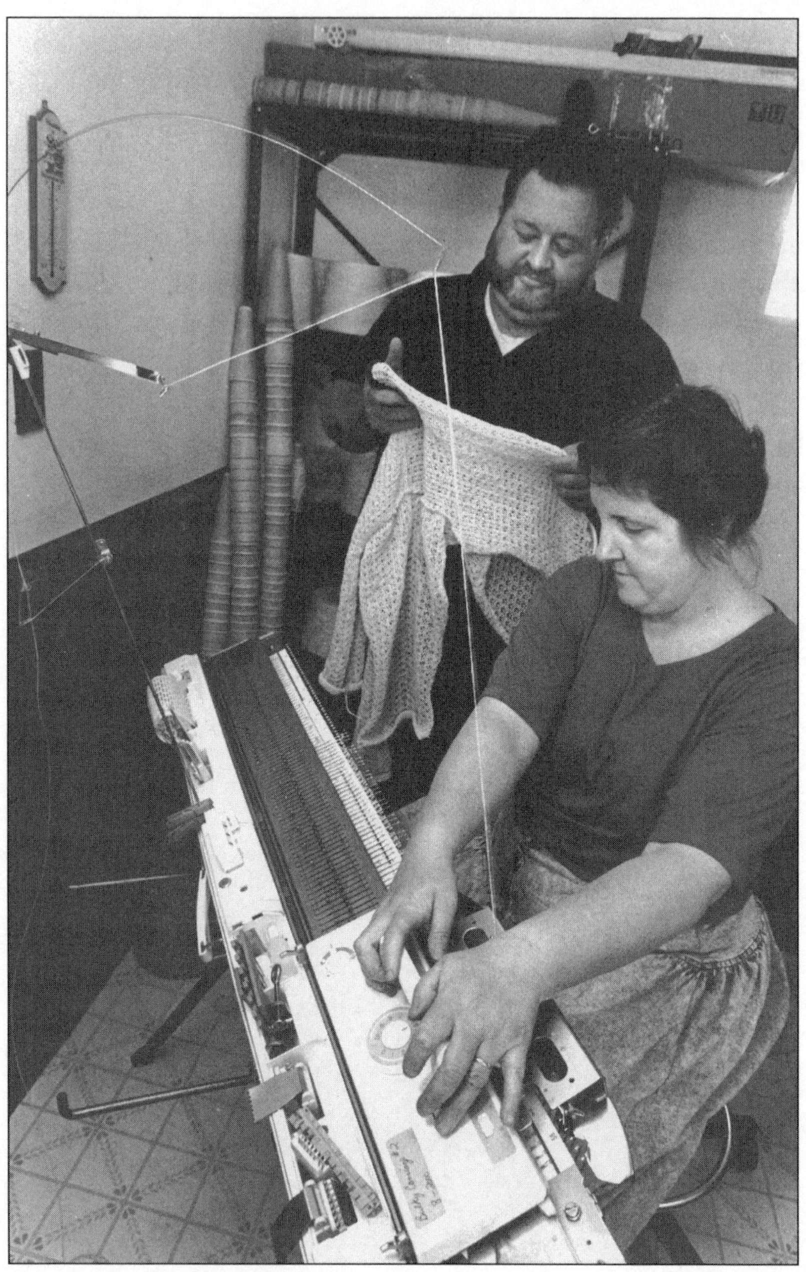

*Electric knitting machines enable Ollie and Rick Barkley to earn a living while supervising the homeschooling of their children.*

chapter 8

# God, Family, and an Electric Knitting Machine
# Ollie Barkley
# Ollie's Mountaineer Knits
# Hillsboro, West Virginia

Ollie Barkley doesn't even have to think about what matters most to her in life. "God and my family," the mother of three says emphatically. "In that order."

For years, Ollie and her husband, Rick, of Hillsboro, West Virginia, struggled to earn a living in a way that would allow them to put their commitment to God and family first. Soon after their third child was born, they moved from Greenbrier County to Pocahontas County so they could be closer to their church and its private religious school. They often worked different shifts so that one of them could be home with the children. When their children's church-run school closed, they took turns staying home so that one of them could supervise their children's homeschooling.

Still, it always seemed as though they were being pulled in too many directions, leaving too little time for the things that mattered most. Even when they earned a good living, much of their income went for commuting and child care, making them wonder just what it was they were wearing themselves out for. And the vagaries of the West Virginia economy meant that jobs came and went, sometimes disappearing altogether to other countries.

Then, a few years ago, Ollie heard about a network of knitters, based in nearby Lewisburg, that was producing hand-loomed sweaters, blankets, and home accessories for retailers around the country. The knitters were making more than the prevailing wage in rural West Virginia. Most appealing of all, they were working from their homes.

In 1996 Ollie took the training offered by the network, which is called Appalachian By Design (ABD). By 1999 she had become the top-grossing knitter for ABD. That year, her earnings from knitting helped moved her family above the poverty line for the first time in six years. Impressed by her earnings, her husband began knitting as well, further increasing the family's prospects for long-term financial stability.

Ollie's development as a businesswoman, with the help of ABD, shows the promise of a particular sectoral strategy in Appalachia, a region of the United States that has, for decades, found prosperity elusive.

## Rabbits and Fireflies

In all of the United States, there are only a few states poorer than West Virginia; in all of West Virginia, there are only a few counties poorer than Pocahontas County, where Ollie and Rick Barkley live. In early 2000, when the United States was enjoying its lowest unemployment rate in three decades—4.1 percent—the unemployment rate in Pocahontas County was 9.8 percent. Times have been especially tough since the mid-1990s, when the county's two major employers, a shoe factory and a leather-processing factory, closed their doors, leaving hundreds of Pocahontas County residents, including Rick Barkley, out of work.

Ollie and Rick moved their three children to Pocahontas County from neighboring Greenbrier County, where they'd both grown up, in 1987. They wanted to live close to a private Christian school and to rear their children in a place where chasing rabbits and catching fireflies were more likely to occupy their time than playing Nintendo. "It's just absolutely beautiful country," Rick brags as he takes a visitor on a sightseeing tour through the Greenbrier River Valley. "It's got rolling hills. It's got woodland with beautiful trees. It's got little towns nestled along the road. And it's got the mountains surrounding it and pulling it all together."

The couple took out a $9,000 mortgage to buy a thirdhand trailer from Ollie's stepmother and move it to land owned by a fellow church member along a one-lane country road a few miles outside of Hillsboro. The site was picture postcard perfect; they could count on two hands the number of cars that drove by on a given day.

"We raised chickens, sheep, and hogs, and each child had a dog of their own," Ollie remembers wistfully. At the time, Rick was working as a laborer for the state highway department, making $7.25 an hour with good benefits. Ollie was a full-time homemaker.

But the highway job took a heavy toll on Rick, who, as a teen, had suffered a neck injury in an automobile accident. He was required to spray tar and patch potholes for up to twelve hours a day, an unpleasant job under any circumstances, but especially when the temperature neared 100 degrees, as it does throughout the summer here. After failing to win a transfer from the Greenbrier County crew to the Pocahontas County crew, which would have saved him two hours of commuting time a day, he and Ollie decided in early 1989 that they would switch roles. She would work, and he would stay home with the children: Joshua, five, Caleb, three, and Launa, two.

Rick quit his job in May 1989, and Ollie went to work as a hand sewer at the Hanover Shoe Company in Marlinton, about thirty minutes up the road from Hillsboro. The job required her to sew together high-priced leather shoes like Bostonians, along with a custom design that Hanover manufactured for the L. L. Bean catalog. She started at a piecework rate that was set to guarantee an income of $4.25 an hour, but by increasing her speed she brought home more than that. "I told Rick that in six months I would be making what he made for the state," Ollie boasts. "It actually took six months and two weeks."

Even so, the family's income fell short of Rick's take-home pay from the highway department job, because he had always worked a lot of overtime, an option that wasn't available at the shoe company. So after just a few months at home, Rick took a minimum wage night job at a sawmill in Marlinton, switching to a better-paying job at Hanover in early 1990. Because both Ollie and Rick were now working full-time, their income that year was more than $24,000, well above the poverty threshold of the time.

With the higher income, though, came home and work conflicts. "Our child care situation was horrible," Ollie says. "We had to drop the boys off with a babysitter in the morning, and their teacher would pick them up there on her way to school. Launa had to go to a different babysitter, because she needed to spend the whole day. The transitions were really hard on the kids."

Rick picks up the story. "One day, we were having lunch together at work, and I said to her, 'Ollie, this is not working out. One of us has got to stay at home. Which one is it?'

"She said, 'Well, I'd like to be the one who works.' And I said, 'Then I'll go home.'" Rick quit working again in May 1991.

## Schooling at Home

The following fall, the Christian school that had attracted the Barkleys to Pocahontas County lacked a large enough enrollment to remain open, so Rick and Ollie decided to homeschool their children, using a fundamentalist Christian curriculum available by mail for about $50 a month. Rick spent his days overseeing the schooling. Joshua was doing third-grade work, Caleb second-grade work, and Launa, kindergarten.

Again, with only one parent working, finances were strained. When a night watchman's job became available at Hanover in October 1991, Rick went back to work again.

"He'd work all night and then come home and try to homeschool," Ollie says. "He'd catch a few hours of sleep after I came home from work and then go back to work himself. He was absolutely exhausted all the time." The Barkleys were back to the work-family conflicts that had distressed them the previous year.

They prayed about it, as they always do when they have a decision to make, and agreed that one of them needed to stay home all the time. They decided that this time it should be Ollie, since she seemed to have more luck getting the children to study.

In February 1992 Ollie quit her job and took over the homeschooling. For ten months, with the help of food stamps, the family somehow managed to live on Rick's income of $4.50 an hour. In December 1992 Rick got promoted to a sole-dying job that paid a piecework rate that produced between $10 and $15 an hour in income, depending upon how productive a day he was having. The next year, he brought home $24,849, a high for the marriage.

## Living in a Tent

Bad times arrived again in the spring of 1994. Doctrinal disputes within the family's Baptist church found Rick and their landlord, the interim pastor, on opposite sides. As a result, the landlord refused to renew the lease on the land on which their trailer was parked, so for two weeks, while they looked for another pad, all five family members slept in a ten-by-fourteen-foot tent at nearby Watoga State Park.

Then the rains came. "Do you have any idea what it's like to try to live in a tent in West Virginia in April, when it's raining?" Rick asks.

Ollie says, "What we did was just try to get through each day."

Finally, they found an open pad in a small trailer park known as Rose's, at the base of Droop Mountain along the main road between Lewisburg and Hillsboro.

The rent for the pad was $60 a month, where it remained well into 2002. It includes water and septic service, a real plus on an income as low as theirs. However, they would now be just a few feet away from the next trailer and no longer have space for farm animals or a garden. Rick later compensated by planting gardens at the homes of several relatives and friends, who let him share the produce.

In the fall of 1994, Ollie began taking correspondence courses in Christian education through the Louisiana Baptist University in Shreveport, with the goal of ensuring that the family's homeschooling plan would continue to pass muster with West Virginia education officials. Rick was still making good money at Hanover, so they could afford for Ollie to continue to stay at home.

But in October 1994, Rick was laid off from Hanover. His unemployment benefits of $269 a week amounted to only about half of what he'd been earning.

When Hanover announced a few months later that it was closing the Marlinton plant altogether and shifting production to the Dominican Republic, any hope of ever again being able to earn $500 a week evaporated. "They said they could get shoes made there by workers who were making $2 or $3 a day," Rick says, with more than a little bitterness. "Our jobs were lost to a foreign workforce."

Under federal trade laws, the closure of the factory because of competition from abroad meant that the displaced Hanover workers—even those, like Rick, who had been previously laid off—were eligible for twenty-four months of unemployment benefits instead of the customary six, provided they were enrolled in a training or higher education program. Rick first took a computer course and then enrolled full-time in an associate's degree program in business at Bluefield State College, which offers classes through the community college in Lewisburg. The state paid his tuition, and he also received a Pell grant of $1,200 per semester, which the family used for living expenses.

With the grant, Rick's unemployment benefits, and Ollie's minimum-wage earnings from a weekend job at the local prison, the family managed to make ends meet. After Rick's unemployment benefits ran out in 1996, with two semesters left in his program, they tightened their belts even more and applied for food stamps. That summer, Rick worked odd jobs—building a stone chimney, digging a hole for a septic tank system—and Ollie took a full-time job, for $4.75 an hour, as a desk clerk at Watoga State Park. It was there that she heard about ABD.

## Praying for a Home-Based Job

While working at Watoga, Ollie became friends with another seasonal employee, Elizabeth Schank. Elizabeth and her husband had moved to the Hillsboro area after retiring from their jobs in New Jersey. "We got to talking about what the Lord wanted us to do with our lives," Ollie says. "I told her that I'd been praying for several years for a job I could work from home, so I could homeschool the kids."

To supplement her pension and seasonal earnings, Elizabeth had begun knitting for Appalachian By Design. "You ought to try it too," she told Ollie. "You could do it while you're home with your children."

Ollie liked the sound of the work. "The more I heard about it, the more it seemed like a perfect fit for what I was wanting to do," she says. "The more you knit, the faster you get, and the faster you get, the more money you can make."

One day after work, Ollie stopped by Elizabeth's house to look at her knitting machine. "She actually sat there and knit a sweater in the hour we were talking," Ollie recalls. "She said to me, 'You can do this,' and I said, 'Yeah, I can.'"

ABD traces its origins to The Appalachian Knitwear Project, a 1992 initiative of the Women and Employment Organization (now called the Center for Economic Options). The organization was a Charleston-based nonprofit committed to "culturally and ecologically sound small-scale entrepreneurship."

The Appalachian Knitwear Project had arisen as a result of attempts by the organization's specialist in community economic development, Diane Browning, to help some sheep farmers start a wool business. While researching potential markets, she had discussions with a designer for the Esprit clothing company.

"The designer asked me if I could round up some organic wool, and then asked, 'By the way, do you know anyone who could knit for us?'" recalls Browning, who had previously founded and helped develop a women's craft cooperative. "I said, 'Oh, yeah, we could do that for you,' thinking of the two people with knitting machines that I knew."

It turned out that neither of the knitters Browning knew was interested in production work, so she had to scramble to find other women in West Virginia who already had knitting machines. It took awhile, but she did. In 1993, revenues from Esprit totaled $134,700 for the Appalachian Knitwear Project's home-based knitters.

For two years, Browning's band of knitters turned out "earth-friendly" sweaters for Esprit's "e-collection" line, which was sold only in Europe. By the time Esprit discontinued the line of sweaters, Browning's West Virginia knitters had produced 800 of them.

As the end of Esprit's orders was approaching, Browning began thinking about how she could keep her knitters knitting. "With Esprit, we had organized entirely around a market opportunity," she says. "Now we needed to find others. We don't have a market here, so we had to look elsewhere."

Browning went to New York to talk with people in the garment industry and found a niche that she knew her knitters could fill. "There's this thin layer in the apparel world of companies that are too small to take an order to a factory," she explains. Browning began coming home from her New York trips with orders from small companies like Anatomy, Branching Habit, George, Blue Fish, and Hot Knots.

## ABD's Most Productive Knitter

In 1995 the Center for Economic Options spun off the Appalachian Knitwear Project as an independent nonprofit organization, with Browning as the president. The new organization was renamed Appalachian By Design. That year, ABD's revenues from contract knitting rose to $143,000.

The contract knitting business had some attractive features, since, with the customer providing the materials, it required minimal investment. It had some disadvantages, though. It was highly seasonal. It was volatile. If a designer bet on the wrong style, his company was soon out of business. (Several of ABD's early customers are now defunct.) Since so many markups needed to occur on the way to the retail market, there was substantial pressure on ABD to keep its prices down.

When ABD's contract sales slumped to $88,000 in 1996, it became hard to retain knitters. So ABD decided to launch its own wholesale line, designing and marketing knit products to home and gift retailers. Demand was less seasonal, which meant that ABD could keep its knitters working year-round. In addition, by directing the design process, ABD could ensure that there were products that could be made by knitters of all skill levels. Pressure to hold down prices was lessened, since only two markups—ABD's and the retailer's—needed to occur along the way to the purchaser.

However, there were some challenges to this approach: the large investment in marketing and raw materials, along with the time needed to establish credibility and brand recognition in national markets. Still, by branching into the wholesale market, ABD raised its total revenues from knitting to $135,200 in 1997. In 1998, as ABD became more widely known, revenues reached $197,000, and in 1999, with the introduction of a baby line, they reached $242,600.

At the end of 1999, the network included fifty-five self-employed knitters, each of whom earned an average of $1,744 from knitting, an important supplement to either their husband's earnings or their own earnings from other jobs. The nine most active knitters earned a substantial income—an average of $7,187 each. Ollie, who had quickly become the most productive knitter of all, earned $11,803.

## Starting Slowly

After Ollie's summer job at Watoga ended in 1996, she enrolled in an introductory knitting class offered by ABD that fall at its headquarters in Lewisburg, about an hour's drive from her home.

ABD's operation fills about a third of a building previously occupied by a Sears catalog store, which had gone the way of the old-fashioned soda fountains and general stores that once filled the storefronts on Lewisburg's main street.

Ollie paid $30 for a forty-eight-hour training class, including forty hours of knitting instruction and eight hours of instruction in business skills. "They tried to instill in us what it meant to be independent contractors, to be self-employed," Ollie recalls, "and they told us how to go about getting microloans."

A knitting machine was required in order to knit for ABD. Since those cost anywhere from $500 used to $2,000 new, ABD recommended that new knitters lease a machine for a few months while deciding whether they liked the work. However, when Ollie's class ended in December 1996, there were no machines available for lease, so she had to put her knitting plans on hold. While she waited for a machine, she worked several weekend jobs, first at a Dairy Queen and then at the state prison near her home, in a special wing for pregnant women prisoners and new mothers.

A knitting machine finally became available for lease in March 1997. She signed a four-month lease—for $25 a month—and brought it home. It was approximately the length of a full-size piano keyboard, and there was no space for it in the trailer's main living area, so she set it up against a wall in the master bedroom, leaving just enough room between the machine and the bed for a folding chair. Ollie went to work.

ABD starts new knitters on simple designs—pillows, baby hats, and baby blankets—while they develop their skills. Knitters are compensated by the piece—for instance, $9 for a rolled-edge pillow, $4.46 for a chenille Christmas stocking, $8.18 for a baby sweater. At the time Ollie started knitting, the piece rate was calculated to produce hourly compensation of $6.75 for a knitter of average ability. (In September 1999 ABD revised its piece rate to provide knitters with compensation of $7 an hour.)

It took Ollie some time to get fast enough to make knitting worth her while. With Rick still in school full-time and the responsibility on her to supervise the children's homeschooling, it was hard to set aside much time to knit. She had kept her weekend job at the prison, so there was little time to knit on Saturdays or Sundays. The first month, she knitted eleven smocked pillows and received $78.65 from ABD; the second month, she knitted only eight and made just $57.20.

"My frustration level was really high at times," she remembers. "Sometimes I'd have trouble with yarns, or I'd take more time than I wanted to learn a new pattern. And it often seemed like the machine had a mind of its own."

But by May 1997, her production was up, and she earned $387.40 for the month. Her revenues were down again in June, partly because she spent a lot of uncompensated time learning a new pattern for a Hot Knots sweater. She spent a day in Lewisburg on design-specific training, and ABD lent her a different knitting machine, called an electronic standard, which uses finer wool and produces a smaller gauge knit than the bulky knitting machine she was leasing. She made $13.28 a sweater, and though the piece rate was calculated on the assumption that it would take almost two hours to knit, after a little practice she found she could knit it in less than an hour and a half.

In July 1997 her billings went up to $629.48, largely because of the Hot Knots orders. "The Hot Knots sweaters have been my basic product since about three months after I started knitting," Ollie says. "I just love them, because it's basically the same design all the time, just in different colors."

Although Ollie had decided that she liked knitting enough to invest in her own machine, she didn't have the money to buy one. With ABD's help, she applied for a loan through the West Virginia Department of Agriculture, which lends money to small businesses at 8 percent interest, a lower rate than they can get from a commercial bank. ABD extended her lease on the knitting machine until the loan could be processed.

It was November before the loan came through and Ollie could buy her own used knitting machine (bought for $1,100 from a former knitter). She took another class at ABD—an eight-hour production class, where she learned how to use tools that could increase her productivity, as well as how to maintain her knitting machine. "It cost me a day's work, but with the production techniques I learned, I've more than made that up," Ollie says. "Taking that class has probably saved me several days' work over the last two years."

Soon after, she took out another loan to purchase an electronic standard demo model for $1,700. With two different machines of her own, Ollie could now handle just about any product for ABD.

## Patching Together Incomes

Rick had graduated from his associate's degree program in May 1997 with a 3.47 grade point average, a remarkable achievement considering that before this he had not set foot in a classroom in twenty-one years.

He put in applications for office work while he continued to take odd jobs. Nothing came through. In May 1997 the unemployment rate in Pocahontas County was 11 percent, with 430 county residents looking for work. Furthermore, with timbering and agriculture providing many of the jobs in the county, there weren't many employers who needed someone with an associate's degree in business.

Frustrated with his unsuccessful job search, Rick and Ollie decided that Rick should take over the homeschooling and Ollie should concentrate on developing her knitting business. She quit the part-time prison job so she could spend more time knitting. Between August and the end of December 1997, Ollie averaged $543 a month in income from ABD, including bonuses. (Every ABD knitter who earns $1,200 in a quarter receives a 2 percent bonus.) The family's income that year was $8,993: $2,173 from Ollie's weekend job at the prison, $4,094 from ABD, and $2,726 from Rick's odd jobs. That placed the family's income well under the 1997 poverty line of $19,380 for a family of five.

Through the spring of 1998, Ollie knitted. In between stints at her knitting machines, she also managed to finish the coursework for an associate's degree in Christian Education from the correspondence school in Louisiana.

Both the knitting and the correspondence courses were isolating pursuits, and Ollie began to feel the need for more contact with other people. So in June 1998, she took a part-time job, for $5.15 an hour, in the office of the family's physician, working every Monday and filling in for absent employees as needed. It was less money per hour than she could make knitting, but she liked being around other people.

## Rick Tries His Hand

Up until then, Rick had stayed out of Ollie's knitting business. With the children needing less direct supervision while they worked on their studies, he decided to try his hand at it. Ollie showed him how to operate one of her machines, and whenever she needed a break, he took over.

"We were mostly making throws for couches then, and I'd work for fifteen minutes or so and knit 100 rows, just enough to give her a rest," he remembers. Eventually, he began sitting down at the machine while she was off working at the doctor's office. He'd knit several blocks of 100 rows, and when Ollie returned from the office, she'd do the finishing work.

To his surprise, Rick found that he liked knitting. Because of his neck injury, he couldn't sit at the machine more than a few hours a day, but in those few hours he could earn $15 or $20. He could take breaks when he needed to and knit as much—or as little—as he pleased.

When the orders for afghans and baby blankets dried up, Ollie taught him to knit baby sweaters, which was a little harder. "I started with just the backs, because it was all straight knitting," he said. "After I did a couple hundred backs, she showed me how to do the fronts, which were harder." Ollie would knit the sleeves and collars and put them together with the backs and fronts. Together, they made $796 in one two-week production period in 1998.

"When I got started, I kind of just wanted to make enough extra money to keep the vehicles up," Rick said. "I set out to average $200 a pay period, or $400 a month. Then, one pay period, I made a little over $400 just doing baby sweaters, and I began to see the potential."

Rick bought his own knitting machine from a knitter who was leaving the area. The West Virginia Department of Vocational Rehabilitation, where his doctor had referred him for services, paid for a $1,300 power drive for the knitting machine to reduce the strain on his shoulders and neck. The agency also paid for a computer, which enabled the Barkleys to computerize their business records and to communicate with ABD in Lewisburg by e-mail, reducing their long-distance phone bills.

It was clear by now that there was not enough room in the trailer for both Ollie and Rick to knit simultaneously. So in the spring of 1999, after they received their Earned Income Tax Credit, Rick and his sons began building a ten-by-ten-foot workshop next to the trailer. They scavenged the siding from an old building on Ollie's father's property, along with several kegs of nails and the two-by-eights they used in the bracing. Although small, the workshop had enough room for Rick's knitting machine and Ollie's two machines.

For Mother's Day 1999, the family presented Ollie with a wooden sign emblazoned with the words, "Ollie's Mountaineer Knits," which Rick installed above the workshop door. "Now that we have it, I wonder how we ever got along without it," Ollie says of the workshop.

### "The Lord Took Her"

With their knitting machines set up in their new workshop, Ollie and Rick fell into a steady production rhythm over the summer of 1999, bringing in an average of $1,000 a month.

But in late September, something happened that would not only derail their production, but their lives. Twelve-year-old Launa got sick, and less than a week later, she died. The cause of death was inflammatory bowel disease. "The Lord took her, and we accept that and go on, but it's very difficult," Ollie says.

Although there are many advantages to being self-employed, there are some major disadvantages. There's no sick pay, for one, or funeral leave.

Concerned about the Barkley family's ability to pay its bills while Rick's and Ollie's production lagged, the board of ABD adopted an emergency benefits policy to subsidize the incomes of any knitter facing a personal crisis. The policy allows knitters to seek compensation from the emergency fund for the difference between their average earnings over the previous six pay periods and their actual earnings during six pay periods following a family crisis.

In the two-week pay period that followed Launa's death, Ollie billed only $129 for knitting, compared with a high of $730 for one two-week period earlier in the year. "There were days, especially in the first few months, when I couldn't work," Ollie recalls. At first, Ollie and Rick were reluctant to tap into the emergency fund. However, as Rick and Ollie watched their income continue to drop as they grieved, they eventually accepted six payments from the emergency fund, for a total of $1,168. The emergency fund payments helped push their joint income in 1999 to $17,825. For the first time in years, their family income was above the federal poverty line.

## "We're All in Business Together"

It's May 2000, the second day of ABD's annual knitters' meeting, and about twenty of the network's knitters have come together in a meeting room at Lewisburg's Carnegie Hall to learn new techniques and hear about what's happening at ABD.

By and large, the other knitters are just like Ollie, drawn to machine knitting because of their desire to work at home. They range in age from their late twenties to their early seventies. Some have young children to care for at home; others are caring for disabled relatives. During the growing season, many devote twenty to thirty hours a week to their gardens and farm animals.

Geography is a far greater barrier to employment here than in many other places—one reason, no doubt, for the lower-than-average workforce participation rate of West Virginia women. Quite a few of the knitters live an hour or more away from any sort of place-based employer, up and down mountain roads that are treacherous to drive in winter months. "By the time I finished paying for gas and the clothes I'd need to wear to work, I wouldn't be bringing much money home if I worked in town," one knitter confides.

Yesterday, the knitters toured ABD's new retail shop at the Greenbrier, a five-star resort in nearby White Sulphur Springs, where many of them saw for the first time the finished versions of the products they knit. They stayed on for tea in the Greenbrier's lobby, a first-in-a-lifetime experience for most, including Ollie.

Today's session is starting off with a brief talk by Diane Browning about the state of ABD, which will have a lot to do with the state of their own families' finances in the coming year. "We're all in business together," Diane tells them, "and the real driver behind this business is our marketing program."

Browning explains that ABD has three marketing strategies, with a fourth on the horizon. The first is contract knitting, which produced disappointing revenues in 1999. One of ABD's steady customers—Blue Fish—went into Chapter 11 bankruptcy, leaving ABD little likelihood of recovering the $6,000 it's owed, and virtually no prospect for new orders.

In addition, ABD's largest contract—Hot Knots—produced only $30,000 in revenues last year, a 70 percent drop. "Hot Knots had a really difficult year," Browning explains. "What they think is that their style of sweater had gone out of style. They've redesigned it, and it's now closer to the body, with a finer gauge." Browning says she expects Hot Knots's orders to stay steady at about $30,000 this year.

The lack of predictability in the contract market has led ABD to put more effort into its second marketing strategy, its wholesale business, Browning tells the knitters. ABD's "Stars and Stripes" line of adults' and children's sweaters has proven very popular with high-end apparel stores.

ABD has also had success with several pillow lines. "We've sold pillows, pillows, and more pillows," Browning says. "Our pillows are unique, and they've found a niche." As a result of a contact Browning made at the New York gift show, furniture retailer Ethan Allen bought 1,200 hand-knit couch pillows to sell through its on-line catalog for $69 apiece.

Then there's the baby line, which ABD added in 1998 because it had inadvertently ended up with too large an inventory of pastel-colored yarn. "We added our baby line almost by accident, and it's turned out to be a really fun and growing part of our business," Browning says. "There's a real market out there for baby gift apparel. A mother won't necessarily spend $90 on a chenille sweater, but a grandmother will."

ABD offers several lines of baby goods, including sweaters, buntings, caps, booties, and blankets, which are sold in gift shops around the country. Each bears the Appalachian By Design label, featuring a bucolic country scene and a tag that says, "This handloomed and handfinished piece was made by a cooperative network of Appalachian artisans. We hope you love it!"

ABD's third marketing strategy is retail, launched just six weeks before at the Greenbrier shop. The shop is ABD's first serious foray into retail sales, and ABD projects sales of $75,000 in the first year.

"Just in the six weeks we've had the shop open there's been a huge amount of synergy with our wholesale line," Browning tells the knitters. "It's going to give us a big opportunity to test-market things before we take them to the wholesale market. We're learning what colors sell, and we'll be able to tell wholesalers with confidence, 'This sells to an upscale market.'"

In addition to its baby items, pillows, and "Stars and Stripes" sweaters, ABD is selling some other gift items and furniture at the shop, along with a sweater, designed by a knitter from Wytheville, Virginia, that's priced at $240 and is selling.

Being able to produce and sell such a high-priced garment has given ABD the confidence to plan a fourth marketing strategy: the production of custom-made knit suits and dresses for career women, with price tags of $300 to $900 each.

"We've talked with the Greenbrier about doing a really fine line of women's suits and selling them through a trunk show at the hotel, maybe during Christmas week," Browning says. "We'll have samples on hand, and take each woman's measurements, and then make them suits to fit. This is going to require a higher skill level than our other lines, so we're talking about creating another knitter level with a higher pay rate." The new piece rate scale, for "virtuoso knitters," would be set to produce income of about $12 an hour.

Browning believes that ABD needs to move aggressively into the high-end market to break even in 2002, its goal. "We did almost $250,000 in business last year, and we're trying to hit $400,000 this year, but we need to be at about $800,000 by the end of 2002," she tells the knitters.

"We're under a lot of pressure from our funders and our bank. Our assessment is that we have the knitting capability to move to a high-end line with better profit margins. What we have to develop is the internal garment finishing and sales management capability. The key is to be adaptable. We think that right now we have a good mix of marketing opportunities for the people in our network, but we're always trying to figure new things out so we can grow to financial self-sufficiency."

## "What Am I Not Doing Right?"

Through the first months of 2000, Ollie and Rick struggled to get their knitting up to speed again. "It's been kind of iffy this spring," Ollie admits during an interview in May 2000. "I keep looking at our checks and asking myself, 'What am I not doing right? I should have more time in there than I do.'

"The problem was that I'd look out that window in my workshop at Red Ridge, which Launa used to like to walk up to, and I'd just lose my focus entirely. I'd see her coming back down with a bunch of wildflowers or a little headband that she'd woven out of flowers, and I would get to feeling really sad. If you can't stay focused, you can't work at home."

At the very least, the Barkleys need to bring in $1,000 a month to pay their bills. Although they've gotten their expenses down to a bare minimum, they still add up. The production goals Rick and Ollie have set for themselves should produce an income of about $20,000 for the year.

One of the things that helped the Barkleys through the spring of 2000 was the $2,250 Earned Income Tax Credit they received after filing their income tax return. They set aside some of it to pay for a headstone for Launa's grave in a churchyard on Friar's Hill, a few miles down the road toward Lewisburg, and used the rest to pay bills and stock up on groceries.

Ollie wishes they'd been able to use some of it to open a savings account. "Maybe next year," she says. During their entire married life, the couple has never had a savings account. If they have an unexpected bill, like for repairs to either of their two old cars, they sometimes borrow from their sons' piggy banks. "If it's going to cost $300 to repair, usually we'll just buy a new car," Joshua, their oldest son, explains matter-of-factly.

As for medical expenses, the children are covered by the Children's Health Insurance Program (CHIP), a federal-state health plan for low-income children, but neither Ollie nor Rick has health insurance. They are fortunate to have an understanding family physician who lets them pay what they can and tries to plug them into charity programs when they need expensive medication (which is how Rick receives his $150-a-month medications). Both are regular visitors to a free clinic run by residents at the osteopathic medical school in Lewisburg. But if either had a major illness or injury that required hospitalization, they'd have no way to pay.

## Delivery Day

It's late in the morning on the fifteenth of the month, one of the two days each month on which knitted goods are due at ABD (the fifteenth and the thirtieth). Ollie and Rick have been at their knitting machines since before dawn, trying to finish a few more sweaters. The boys put a few hours into their studies before turning to their delivery-day chores: tying off loose ends of yarn on Rick's baby sweaters and attaching tags to Ollie's Hot Knots sweaters. (Their parents pay them ten cents per sweater for their efforts.)

By 11 A.M., when Mayes Jackson, the so-called truck driver preacher, comes on the radio, all four family members are at the kitchen table readying the deliveries for ABD.

When Rick goes out to the workshop to get more sweaters, Joshua holds one of Rick's baby sweaters up to show Ollie. "Mommy, this doesn't look right," he says. The pink buttonhole band is joined incorrectly to the lavender frontispiece.

Ollie takes a look. "You're right," she tells him. "Let me take this out to the shop and see if he can fix it. The bands are only three rows wide. It'll take him five minutes to repair it."

Ollie takes it out to Rick, and when she comes back into the trailer, she's laughing. "He wasn't happy," she says. "He kept saying, 'It's all right the way it is.' I had to tell him, 'Well, it isn't all right. They'll send it back to you.'"

This isn't the first time Rick has had to redo a sweater, and Ollie's glad to have caught it before ABD's inspectors did. Earlier this year, ABD sent back twelve sweaters on which Rick had reversed the sleeves, and he had to redo them all.

Ollie is by nature a perfectionist and can't stand turning in work with loose strings or missed stitches. She also knows that knitted goods rejected by ABD mean lost income for her family. Earlier this year, she lost a whole week's worth of work—$258—when ABD rejected a batch of ivory Hot Knots sweaters she'd knitted. "When I finished them, they were half an inch too long, which is reasonable, because they shrink," Ollie says. "But when they blocked them at ABD, they were an inch and a half too short."

For a week, Ollie alternated being angry at ABD and at herself, first blaming the yarn ABD had given her and then her own stupidity for failing to make a sample and adjust her gauge. "What it means was that instead of a $600 payday, like I normally strive for, I only got $342," she explains. "I worked extra hours the next week to make up for it. Believe me, it was rough making those replacements."

When Rick comes in from the workshop, he's still upset over having to redo the button binding. "If we didn't have a visitor, we'd be screaming and yelling at each other," Ollie says. "One of our main arguments is over Rick's favorite statement, which is, 'If it were your sweater, you'd let it go.'"

Ollie and the boys head into Lewisburg in the family's '84 Delta Eighty-Eight, which they bought for $300 a year and a half ago. Although Rick often goes along to deliver his sweaters, today he's staying behind to see whether he can figure out what's wrong with the family's other vehicle, a '79 Dodge van that one of his brothers gave them.

Rick is sending in seven sweaters, less than a quarter of the goal he had set for himself for the week. He tries to knit four sweaters a day, which, if he succeeds, would produce between $30 and $36 in daily income for him, depending upon the piece rate, which varies by color and design. Ollie prefers to set a monetary goal each day of $60.

If both Rick and Ollie reach their production goals, their income from ABD should be about $900 every two weeks.

Ollie delivered most of her finished sweaters earlier in the week when she went to town for the annual meeting, but this day she is bringing in one Hot Knots cardigan sweater and six Hot Knots vests.

At ABD, the production staff is busy accepting deliveries from knitters and packing up yarn for the orders the knitters will be filling in the next two weeks. Knitted goods received today entitle knitters to receive compensation for them in the next pay period. Although many knitters drive their products to Lewisburg, those who live far away ship them by UPS.

Ollie looks forward to her trips to ABD because of the opportunity to socialize. "I love the atmosphere at ABD," she says. "They're really good to the knitters. Any question that I have ever asked, someone was willing to find the answer for me."

Pam Bowes, production manager, and Dolores Sanford, production assistant, are Ollie's main points of contact at ABD. They exchange pleasantries with her while they inspect her finished work and give her new orders. Ollie is taking home orders for three Hot Knots jackets, four tunics, and four vests, and expects to receive more orders by e-mail later in the pay period.

Rick's orders for next week include seven blue stripe blankets, a dozen baby hats, and a dozen baby sweaters, for which he'll make a total of $161.76. That's less work than he'd like to have, but ABD has a lot of inventory right now, so there's not much work for him.

After they leave ABD, Ollie and the boys head eight miles up the road to the Greenbrier so the boys can see ABD's new shop. The boys have never been to the Greenbrier before, and for the occasion they've dressed in their best outfits, complete with cowboy hats, Western-style shirts, boots, and lanyard ties.

The shop is cute and colorful, with ABD's baby sweaters and color-coordinated accessories artfully displayed. Joshua and Caleb do a double take when they look at the price tags on the items they've seen their parents knit at home. Since Ollie was here once already, during the annual meeting, she's had a few days to get used to the retail markup. "There isn't an item in this shop that I could afford to buy," she observes.

## Dreaming of Their Own Line

The couple dreams of someday supplementing their income from ABD by developing a retail line of their own under the label

Ollie's Mountaineer Knits. Several of ABD's other high-production knitters produce apparel of their own design for sale through crafts shops, including Tamarack, a state-operated store along the West Virginia Turnpike that draws tens of thousands of visitors a year. Ollie hopes to produce hand-loomed socks, mittens, ponchos, and coverlets for sale at outlets like that.

To that end, she's applied for a grant from the West Virginia Commission on the Arts to enable her to purchase Design-a-Knit computer software, which would enable her to create her own patterns. She's also asked for money to buy a special carriage that would permit the knitting of coverlets and extra regular carriages for each of her knitting machines, to prevent lost knitting time due to breakdowns.

Ollie hopes she has produced a winning application by emphasizing her intent to incorporate Appalachian themes into her knitting. In her application, she's written, "Knitting has been a part of Appalachian heritage for centuries. The knitter makes products for use by their families, friends and visitors to the region. Each article is a piece of Appalachia. As a new artist, I want to continue this knitting heritage and work toward preserving the skills necessary for this craft."

She explains, "I do a lot of listening when I'm at ABD, and I've learned that a lot of successful marketing is around a 'feel.' The design should suggest a pleasant experience, maybe even a particular aroma that most people like."

Last winter, Ollie and Rick test-marketed some mittens of their own design by giving a pair to each of their relatives as Christmas gifts. The most popular version was knit in flame orange acrylic, perfect for hunters.

"Hunting's really a very big to-do around here," Ollie says. "We've got squirrel hunting, followed by bow-hunting for deer, and then turkey season, so the season is nice and long. Our first products will probably be wool socks and mittens for hunters. I think we could sell them for about $8 or $10 a pair, which would give us a nice little profit."

Ollie plans to start small by placing hand-loomed items for sale in a convenience store operated by one of Rick's sisters and her husband, and perhaps in the crafts shop in Hillsboro and the gift shop at Watoga State Park. "Eventually, I would hope we could design our own sweaters and get them sold at Tamarack and at ABD's shop at the Greenbrier," she says. "Their high-end clientele wouldn't think twice about spending $100 or $200 for a sweater." Selling through the internet is also something the couple would like to explore.

But the only way that Ollie's going to be able to take time to work on her own designs is if Rick takes on more of the ABD orders. "I'm never going to be a full-time knitter, but I'd like to get to the point where I'm able to knit more each week so that Ollie can set aside a whole day to work on her own retail line," he says.

Originally, the couple's goal for 2000 was for Rick to earn $6,000 in income from ABD and Ollie to earn $14,000, which would have given them a joint income of $20,000, about two-thirds of the median family income in Pocahontas County. Rick ended up exceeding his goal, pulling in $7,608 in compensation from ABD. However, because of the slowdown in her productivity in the months following Launa's death, Ollie fell a few thousand dollars short, earning just $10,232 from ABD.

## "We Have the Control"

Even so, they're content with their lives. Working at home allows them to spend as much time with their children as they wish, a privilege they hold especially dear since Launa's death. "It gives us the freedom to do what we want to do, to be available for family and friends should the need be there," Ollie explains. "If there's a family crisis, we don't have to ask for time off. Like, for instance, when my mother-in-law was dying and they called the family to Charlottesville, we didn't have to call our bosses and say, 'We need a few days off.'"

It doesn't take a crisis for them to take a break, Ollie points out. "Our anniversary was last week, and we all took a day trip together," she says. "Myself and Caleb took a boat out for an hour, and we just loved it. And during the hunting seasons, we take off when we want to. We're going to take a week of vacation the first week of deer season. And Rick and the boys will also take a few days during muzzle-hunting season and bow season, and the squirrel and turkey seasons too.

"We do a great deal together. We've always made everything we do a family thing. In so many families, the women go shopping and the men go hunting. Our family is so close that we all take part in what everybody is interested in. We're in no way deprived by the way we've chosen to live our lives."

Whether or not they are actually able to launch their own retail line, Ollie now regards knitting as her career. "Personally, I feel that we're a great deal better off than we were when we had jobs, even though our income is lower," she says. "We have the control now. We're not depending on somebody else pulling the strings. And we're really not dependent on the local economy anymore. ABD sells what we knit all over the country. And if ABD disappeared, I have the skill level now that I could knit for other contract knitting operations."

Even if her own line takes off, Ollie wants to continue knitting for Appalachian By Design. "They are the ones who gave me the start, and I don't want to ever forget that," she says. "I want to make sure that the opportunities ABD provides always remain available for other women.

"Who knows?" she muses. "Maybe my own business will get so big that I can use some of the knitters from ABD to handle my excess orders. I've got a lot of ideas in my head."

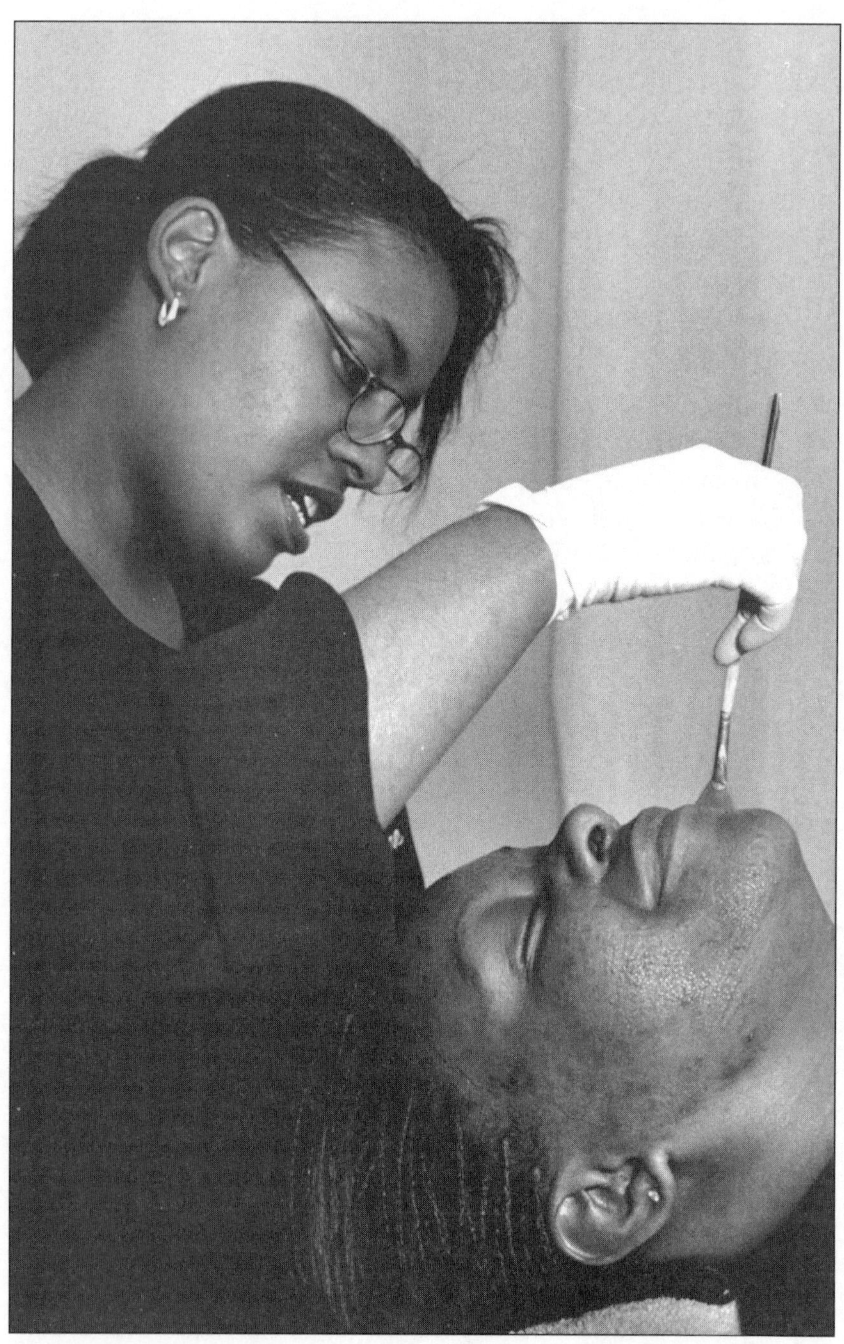

*Danielle Franklin is a bundle of energy: "I'm like a sales team and marketing team and financial team, all wrapped up in one person."*

chapter 9

# "Life Happens" Danielle Franklin Danielle's Touch Oakland, California

When she was twenty-three years old, which seems like a lifetime ago, Danielle Franklin thought she knew exactly how her life would unfold.

She was happily married to Terrace "Terry" Franklin, a barber. They had an adorable two-year-old girl, Samyiah, and were planning a second child. They lived in a little cottage in a nice section of Oakland while they saved up to buy a house of their own.

All that changed on January 6, 1994, when Terry died suddenly. Overnight, Danielle became a single mother.

Since Terry had been the primary breadwinner, Danielle was forced to go on welfare. For months, she was paralyzed with grief. "That whole period is a blur," she says.

After six months, she began to emerge from her depression. "One day, God spoke to my spirit," she says. "I realized it was time for me to get up and make a move and not just wallow in my loss. I had to get myself up and out. I had a child to raise and a life to live."

Years before, Danielle had considered pursuing a career in aesthetics (facial beauty treatments), but her family had discouraged her. Terry's death made Danielle realize that life was too short to live out someone else's dream. She enrolled in beauty school to become a licensed aesthetician.

Seven years later, Danielle owns and operates Danielle's Touch, a thriving skin care and body care salon in downtown Oakland that counts among its clientele judges, City Council members, and the area's business elite. Her salon has been featured in *Heart & Soul*, a national magazine that caters to African American women; the *Oakland Post*, a weekly newspaper; and the netnoir.com, soulofamerica.com, and blackenterprise.com internet sites.

A born marketer, Danielle has nevertheless had to struggle with numerous challenges as she's transformed her business from a rented station in someone's else's shop to her own freestanding salon on one of Oakland's busiest pedestrian streets. She credits Women's Initiative for Self-Employment, a nonprofit microenterprise development group, with giving her the capital she needed to finance a move, as well as the technical know-how she needed to help her business grow.

It's helped, too, that she's imbued with an extraordinary amount of energy, a creative streak, and a zest for life. "I'm like a sales team and marketing team and financial team, all wrapped up in one person," she says. "That's my personality."

And then there's the unquantifiable benefit of her relationship with God. "I pray for my salon every night when I close up," she says.

## A "Girlie Girl"

With the insight that comes with hindsight, it's hard to imagine Danielle ending up in any other career than beauty treatments.

As a teenager, she was a self-described "girlie girl," obsessed with the latest fashions, makeup, and hairstyles. When she was sixteen, she persuaded her parents and grandfather to pay for finishing school, and at seventeen, she made a formal debut.

As a senior in high school, she earned spending money by working as a makeup artist at several Oakland salons. "At this point, I didn't have any formal training," she says. "I just absorbed everything I read and watched on TV. And I guess I have a natural instinct for it."

However, Danielle's family discouraged her from pursuing a beauty career. "'Beauty college? No way,' they said," Danielle remembers. "They wanted me to go to a four-year college. But I felt it was a waste of money to go to a four-year school right out of high school. I told my mother I wanted to go to junior college while finding my way. My parents were very disappointed."

Danielle enrolled in Samuel Merritt College, a two-year college in Oakland. While going to school, Danielle also worked part-time. She got several good-paying jobs, which made completing college seem less important, and she left Samuel Merritt without a degree. "I didn't walk the stage, but I have enough credits for an associate's degree," she says. "I probably would have gone on to a four-year college eventually. But life happens."

For one thing, by nineteen, Danielle had met Terry. She gave birth to Samyiah two years later, and she and Terry married on September 25, 1993. She was a full-time mom until Samyiah was sixteen months old, when she took a part-time job, through a temp agency, in the accounts receivable department at the Port of Oakland.

When Terry died less than four months after the wedding, Danielle says, "it seemed like the end of my world. It had been my first serious relationship, and I wasn't just losing my husband, I was losing my best friend. I was incoherent for about two weeks, and after that I had a breakdown and had to go on disability because I was not able to hold a position. I couldn't take a lot of stress."

Danielle and Samyiah moved in with Danielle's mother, both for emotional and financial reasons. "I was like a zombie," Danielle says of that period of her life. "I was in the house with my daughter day in and day out for months after Terry passed.

The only time I went out was for therapy. Those first four months, you would never believe I'd have been able to go to school again.

"But one day I woke up, and God said to me, 'Okay, what are you going to do, kiddo, stay like this for the rest of your life or do something with it?'

"I realized I needed to get out and get around some people," she continues. "I made the announcement at home that I was going back to school. My mother said, 'You have not been out of the house for more than a few hours for months. How are you going to do this?'

"I knew I could not possibly go back and work in the accounting field anymore because it was too stressful, with all the deadlines and everything. I needed to find something in a controlled and calm environment, without a lot happening that would upset me. I started researching options and applying to programs."

Danielle decided to try to make a career out of her lifelong interest in beauty treatments. In August 1994, eight months after Terry's death, she enrolled at Alameda Beauty College. The state's disability program paid her tuition, and the state welfare program continued to send her a monthly check and provide health insurance.

In December 1994, after 600 hours of training, she was certified as an aesthetician. "I knew I was going to be doing something with my life, not just sit back," Danielle says. "I knew I would eventually have my own salon."

## From Fruitvale to City Center

After finishing at Alameda, Danielle went to work early in 1995 at Beauty and Health Cultivations, a salon in Oakland's largely low-income Fruitvale neighborhood. Initially, she worked on a commission basis, giving facials and waxing away unwanted hair. She had developed a following while at the beauty college, which offers discounted treatments to clients willing to let students work on them. "A lot of them followed me to Fruitvale, which was really a blessing," Danielle says.

As her clientele grew, she rented her own booth in the salon, which helped increase her income. In her spare time, Danielle shopped sales and began stockpiling the white towels and other supplies that she knew she would need when she had her own salon.

After seven months at Beauty and Health Cultivations, Danielle figured out that for what she was paying to rent a booth, she could operate her own salon. She moved into a small space in an office building on MacArthur Boulevard. Danielle's Touch was born.

"I didn't really make much money, but I didn't have many expenses, either," she says. Her rent was a little over $300 a month. Near the end of 1995, only five months after she'd moved to her own salon, the landlady told her that she'd have to move out by the following weekend because she needed the space for a thrift shop. Still a novice at business, Danielle had set up shop without signing a lease. Losing the space was a traumatic experience, but, looking back, she calls it "a very good learning experience."

"It was a bad decision I made, just making a verbal agreement," she continues. "Since then, I don't generally do stuff with people based on their word. I want something on paper saying, 'This is what we're going to do.'"

Danielle contacted a real estate broker to help her find a new space. He advised her to move downtown. "But I was afraid to go downtown," she remembers. "I thought the rent would be really high.

"He said, 'Oh, no, there's a building downtown that has never been really full since the earthquake in '89. I can get you a good rent.' It was like God gave me the nudge to move forward."

The broker delivered on his promise. In January 1996 Danielle rented a small office on the second floor of a professional building on Franklin Avenue for $485 a month, not much more than the rent at her old place, which had been in a less-desirable neighborhood. "I knew my clientele was growing and that I'd be able to handle it," she says of the increase.

The landlord paid for the build-out necessary to turn the office space into a salon. Danielle was back in business within two weeks. At her new location, her clientele grew slowly but steadily, mostly through word of mouth or in response to promotional flyers.

A few months after she moved in, she heard about Women's Initiative for Self-Employment, a nonprofit group that helps low-income women start or expand their businesses. "I was looking for guidance," she says. "I had no focus, no direction. I was trying to grow my business and do well in it without really knowing what to do."

Over the succeeding months, Danielle took two classes from Women's Initiative: Business Planning 1 and 2. "They helped me understand how to take the things that were in my head and put them on paper," she recalls. "They taught me how to do a business plan. It was easy for me to put it together because I already had it in my head."

By the end of 1996, the salon's first year on Franklin Avenue, the gross receipts for Danielle's Touch came to $14,343, more than double the previous year's receipts. Although the income covered all of her business expenses, there wasn't much left over, and Danielle and Samyiah still needed welfare checks to pay their day-to-day expenses. However, Danielle felt confident enough about the business's prospects for growth that when she renewed her lease, she rented a parking space and an extra room, which raised her monthly rent to $700.

## The Best-Laid Plans

Danielle had grand plans for the second room. She intended to use it primarily as a classroom. "I'd gone to some skin care shows, which are really motivating," she says. "You see new products there, and you can take courses about how to build your business. At one of them, I'd heard a talk about how you can build your clientele by educating them. So I decided that if I put them all into a classroom together, it would save a lot of my voice time during facials. I started offering classes on different topics and having events."

Danielle's first event was "an eggnog sip," which flopped. "It was a bad evening, with terrible weather," she recalls. "Three people showed up, my mom, my aunt, and one client. I was so devastated I cried and cried. I had bought all this food and put all this effort into it."

Danielle also held several skin care classes for new customers, but they weren't much of a success either. Eventually, she ended up using the room for storage space. But she learned a valuable lesson from the experience. "The one thing that can put a small business owner out of business is to assume that our event is going to be a great success just because we think it's a good idea," Danielle says.

Danielle's disappointment in the response to her workshops was mitigated by her selection as a speaker at Women's Initiative's annual "Showcase of Enterprising Women" in the spring of 1997. She received a standing ovation after her talk, and later met San Francisco Mayor Willie Brown. "It was my great pleasure to meet you," the mayor wrote her afterward. "I applaud and admire dedicated entrepreneurial businesswomen such as yourself."

## Another Move

In the summer of 1997, Danielle's salon was burglarized twice, shaking her confidence in her building's security. "I came in one day and found that someone had taken the stereo system," Danielle says. "The next time, they took my fax machine and telephone, which was brand-new. After that, I moved my computer out. I complained to the landlord that it had to be someone with a key. The management said it wasn't possible. Then there was a third attempt."

At her wit's end, Danielle consulted several lawyers who were among her skin care clients. "One of them advised me to go and buy a book about how to file a small claim," she says. "I read the whole thing, and I sued the building and won. I didn't quite get all of the money I should have to cover the losses, but the judge said I could break the lease."

Although Danielle was happy to be able to move, the decision brought with it a new problem: where to go. "I was walking down Franklin one day, depressed because of everything that had happened," she said. "I was praying, trying to move myself away from thinking about the frustrations in the salon. Suddenly, I saw the space I have now. It was just a blessing the way it worked out."

The new space was not only in a nicer building, but it was on the ground floor, which increased the likelihood of attracting walk-in customers. In addition, the rent was $150 less than Danielle had been paying down the street.

She put a deposit on the new space, which was to become available in December 1997. The landlord wasn't willing to pay for the costs of build-out, as her previous landlord had done, so she faced several thousand dollars' worth of expenses for renovations, including the addition of a sink and a wall. She talked to Colleen Tiffenson, her counselor at Women's Initiative, whom she'd come to regard as a mentor.

Tiffenson suggested that Danielle apply for a loan from the organization. Women's Initiative runs a revolving loan fund that disburses loans of up to $10,000 for first-time borrowers (and up to $25,000 for repeat borrowers). At first, Danielle was reluctant. "I thought if you got a loan from someone and you couldn't pay them back, they could take your business from you," she says. "I have such a personal attachment to my business. It was my change of life experience. I didn't want anyone else to have any kind of ownership."

Tiffenson reassured her that taking out a loan wouldn't put her business at risk, so Danielle applied for $2,000. "I was really stressed about whether they'd give it to me or not," she says. "My credit wasn't so great, because after my husband died, I'd had all sorts of expenses and missed some utility bills."

Women's Initiative specializes in loaning money to women with backgrounds like Danielle's, so her past credit problems weren't insurmountable. The organization offered Danielle a one-year loan at market-rate interest. With the lower rent at the new location and the prospects for increased business, she calculated that she could easily manage the payments. She found a contractor for the renovations through *Classified Fleamarket*, a free-distribution newspaper. "He gave me a really good quote, and he knew the kind of business I was in," she says. "Plus, he turned out to do excellent work. That's when you know that God is involved."

In late December 1997, Danielle closed the door at her old salon for the last time and moved all her equipment and inventory to the new location, less than a block up the street. She was unable to find a mover who would take on such a small job, so her father and brothers moved everything for her. "They just strolled it up the street," she says. Three weeks later, with the renovations finally finished, she was back in business again.

From the start, the new location was a success. "The space is smaller, but it's nicer," Danielle says. "And more people notice me when they're walking by." In 1998, the business grossed $39,359, almost three times as much as in 1996. Danielle and Samyiah no longer needed monthly welfare checks to help pay their bills. In 1999 the salon's gross rose to $46,590.

## Facials, Waxings, and a Sink Problem

It's a typical weekday in early December 2000. Danielle has been up since before dawn to complete her daily Bible lesson. "Last week I did the book of Esther, and this week I'm doing Ephesians," she explains. Afterward, she'd made breakfast for her daughter, who's now nine, and helped her get dressed for school.

In 1997, Danielle and her mother moved into a house about thirty minutes from downtown Oakland in an area that feels quite suburban. It's a comfortable, stylishly decorated ranch-style house with three bedrooms and a nice yard. They split the expenses down the middle, which helps keep Danielle's monthly living expenses well below $1,000. Because both women work downtown, they usually commute together, which saves on transportation costs. Today, as usual, they've dropped Samyiah off at her elementary school before heading downtown.

Danielle's first appointment isn't until noon, but she likes to get to the salon early so that she can take care of walk-ins, most of whom are seeking a quick brow or lip wax.

Danielle's clientele is diverse, ranging from service workers for whom a facial is a once-a-year splurge to professional women who spend $300 to $400 a month for salon services. Although most of her clients are African American, like Danielle and the majority of Oakland's residents, she has clients of just about every ethnic and racial background. Most are women, with a smattering of men. A few are transgender. "They're all equally valuable to me, because they all have chosen to come to Danielle's Touch," she says. "I appreciate that they have come to me. And I think it's because they get a real quality, customer-oriented service from me. And that's what people are looking for today."

There's only one walk-in this morning, a woman seeking a brow wax, so Danielle spends most of the morning catching up on paperwork and working on her newsletter, which she produces herself on a two-year-old computer. Although entirely self-taught, Danielle is quite adept at turning out attractive publications, complete with graphics. The newsletter provides her with a vehicle for promoting customer loyalty and publicizing specials.

"One of the tricks in my business is turning the casual customer into a regular customer," she explains. "How do I do that? Mainly by providing quality customer service. Last weekend I had a lady come in for a hand and foot treatment, and now she's going to come back for a facial. Another woman came in for a brow wax, and now she's coming back for a facial and a glycolic treatment on her back."

As noon approaches, the appointment time for her first client, Danielle looks around the salon to make sure everything is in order. She'd put up Christmas decorations for her post-Thanksgiving sale, so the salon looks even more inviting than usual. Lights twinkle in the wall-size window, which looks out on the building's lobby. Christmas cards add color to the pale pink walls, and her CD player is playing Christmas music. Ominously, though, the sink in her treatment room is making gurgling noises. Danielle's worried that she's got a blockage somewhere in her line.

Her noon customer arrives a few minutes early for her facial. "Come on in, Miss Gail," Danielle says, greeting the woman, as she does all her older female customers, by appending "Miss" to her first name. "You having a good day at work?"

"Yes, I am," Gail responds. "It's been so busy though. I'm doing a lot of paperwork."

While Gail changes into a treatment gown, Danielle removes the Christmas CD from the player and replaces it with some jazz, which she knows this customer prefers. When Gail announces that she's ready, Danielle goes into the treatment room and fills the face steamer with distilled water. Gail is lying on the treatment table with a pink sheet pulled up to her neck. Danielle puts a headband on Gail's head to protect her hair from the face-care products.

From her perch on a stool at the head of the table, Danielle mixes together a chamomile skin cleanser, dons latex gloves, and begins working the concoction into Gail's skin. The aroma of chamomile perfumes the air as Danielle and Gail chat about the merits of various skin care products.

"You know what I've noticed about the Lipogen?" Gail asks, referring to a product she'd bought here the month before. "When I used it at night, which you recommended I do, it seemed to make my skin dry. It's almost like it made my skin exfoliate."

"I think the weather has been really hard on everybody's skin recently," Danielle responds. "Are you still using your sunblock?"

"Oh, yes," Gail says. "Ever since I started coming to you, I've been wearing sunblock."

Danielle is now massaging Gail's face. Gail's eyes are closed, and her shoulders are noticeably more relaxed. Danielle takes her cue from the client and stops talking.

A few moments later, after the massage has ended, their banter resumes. "How's your mom doing?" Gail asks.

"She is doing good," Danielle responds. "Thank you for asking."

"And your daughter?" Gail continues.

"She is growing up too fast. She needs to slow down."

"She's nine, right?"

"That's right. And Abigail, she's about eight, isn't she?"

"Yes, she's almost eight. She's doing fine. She wants to have a sleepover for her birthday. I know you did that for your daughter, so I wanted to ask your advice."

As she answers, Danielle wipes the cleanser off of Gail's face. "Just think of a theme," she advises. "That'll make it easier for you. One year, I did a Mexican dinner. I decorated the whole house Mexican style, and I made them those virgin strawberry daiquiris and gave them each a little menu with a choice of tacos or enchiladas. It was just like being in a restaurant. It took them about two and a half hours to eat dinner. Afterwards I did something active with them, to burn off energy. I think we played Twister. And after that we put on a video."

Danielle is now using a paintbrush to apply an enzyme peel to Gail's face. "And then last year we did a slumber party with a disco theme," she continues. "The girls came all dressed up, and they danced until midnight. They acted like they were at a club. Then they went to sleep, and the next morning I cooked a full breakfast with eggs, bacon, sliced ham, grits, and pancakes. I always go all out.

"The next one we're going to do will be a PJ fashion show. I'm going to tell them to wear their best PJs, and we're going to set up a runway, and I'm going to videotape it."

"It sounds like a lot of work," Gail observes.

"You don't have to do all that," Danielle assures her. "A slumber party can be as simple as calling up a few friends to spend the night."

Danielle aims the steamer at her client's face. It blows warm moist air on her face to aid the action of the exfoliant.

The conversation turns to their respective Thanksgivings. "We had a really small Thanksgiving this year," Danielle says, "the smallest one since you've known me. It was just my immediate family. It's the first time in a long time we've done it that way. We usually have a really big gathering for the whole extended family."

"Your family sounds a little like mine," the client responds. "We have a whole tribe. You can't just invite one or two. You have to invite them all or none of them."

Danielle takes a warm wet facecloth from the Crock-Pot where it's been heating and wipes the exfoliant off Gail's face before beginning a pore-by-pore search for impurities that need to be extracted. The conversation returns to the dryness of Gail's skin.

"I have to admit that I haven't been good about drinking water," Gail says. "I'm not a big water drinker."

"If you don't drink water, what do you drink?" Danielle asks as she spritzes Gail's face with a hydrating facial tonic.

"Aronaberry juice," Gail replies. "It's like cranberry juice. I buy it by the case at Costco."

The conversation turns to the bargains to be found at Costco and then to salmon recipes, as Danielle massages Gail's face, neck, shoulders, and arms with chamomile oil.

"It smells so good," Gail comments. "It's like aromatherapy."

The next step in Gail's treatment is the application, again by paintbrush, of a hydrating mask infused with frankincense and myrrh. "It's a very expensive mask," Danielle says, "but you're a special customer." And off the discussion goes to the qualities inherent in various Biblical herbs and essences.

After Gail's mask has set, Danielle uses a soft wet cloth to remove it and then massages a daytime hydrating cream into Gail's skin as an extra precaution against dryness.

"Everything you've done has felt heavenly," Gail says as she climbs down from the table. "I'll have to come more often."

It's 1:25 P.M. The treatment has taken twenty-five minutes longer than usual, but the charge is the same: $55. Gail includes a $5 tip in her check. "So, Danielle, I'm off," she says. "Happy holidays. Let me give you a hug." The two women embrace.

## Creating a Regular Customer

After Gail leaves, Danielle puts the Christmas CD back on the player. She has just enough time to scarf down some take-out Chinese food before her 2 P.M. appointment arrives, a new customer who's coming in to have false eyelashes glued to her eyelids. The customer usually goes to another salon, but she thinks that the glue the other salon uses is making her own lashes fall out. Danielle's determined to turn her into a regular.

The woman, who's on her lunch break, lies down on the treatment bed. For ten minutes, Danielle bends over her, using a pair of tweezers and eyelash adhesive to attach perhaps a dozen clusters of false lashes to each upper lid. Each cluster contains fourteen individual lashes. The end result is startling. The woman looks as though she has about ten times as many eyelashes as she had before.

She asks Danielle if she has time to wax her eyebrows as well. Danielle obliges. When she's finished, she hands the woman a hand mirror.

"So, do you like it?" she asks the customer.

"I sure do," the customer says. "I'm going to make an appointment for next week. Not only are you less expensive than the other place, but you asked me how I wanted it done. The other lady I've gone to just does everybody the same. How much do I owe you?"

Danielle charges her $27—$15 for the false eyelash application and $12 for waxing.

She has a few minutes to spare before her 2:45 P.M. appointment with Beverly, a woman who comes every two weeks for a brow, chin, and lip waxing. The sink is still gurgling, so she calls her plumber and leaves a message on his answering machine. Tomorrow is Saturday, her busiest day, and if her sink is blocked, it's going to be impossible to do facials. "I've got customers coming from 8 A.M. to 7 P.M., so I have to have my sink," she says. "This is a big problem."

The building manager told her earlier in the day that it sounded as though the drain needed to be snaked, which his maintenance crew couldn't do. If Danielle wanted her sink attended to, she'd have to find someone herself.

When she turns her attention to Beverly, there's nothing in her demeanor to suggest that she's worried sick over the plumbing problem. "This wax is so wonderful," Beverly says as Danielle paints hot wax under her eyebrow. "I wish you'd tell me the name of it."

"Well, then, you'd go and do it yourself, and I wouldn't have any business," Danielle retorts playfully as she pulls the cooled wax off the customer's face with no apparent discomfort to her. "And give me some credit for the technique. It's not just the wax."

The treatment, which takes fifteen minutes, costs the customer $25. She gives Danielle $30 and tells her to apply the $5 in change to a ticket for the holiday raffle that Danielle's holding, with a computer as the prize.

Danielle has thirty minutes before her next client is scheduled to arrive. She tries again to reach her plumber, but can only leave a message. Five minutes before her next customer is expected, he calls back.

"Greg, I am so stressed out," she tells him. "I have a full schedule tomorrow, from 8 A.M. to 7 P.M., and I need my sink. If you could do anything for me tonight, I'd be really grateful. The building manager told me he thinks it needs to be snaked out, but I'm not sure that's the case. You've already replaced some of the pipes so that this shouldn't happen, and I don't put anything down it that would stop it up. It's really important for me to get my sink fixed before tomorrow." Greg agrees to come around 5 P.M.

At 3:30 P.M., Danielle's cousin, Myisha, walks in the door for her waxing appointment. This time, the conversation is about the high rents in the Bay Area. Myisha has just been hit with a rent increase—to $675 from $610—and is thinking of moving.

Myisha's waxing costs $10. She and Danielle exchange family news before Myisha heads off to her night shift job at UPS.

Danielle gives another facial at 4 P.M., which takes a little less than an hour this time, since the client doesn't like to chat. "Some people are talkers, some people are sleepers, and some people are observers," Danielle comments afterward. "I take my cue from them."

The plumber arrives just before 5 P.M., and after a few minutes of action with a plumber's snake, the drain is working just fine. The 5 P.M. client arrives ten minutes late, unaware of the drama that's preceded her arrival.

Danielle's take today is $265, somewhat less than she would like, but respectable for a weekday. One reason it's lower than it could be is that she's sold no beauty products today. The first facial customer had stocked up the previous month, and the other facial customers didn't feel they could afford to buy anything right now, with Christmas approaching. Waxing customers don't usually buy much.

Danielle needs to sell beauty products for income, but she's a strong believer in them as well. "I hate when people come in and they expect a major improvement but they don't want to purchase the proper home care items, or if they purchase them, they don't want to use them," she says. "I think people need to own up to their own responsibility for their skin too. I'm quick to tell people that they've got to do their side of the skin care business for me to be able to do mine.

"This was a slow Friday," she concludes. "But tomorrow will make up for it."

## A Flare for Special Events

Ever since she moved into her current space, Danielle has been integrating more special events into her business, not only because she wants to increase her income and build customer loyalty but because she loves planning them. "I think the events business must be in my blood," she laughs.

The disastrous "eggnog sip" that she'd thrown in her first year of business has evolved into an annual Holiday Savings

Celebration, complete with free chair massages and refreshments, on the day after Thanksgiving. In 2000, she made $1,500 in profit from that event, which cost her about $200 to stage. "I decided to change the flow," she says. "I looked at how it had worked the previous years and saw what it was that people really wanted to buy. I sold mostly old product, gift certificates, and coupon books, so most of what I took in that day was profit. It was a great event. It evolved into what it needed to be."

For a Mother's Day promotion, she came up with the idea of offering a "glamour photo session" on the preceding Saturday. For $19.95, each participant receives a makeup application and a ten-by-thirteen-inch portrait. The event attracts mothers and daughters; mother, daughters, and grandmothers; and even mothers, daughters, grandmothers, and great-grandmothers.

Then there's Luau Night, held on a balmy evening in June. As they enjoy tropical refreshments, a dozen attendees watch Danielle demonstrate a mango body polish/seaweed body mask application as well as a glycolic hand and foot treatment with paraffin mask.

One of Danielle's most ambitious annual special events includes a fancy dinner with bottomless glasses of champagne, shopping, and one-on-one makeup consulting at an upscale cosmetics store in San Francisco, with transportation via limousine. Despite its high price—$125—the event sells out each year.

Besides special events, Danielle sponsors regular promotions as well. For instance, one of the ways she rewards customer loyalty is through her Referral Club. A regular customer who refers a new customer gets a ticket for Danielle's monthly raffle. A typical prize is a $50 gift certificate at a restaurant.

Then there's Waxy Wednesday, a weekly or semiweekly promotion that she came up with after a trip to Atlanta the year before. "While I was there, I went to The Limited, because that's the kind of clothes Samyiah likes," Danielle says. "Someone there handed me a card, and she said, 'You have to come back tomorrow, because this is so much fun.' The card advertised 'Wacky Wednesday.' So I went back, and they had blaring music, and these girls wearing funny hats and goofy clothes, and balloons and entertainment, and fashion shows for the kids. Credit cards were flying everywhere, whereas the day before there hadn't been anyone else in there but me and two other women.

"So when I got home, I thought, 'What's my bread and butter service?' The answer was waxing. So I came up with Waxy Wednesday, discount waxing all day on Wednesdays. A $12 brow wax on Waxy Wednesday is $8. That sounds like a $4 loss, but on any given Wednesday I can now make more money than on a Saturday, which is a big day. The average time it takes me to do a brow wax is between three and five minutes. If I work eight hours a day, I can do a lot of three- to five-minute waxes. Do you know how much money I can make? I can guarantee that I'm going to make $200 on a Wednesday, and if I don't make more than that, I'm mad."

Over the years, Danielle has improved her sense of what works when and how to tailor specials to the season. This winter, for instance, she's reduced Waxy Wednesdays to a biweekly event, since the demand for waxing falls in the winter months. In the summer, when people worry more about how their bodies look, she publicizes her back facials.

June brings Father's Day promotions aimed at men. In July, typically a slow month because of vacations, she offers "Christmas in July" specials of four facials for the price of three, and 15 percent off all beauty products. July customers who schedule their next visit before they leave the salon also receive 20 percent off their next service.

At the moment, Danielle is thinking about staging what she calls Pamper Parties. "The idea behind the Pamper Parties is providing spa services in your home for you and your guests, a minimum of three people and a maximum of five," she says. "It'd be a lot of work to organize, but it can be done. I could take along a massage therapist and a manicurist.

"Everybody asks me where I get my ideas for marketing," she continues. "I think a lot of it comes from God. And I look at what other people do and I learn from them. I've taken some classes to get more ideas. Plus there's this creative streak in me. I have so many ideas. Too many, really."

Experience has taught Danielle to cancel an event if advance reservations suggest that she's not going to be able to cover her costs. For instance, early in the summer of 2000, she'd begun planning an "Invest in Yourself Weekend" for women at a charming inn in Oakland. The two-day event, set for mid-August, was to feature talks on financial investments, stress relief, and spirituality, along with a lovely buffet luncheon, a champagne reception, and a gospel brunch. She set the price at $100 and pledged a portion of the profits to Potters House, a group home for at-risk teens. But by late July, not enough women had signed up to cover her costs. She pulled the plug on the event before the deadline ran out for getting her deposits back.

Danielle has learned other valuable lessons during her six years in business. In 1999 she got into a dispute with the company from which she was leasing a credit card verification system. She'd opened a new bank account, and her bank had assured her that it could switch her funds over with no gap in her access.

"Well, that didn't happen, and I ended up having a debit charge rejected to the credit card company," Danielle says. "The one thing I have to work on is, I get mad. I got mad at the credit card company, and I said, 'Well, I'm not paying you anything.' They ended up putting a lien on my business account for the entire cost of the equipment I was leasing, about $1,000. It started out being their fault, but I made it worse by how I responded. I ended up having to get an attorney to fight the lien.

"It was a growing experience for me," she continues. "Now I'm very particular and suspicious about contracts, especially the fine print. A $1,000 bill can put a small business under. My gross annual income is only in the thousands, and if you start taking away $1,000 here and $1,000 there, that's a lot."

Also, in 2000, Danielle hired a publicist, a move she later came to regret. The publicist was to place articles about Danielle's Touch in publications and develop a plan for Danielle to market herself as an inspirational speaker. At first the arrangement seemed to pay off, since the salon was mentioned as one of twenty-five black-oriented day spas in the August/September 2000 issue of *heart & soul*, and then soon after got mentioned on two websites that cater to African Americans. But Danielle came to believe that the publicity resulted from her own efforts, rather than the publicist's, and terminated the arrangement a few months later.

## From Prayers to Promotions

It's 7 P.M. on a chilly night late in 2000. Although Danielle's day started at 5 A.M. with prayers, and she didn't finish her last facial until 5 P.M., she's looking fresh and alert as she stands in front of a class of about a dozen aspiring women entrepreneurs who want to know the secret of her success. Danielle is the guest speaker at a workshop on marketing strategies for the fourth meeting of a Women's Initiative class called "Managing Your Small Business."

Danielle often speaks to Women's Initiative classes as a way of giving back to an organization that she credits with helping move her business to a higher level. She's also taken part in a panel of successful women entrepreneurs who talked to teenagers attending Camp $tart-Up, an entrepreneurship program sponsored by Independent Means, Inc., in Santa Barbara, California. She loves public speaking, and she's pretty good at it.

The women gathered at the horseshoe-shaped grouping of tables are in various stages of thinking through their business concepts. Some of their ideas include painting custom wall murals, operating a group home for abused children, opening a bridal accessories shop, and offering body work healing treatments over the phone, the latter clearly an only-in-California type of concept.

Colleen Tiffenson, the Women's Initiative staff member who taught the classes Danielle took, is teaching this class too. She introduces Danielle. "I am really proud to introduce Danielle to you because Danielle went through 'Managing Your Business,' just like you are," Tiffenson says. "This could be you. That's why I thought it was so important for her to come in and share some of her strategies. She's going to talk about what you can do to get your product or service to your market in an efficient and wonderful way."

Danielle begins to spin her story. "I got into my business through a tragedy," she tells the women. "I was a widow, and I had a little girl to support, so I had to earn money. My husband had made good money, and I had the habit of going shopping. That has always been my struggle, my shopping. So I knew I had to develop a business so I could afford to shop." The women laugh. "And now I don't have time to shop.

By now, many of the women are taking notes. Danielle picks up a colored marker and writes "Referrals" on the white board behind her.

"Referrals are the most important thing to my business," she says. "My bread and butter is my referral program."

Now she's writing "Bread & Butter" on the white board. "A person who's referred to you costs you no money," she explains. "A referral is a free advertisement. Someone is planting a seed for you and watering it. A person walks in the door ready to hand you money. That sale is closed. You don't have to advertise. You don't have to do anything. But you don't want to just take that referral and go, 'Whew.' You have to make that referral work for you.

"How you do that is you make deposits and withdrawals to your customers." She writes "deposit/withdrawals" on the white board. "When your customer comes to you, they're tuned into one radio station, WIFM, which stands for 'What's in it for me?' Write this down and remember it." She writes WIFM on the board.

"Whenever I do a promotion, a flyer, a brochure, a business card, I'm always thinking about my customer thinking about that. 'What's in it for me?' My business card says, 'Experience the difference,' which tells the customer what's in it for her. I'm competing with the Claremont Hotel spa, with Sunset Cosmetics, with Solutions. I'm surpassing them because I understand that customers are asking themselves, WIFM."

Danielle has already heard each of the women give a thumbnail description of her business idea, and now she singles out a few so she can provide some concrete illustrations.

"Where's the bridal veil lady?" she asks. A hand goes up. "What's the name of your business?"

"Wedcessories," the woman tells her.

"Okay, we're going to talk about Wedcessories, and we're going to talk about bridal veils," Danielle says. "When we hear bridal veils, what do we think about?"

A few words are thrown out. "Delicate." "Beauty." "Lace and beads."

Danielle interjects: "Quality. What do most brides want to do with their dress and veil after they get married? They want to bag it and keep it. I don't want to get a little $50 veil, because when I pull it out fifteen years from now it's going to look like nothing. Quality should be the first word in her ad," she says, writing "quality" on the board.

"And then 'archival.' That's a new word in scrapbooking, which I do as a hobby. Use that in your ad too. If somebody told me a veil was archival, I would buy that veil, even if it was $500, because she had shown me the benefit of that veil. She had shown me what's in it for me."

Danielle zeroes in on a striking woman wearing an African turban. "What kind of business do you have?" she asks.

The woman mumbles something about herbal treatments. Danielle interrupts. "You have to speak up and speak firmly about your business if you want to be successful," she says. "The first thing about marketing and promoting your business is not that flyer you hand out. It's you. You are a walking billboard. You have to speak confidently about your business. When Bill Gates was in school and the students in the room were asked to respond to questions, Bill Gates was probably the first one up every time. I always speak confidently. You have to all the time.

"So now, what's your business again?"

This time, the woman says her business is "bathology," which, she explains, "is the art and science of performing herbal baths in conditioning massage."

Danielle presses her. "So what exactly do you do?"

The woman continues, "Bathology is a word you might not have heard before. It's like aromatherapy, just a different word for treatments that help you relax or energize you."

Danielle says to the class, "The first thing we're going to help her with is to make sure that when she talks about her business, the consumer has to understand what she means." Danielle heads off on a riff that illustrates the point she's trying to make.

"Two years ago I was sitting in my office and praying," she says. "I was trying to come up with a promotion. I knew it had to be something I could do constantly, because I hated having to come up with a new promotion every month.

"I said to God, 'Okay, Lord, I need to come up with something that is going to bring me money, that's not going to cost me a lot, and that is going to be ongoing.' The secret to a good promotion is something that costs you the least amount of money, reaches the largest amount of people, and brings you the greatest return—when people come back for it not twice, but six or seven or eight times."

She writes "least amount $," "largest # people," and "greatest return" on the board. And then she tells the class about Waxy Wednesdays.

"What each of you needs to come up with is a promotion that gives people something they want badly, that they can't do without, and that they're willing to tell other people about. I don't advertise Waxy Wednesdays. I did one bunch of flyers, and when they ran out, that was that. Now it's all word of mouth.

"My bread-and-butter promotion is Waxy Wednesday. When business gets bad, I can boost my bread-and-butter promotion by calling up some of my customers and saying, 'Did you remember that Waxy Wednesday is coming up?' It's gotten so when I walk into the coffee shop down the street, I hear women whispering, 'That's Danielle Franklin, and she's got a salon, and she does something called Waxy Wednesday.'

"Okay, back to you. So what's the name of your business again?"

"Bathology."

"So, on her flyer she's going to put 'Bathology,' and italicize it, and then put 'equals' and define it." Danielle writes on the board: "Bathology = the art of herbal treatment to relieve stress."

She turns to the class. "Who made the most money off of aromatherapy?" she asks. "Aroma Vera. And why? Because they put 'Aromatherapy' at the top of their flyer and defined it. If you just put your name there, 'Bathology,' people are going to throw your flyer out. Who are you, how much do you cost, and where are you is all I care about. That's why you have to put, 'Bathology is what I am, this is what I cost,' and then the name and address of your business.

"Okay, ladies, what do you want to buy from her? We know that she'll relieve stress. We maybe get some massage with this treatment and some exfoliation.

"What is the one thing we really need because we're stressed out today?" she asks, as she closes her eyes to aid in visualization. "We're in her facility, and we're sitting in the chair. We're sitting here and looking at the menu. There's just one thing on the menu we're going to get from her. Maybe a neck and shoulder massage. We don't want to get naked with this lady yet because she's a stranger.

"Do I want to drive all the way out to her place for a neck and shoulder massage? What would really be convenient is if she came to me. But it's not going to benefit her to have to drive forty miles to my house. But what about if she made office visits? Has anybody here ever experienced an office visit massage?" Only the teacher raises her hand.

Danielle writes on the board: "Create a healing environment in an office space."

"Aren't we getting a better understanding of what she offers?" she asks. "She thought everybody knew what bathology was. She told us, 'It's like aromatherapy. It's just a different word.' But suppose I don't know what aromatherapy is. You have to put yourself in the other person's shoes.

"Okay, so this is a bread-and-butter promotion—bathology treatments in an office setting. Now we're going to go on to a seasonal one."

Danielle gives a few other aspiring entrepreneurs ideas for seasonal promotions specific to their businesses. Six women have their hands in the air, seeking her advice, when Tiffenson calls an end to the class.

"Danielle really gives back to Women's Initiative," Tiffenson says in her concluding remarks. "She leads some of the networking events. You have her card. Call her.

"I hope a lot of things she said penetrated, like details, details, details. Don't just tell me you're doing a direct mail. Don't just tell me you're printing up a flyer. Give me details. Your first assignment for next week is to pick some strategies for bread-and-butter promotions and also quarterly or seasonal."

The class concludes at 9 P.M., half an hour after Danielle had been due at her church for a meeting. She's clearly not going to make it, but she feels her time has been well spent.

"Ultimately, I want to do more public speaking, teaching people how to build their businesses, and I want to get paid for it," she says. "This is good practice."

## Thinking About the Next Step

As 2001 began, Danielle's biggest challenge was figuring out how to raise her revenues. Her gross for 2000 turned out to be about the same as in 1999, which suggested to her that she needed to change her business practices if she was to maximize her business's potential and raise her personal income.

Danielle has been working with an accountant to figure out how to make the most out of the forty hours a week that she spends in her salon. "My accountant helps me figure out how much to charge for everything," she says. "My goal is to bring in $55 an hour. A facial takes an hour, so that's what I charge for one, and all of my other pricing is based on that figure too. So, for instance, brow waxings cost $12, because I can do more than four in an hour. And for some procedures we charge more than $55 an hour because of the cost of the product."

In 2000, she brought in an average of $35 an hour, $20 an hour less than her goal. She knows she could be earning more. She needs to figure out how to better fill the holes in her schedule, since she's reluctant to raise her prices.

"I made a vow that I would not raise the cost of my facials," she says. "Being a single mom, I can look back at my life before I was making a profit. It's tough on single parents. I want women like myself to be able to enjoy the luxury of having a good facial. It's something for low-income moms to aspire to."

One strategy she's considering to increase her revenues is to contract with two massage therapists to provide massages in her treatment room when it's not in use. "When a customer wants a massage, I could call one of the therapists and rent my room to her," she explains. "She charges $45 for a massage, and I charge the customer $60, so that's a $15 profit for me. That enables me to sit in my outer room and do my book work and basically get paid $15 an hour for doing it."

Danielle is also looking for a manicurist who could work out of a corner of her outer room and either share her fees or rent the space. That would provide additional revenues to the business without additional work on her part.

For several months in 2000, Danielle gave serious thought to expanding, which would have required her to move to larger quarters. "My customers put ideas in my head," she says. "They'd say to me, 'You really should expand. You need a spa room.'

"You have to listen to what the customer is saying, because when they suggest something, it means there's a need there. But you have to be mindful and think about whether it's a need you'll be able to fill. I was worried that I'd go and spend all my money on that sort of thing and then they wouldn't utilize it.

"I never do anything without praying, and God was sitting right by my shoulder, putting his hand on me, and saying, 'This is not the time to move.' The Bible talks about different seasons, and I think it's not my season for expanding now."

A better time to expand, Danielle thinks, might be in 2003, when her mother retires from her job with Alameda County. "She would be an ideal staff person for me, to do the hiring and firing and make sure the books are balanced every evening," Danielle says.

With expansion would come trade-offs, Danielle realizes. "It would be a magnificent thing if I could bring in $10,000 a month," Danielle says. "But then I think about all the sacrifices I'd have to make and all the extra work I'd have to put in."

At the moment, Danielle's income from her business covers all of her living expenses, her expensive scrapbooking hobby, and a few short vacations with her daughter each year. She also manages to save, and in 2000 she put some money into the stock market for the first time.

One expense she hasn't been able to pay out of her business income is health insurance. For a while, Samyiah was covered by a state program, and Danielle simply did without. But early in 2001, Danielle took a part-time job at Fed Ex, working twelve to seventeen hours a week, at night, for $11.65 an hour. Her primary reason for taking the job was to gain health coverage for herself and Samyiah. The money she earns goes right into her savings account.

Although Danielle often speaks to women's groups about how she's built her business, she says there's nothing magic about her formula. "If you have a vision and dream you want to go after, then you need to go after it," she says. "Be willing to work hard. And don't be foolish. Don't think you're going to take your $50 investment and make $5 million tomorrow. Listen and observe, but in the end, you need to follow your intuition, because your intuition is always going to lead you in the right direction. And intuition is nothing but God talking to you."

Danielle believes her attitude toward her business has matured over the last seven years.

"I've learned that you have to make sure you have balance in your life," she says. "You have to have a personal life. You have to have a family life. You have to have a spiritual life. You have to have a professional life. And you have to have time to spend on things that you do for you.

"Today, my life revolves around my spiritual walk with Christ, my daughter, and my work. But when I first started my business, it was all business, no play. The business was all I thought about. Then it became all business and all family. Last fall, I decided to take off one Saturday a month to spend more time with myself and my daughter. Plus, I began closing my shop earlier on certain days so I could pick her up from school.

"It's just been in the last year that I learned I need time for me. I try to go to prayer meeting on Monday mornings. Tuesday nights I have Bible study, and Thursday evenings, I have my Young Adult committee meeting. With all I've overcome in my life, my walk with Christ has been really important to me. And for fun, I belong to three different scrapbook clubs. When I'm with my scrapbooking friends, I don't do any business at all. I don't even bring along business cards."

Although she wants to be financially comfortable, getting rich has never been the standard that Danielle has set for measuring her success. "Everybody else looks at finances first, but I look at success more in terms of having a good wholesome reputation and a stable income, through a solid small business that provides good customer service," she explains. "The Bible says a righteous life is greater than all riches. I don't want to go broke, but I don't need to be making millions and millions. I went into business myself not because I didn't like working for other people or because I wanted to get rich, but because I wanted to be spiritually prosperous. And being a single mom and a widow, I needed to be able to spend more time with my daughter.

"I feel very successful right now, even though I don't have fame or fortune," she continues. "I own my own business, and I'm recognized as the top of the market. I spend a lot of time with my daughter. We can afford to go places, like a weekend in LA for her birthday or a weekend-long spiritual retreat.

"And I'm happy. I smile a lot. The weight of the world is not on my shoulders. I'm enjoying every facet of my life. I'm very blessed."

# Conclusion: Building Businesses, Changing Lives

As these stories make abundantly clear, starting their own businesses has led to momentous changes in each of the lives of the eleven low-income women profiled in *Kitchen Table Entrepreneurs*.

In most cases, their enterprises are generating enough revenue to greatly ease, if not eliminate, their financial worries. Some, like Jeanette Bradshaw, Lucille Barnett Washington, and Sheela Drummer, are even creating jobs for others in their communities. The women are spending more time with their families, and several—such as Jackie Clark, Ollie Barkley, and Lucille Barnett Washington—have taken on a spouse or children as business partners. Each is deriving deep satisfaction from being her own boss and doing work she *chooses* to do instead of *has* to do. Each is enjoying the pride and blooming self-confidence that come from testing one's mettle and finding it up to every challenge. Too, the businesses are becoming assets that the women will be able to pass down to their children.

These eleven microentrepreneurs didn't reach this point on their own, of course. Nonprofit organizations such as the Detroit Entrepreneurship Institute and the Lakota Fund provided them with guidance, training, and support (both financial and emotional) every step of the way. As Roselyn Spotted Eagle said, "At the Lakota Fund, they're always there for me, encouraging me on, telling me I'm doing good. I don't know what I'd do without them." These groups continue to help individual women get a firm grasp of skills they struggle with, such as record keeping and pricing, as well as to tackle new issues that arise as their businesses grow.

About 500 such programs around the country provide training and credit services to about 100,000 people each year.[1] The Aspen Institute estimates that there are at least 2 million low-income people operating microbusinesses.[2] Other studies indicate that many more would choose this strategy if support services were available.[3]

As we explain in more detail in Appendix A, several studies have demonstrated the potential of microenterprise as a route out of poverty for a small, but significant, percentage of low-income families. For example, the Self-Employment Learning Project (SELP) of the Aspen Institute found that:

- Almost three-fourths (72 percent) of the low-income microentrepreneurs in the study increased their household income over five years, by an average of $8,484 (from $13,890 to $22,374).
- The low-income entrepreneurs increased their household assets by an average of $15,909 over five years.
- More than half (53 percent) moved out of poverty.
- Reliance on public assistance decreased by 61 percent.[4]

In this chapter, we will discuss how public and private funding, government policies, and individual action can help microenterprise development programs improve and expand their services to assist entrepreneurial women in moving out of poverty.

## Public and Private Funding

Since 1992, federal and state funding for microenterprise development has increased dramatically, demonstrating the growing support for microenterprise development among policymakers. In 2000 annual federal funding specifically targeted to microenterprise development totaled about $54 million, with state and local governments adding somewhere between $10 million and $20 million.[5]

So that microenterprise programs can continue to provide quality services to their existing clients and expand to reach latent demand, public funding should be not just sustained, but increased. Around the country, the groups working with struggling businesses have identified increased funding for training and counseling as a priority. As the profiles show, training classes and one-on-one counseling greatly increase the prospects for business success in our sophisticated economy. A case in point is the intensive business counseling that West Company provided to Jackie Clark; while expensive, it was essential in helping her business weather real and proverbial storms.

Private foundations were the pioneers in seeding and funding microenterprise programs in the United States, and continue to provide significant support. In the mid-1980s, foundations such as Ms., Ford, and Mott gave fledgling microenterprise programs in this country their first grants. Corporate philanthropies, such as the Levi Strauss Foundation, soon joined suit. Although the figures are difficult to calculate, we estimate that foundations and corporations have contributed at least $90 million to the microenterprise field in the United States since the 1980s.

Even though annual government support for microenterprise programs now exceeds that of foundations, it is crucial for the philanthropic sector to continue to provide local organizations with funds to experiment with new program designs that can best meet the needs of low-income entrepreneurs. Foundations can also improve the quality of programs by supporting research on outcomes and best practices. Finally, it is important that local programs and the national groups that support them have the resources available to advocate for increased public funding and for policies that facilitate business development among the poor.

Increasingly, banks are attracted to microenterprise programs and have become major supporters. Banks see microentrepreneurs as potential new customers. They also assist microenterprise programs as a way to fulfill requirements under the Community Reinvestment Act.[6] More banks should support microenterprise development by making loans—either directly to the microentrepreneur or to the program's loan fund—by making grants to programs, or by providing in-kind services, such as encouraging bank staff to sit on nonprofit organizations' loan review committees.

## Mainstreaming Microenterprise

In this country, where starting a business has always been an integral part of the American dream, one would think that government programs that serve the poor would embrace microenterprise. However, many programs actually create barriers to business development among low-income people. So that low-income people are not excluded from the opportunity to start a business, policymakers need to remove such obstacles and mainstream microenterprise into the welfare, job training, unemployment insurance, and other systems.

Let's look at two examples of current barriers. When Congress passed the Personal Responsibility and Work Act of 1996 (commonly known as welfare reform), it mandated that most welfare recipients work at least twenty hours a week to continue to be eligible for benefits. But it left it up to the states to decide whether microenterprise training and operating a business could even count as work. Given the long hours the women profiled here put into their businesses, it is hard to believe that anyone would think of their effort as anything but work. Not all states agree. Even when policies decree that self-employment should count as work, caseworkers often tell women on welfare that they must get a wage-paying job.[7] The reauthorization of the welfare reform bill in 2002 presents an opportunity for federal and state policymakers to expand the definition of work to include self-employment and microenterprise training.

In addition, states currently have the option of allowing laid-off workers to collect unemployment insurance benefits while they work full-time on starting a business instead of looking for a wage job. Despite promising results to date, however, only eight states have implemented such programs.[8] More should do so.

## Building Assets for the Future

Of course, moving out of poverty takes more than just increasing income. Historically, families have left poverty in this country by building assets that they can rely on in times of crisis and can also pass on to future generations. Starting a small business is one way low-income families can build assets for the future.

Even if their incomes are modest, many microentrepreneurs are able to save, increasing their long-term prospects for financial stability. For instance, America Ducasse has saved several thousand dollars from her earnings as a home-based child care provider. She also contributes regularly to an Individual Development Account (IDA), a matched savings account dedicated to investing in a home, business, or education. Although Ollie and Rick Barkley have never been able to save, they transformed their Earned Income Tax Credit, a refundable tax credit, into a business asset by using it to build a knitting workshop. And, as Lucille Barnett Washington's and Sheela Drummer's story shows, a small business is itself an asset that can be passed down from one generation to the next.

Government policy can go a long way in helping low-income business owners save and accumulate assets.

First, federal and state governments can continue to support IDA programs, such as the one America is using to save money to buy a computer for her business. Here's an example of how an IDA works. A low-income businesswoman may calculate that if she really scrimps and saves, she can put away $25 a month. At the end of three years, she would only have $900, perhaps not enough to motivate her to save consistently. However, if she joined an IDA program, her $25 would be matched at a rate of, say, two to one. Each time she put $25 in the bank, the federal government, her state, private foundations, or banks would put in an *additional* $50 a month. At this rate, in three years she could accumulate $2,700 to invest in her business, use as a down payment on a home, or spend on education and training.

Second, federal and state governments can raise the asset limits for people who receive public assistance, such as welfare, food stamps, or Medicaid. Asset limits pose special problems for microentrepreneurs who are building up their businesses, since they must generally accumulate business assets, such as a computer and operating capital, before the businesses begin to generate income. It is, therefore, important for public assistance programs to view business and personal assets separately, and to allow aid recipients to accumulate a reasonable level of business assets.

Under welfare reform, for example, states can set asset limits at any amount and determine which assets are countable toward the limit. Several states have made it easier for low-income people to continue to receive crucial income support, in the form of welfare payments, while building up their businesses. Some states do not count business inventory as assets, others exempt funds in business bank accounts, and others don't count business property and loans.[9]

## The Challenge of Health Insurance

Most of the women profiled here share one of the same challenges as self-employed people of all income levels: the difficulty of acquiring affordable health insurance. Purchasing health insurance outside of an employer-based plan typically runs an average of $1,000 per year for a single individual and $6,000 for a family—costs that are out of range for women like America Ducasse and Ollie Barkley.[10] Even Danielle Franklin, whose skin care salon generates a modest income, decided to take a part-time night job at FedEx to obtain health insurance coverage rather than pay individual premiums herself.

Over the last few years, there has been a welcome expansion of health insurance coverage for children through Medicaid and the federal Children's Health Insurance Program (CHIP). However, unless the parents meet adult eligibility requirements for Medicaid, which in many states is below the official poverty level, they themselves do not qualify.[11] As we saw in the profiles, government programs cover both America's and Ollie's children. But the parents go without, generally relying on the generosity of local doctors, forgoing preventive care, and hoping against hope that a medical crisis won't propel their families into financial crisis.

The best way to ensure health care coverage for low-income entrepreneurs, as well as millions of other uninsured Americans, is to establish a universal health insurance system in this country. Short of that goal, however, national and state governments should expand Medicaid and CHIP eligibility to cover low- to moderate-income working and self-employed adults as well as children.

Another way states can help is to require insurers to make affordable policies available to small businesses. For example, New York now requires health maintenance organizations (HMOs) to offer health benefits packages at subsidized rates to businesses employing fifty or fewer employees and to sole proprietors with household incomes of less than 250 percent of the poverty line (for instance, $44,136 for a family of four).

State governments can also provide health insurance coverage to small business owners working in state-subsidized sectors, such as child care. In Rhode Island, a local group successfully lobbied the state to cover child care providers who care for children in state-subsidized programs. As we go to press, the Acre Family Day Care Corporation and other organizations in Massachusetts are advocating for similar coverage for child care providers in their state.

## How Can You Help?

Many readers may be asking what they can do to help make the dreams of women like Sharon Garza and Roselyn Spotted Eagle become realities. In addition to providing financial support to microenterprise programs, there are many things individuals can do to make a significant difference.

Here are some suggestions:

- Tell your local, state, and congressional representatives that you want them to support microenterprise development. By visiting the websites of the Association for Enterprise Opportunity (AEO) and your state's microenterprise association (see Appendix B for website addresses), you can find out their policy priorities and how to support them.
- If you are a businessperson or have skills in a particular industry sector, contact local microenterprise programs and volunteer to serve as a mentor. Again, you can find out about local programs on AEO's website.
- If you work for a bank or serve on the board of a bank, corporation, or community group, encourage these institutions to support microenterprise programs.
- If you belong to your local Chamber of Commerce, make sure that the small business policies it promotes will help the smallest businesses.
- Finally, when buying cakes, fixing your car, or getting a facial, patronize women-owned microbusinesses. Local programs can often give you directories of the businesses they have assisted in your area.

As part of a broader antipoverty agenda, microenterprise development is a promising strategy that appeals to policymakers on the right and left, to foundations that want to improve the livelihoods of families and communities, and to individuals who want to make a difference in other people's lives.

The Ms. Foundation urges both the public and private sectors to support microenterprise development as one of many strategies that create paths out of poverty for low-income women.

## Notes

1. John Else, "An Overview of the Microenterprise Development Field in the U.S.," in John Else et al., *The Role of Microenterprise Development in the United States* (Geneva, Switzerland: International Labor Organization, 2001), 5.

2. Peggy Clark and Amy Kays, *Microenterprise and the Poor: Findings from the Self-Employment Learning Project Five Year Survey of Microentrepreneurs* (Washington, D.C.: The Aspen Institute, 1999), 78.

3. Using data from two U.S. Department of Labor studies comparing unemployed people given microenterprise development services with a control group that did not receive services, microenterprise expert John Else estimates that making support services available would increase by 40 percent the percentage of unemployed people who would choose to start a business. John Else, "Microenterprise Development in the U.S.: Is There a Case for Public Support?" in *The Role of Microenterprise Development*, p. 54. According to the *Women's Voices 2000* poll, a survey of 1,576 adults, 26 percent of women and 34 percent of men say they would like to own their own businesses. Center for Policy Alternatives and Lifetime Television, *Women's Voices 2000* (Washington, D.C.: Center for Policy Alternatives, 2000), 25.

4. Candace Nelson, *Microenterprise Development Works! Outcomes for Clients*, Microenterprise Fact Sheet Series, Fall 2000 (Washington, D.C.: The Aspen Institute, 2000), 4.

5. John Else, "An Overview of the Microenterprise Development Field in the U.S.," in *The Role of Microenterprise*, p. 9.

6. The Community Reinvestment Act, enacted by Congress in 1977, requires depository institutions to help meet the credit needs of the communities in which they operate.

7. Lisa Plimton and Mark Greenberg, *TANF Policies in Nine States: Implications for Microenterprise Initiatives* (Washington, D.C.: Center for Law and Social Policy, 1999), 8.

8. As of early 2002, the eight states were California, Delaware, Maine, Maryland, New Jersey, New York, Oregon, and Pennsylvania.

9. Plimton and Greenberg, *TANF Policies*, p. 14.

10. Kaiser Commission on Medicaid and the Uninsured, *The Uninsured: A Primer* (Washington, D.C., 2001), 1.

11. H. Sklar, L. Mykyta, and S. Wefald, *Raise the Floor: Wages and Policies That Work* (New York: Ms. Foundation for Women, 2001), 124–125.

# Appendix A:
# What the Research Tells Us

Since 1988, several evaluations have been conducted on microenterprise programs that shed light on the characteristics of people served and on program outcomes. In the summary below, we will draw on the following national studies:

- The Self-Employment Learning Project (SELP) of the Aspen Institute, a five-year (1991–1996) longitudinal survey of 405 clients sampled from seven microenterprise programs. The Aspen Institute also analyzed a subsample of 133 low-income clients (defined as those with household incomes below 150 percent of the poverty line).[1]
- The Self-Employment Investment Demonstration (SEID), a study of 1,316 welfare recipients who participated in microenterprise programs in five states from 1988 to 1992.[2]
- A study, released in 1998, by ACCION International of 1,957 borrowers from six ACCION programs throughout the United States.[3]
- The Welfare to Work demonstration project of the Charles Stewart Mott Foundation, conducted by the Microenterprise Fund for Innovation, Effectiveness, Learning and Dissemination (FIELD) of the Aspen Institute, supporting ten microenterprise programs serving welfare recipients under the Temporary Assistance for Needy Families (TANF) program. (This study began in

1998 and has so far only released baseline data on client characteristics.)[4]

- Findings from MicroTest, a national effort coordinated by FIELD that collects performance data on microenterprise programs around the country.[5]

## The Characteristics of Clients Served

Major findings:

- A significant proportion of the clients of microenterprise programs are women and minorities. Over half (56 percent) of the clients of the forty-three programs participating in MicroTest as of May 2001 were women, and over a third (38 percent) came from minority communities.
- Microentrepreneurs are relatively well educated. In the studies of low-income entrepreneurs (SELP, SEID, and Welfare to Work), 74 to 88 percent of participants had completed high school or equivalency degrees. About half (44 to 50 percent) had pursued some education past high school. This compares to 55 percent of the poor population overall with high school diplomas or equivalency degrees, and 22 percent with additional years of education.[6]
- Microentrepreneurs are mature in age. In the SEID and SELP studies, the vast majority of program participants were over 30 years old (70 percent of the SEID participants were over 30, and 74 percent of the SELP participants were over 35). While the Welfare to Work group was younger (47 percent were over 35), this cohort is older than the general welfare caseload, in which 27 percent were over 35 in 1997.
- Large numbers of microentrepreneurs patch income from multiple sources. Nearly half (43 percent) of the low-income entrepreneurs in the SELP study reported at least two different sources of individual income in the first year of the survey. On average, 28 percent of household income came from the business, another 28 percent from public assistance, and 15 percent from the entrepreneurs' second job.

## Business Characteristics

- There is a wide range in the size and type of businesses run by clients participating in microenterprise programs. A typical microenterprise in the first year of the SELP study was a sole proprietorship that had been in operation for two or more years with sales of $12,000 per year. In contrast, for the participants in the Welfare to Work study who had businesses when they enrolled with the microenterprise program, the typical business was one year old with $5,000 in annual sales.

  The percentage of businesses that were home-based ranged from 39 percent in the ACCION study to 84 percent in the Welfare to Work study.
- Microbusinesses are concentrated in the retail and services sectors. The vast majority of microbusinesses in the SELP, ACCION, and SEID studies (74 percent, 82 percent, and 93 percent, respectively) were in the retail or services sectors.

## Outcomes

- Microbusinesses grow and become profitable over time. ACCION tracked clients who received one, two, and three loans. The most significant increases in profits occurred among low-income entrepreneurs who had taken out three loans over an average of two and a half years. Their average monthly profits nearly doubled, from $239 at time of entry to $468 at the time of their fourth loan application.

  SELP findings show that among the businesses that remained open for the full length of the study, profits doubled over the five-year survey period.
- This growth fuels increases in business earnings and household income among low-income entrepreneurs. For low-income entrepreneurs in the ACCION study, their take-home income from their business increased by 29 to 54 percent, depending on how many loans they took out. The most significant change, of $515 in monthly owners' draw, occurred among clients who had taken out two loans over a period of about one and a half years.

ACCION found that business income contributed nearly two-thirds of household income for the low-income entrepreneurs. Again, depending on the number of loans taken out, household income rose by 40 to 58 percent for this group. The most significant change, of $886 in monthly household income, occurred among clients who had taken out two loans over a period of about one and a half years.

Over the five years of the SELP study, 72 percent of the low-income microentrepreneurs increased their household incomes by an average of $8,484, from $13,890 to $22,374 (adjusted for inflation).

More than half of the low-income SELP entrepreneurs (53 percent) moved out of poverty.

- Microentrepreneurs significantly increase their household and business assets. Over five years, low-income participants in the SELP study increased their household assets by $15,909 on average.

  Similarly, over four years, SEID participants who started businesses increased their household assets by $8,738 and their business net worth by $4,867 on average.
- Survival rates of microbusinesses compare favorably to national business survival rates. In SELP, 57 percent of all businesses survived the full five years of the study. For low-income microentrepreneurs, the microbusinesses survival rate was 49 percent after five years. These figures compare favorably to national business survival rates of 47 percent over four years.[7]

  At the time of the final evaluation, 79 percent of businesses started by participants in the SEID study were still operating. These businesses had been in operation for an average of 2.6 years, ranging anywhere from one month to eight years.
- Microentrepreneurs reduced their reliance on public assistance. On average, low-income entrepreneurs in the SELP study reduced the amount of public assistance (such as welfare and food stamps) received by 61 percent, from $2,733 the first year to $1,054 the fifth year. Among the SEID participants who had started businesses, welfare payments declined from 74 percent of personal income to 26 percent, a decrease of 65 percent.

## Notes

1. Data from the SELP study are drawn from:

Peggy Clark and Amy Kays, *Microenterprise and the Poor: Findings from the Self-Employment Learning Project Five Year Survey of Microentrepreneurs* (Washington, D.C.: The Aspen Institute, 1999).

Candace Nelson, *Microenterprise Development Works! Outcomes for Clients*, Microenterprise Fact Sheet Series, Fall 2000 (Washington, D.C.: The Aspen Institute, 2000).

*SELP Longitudinal Survey of Microentrepreneurs: Major Findings over Time* (Washington, D.C.: The Aspen Institute, 1998).

2. Data from the SEID study are drawn from:

Robert Friedman, Brian Grossman, and Puchka Sahay, *Building Assets: Self Employment for Welfare Recipients* (Washington, D.C.: Corporation for Enterprise Development, 1995).

Salome Raheim and Catherine Foster Alter, *Self-Employment Investment Demonstration Final Evaluation Report, Part I: Participant Survey* (Iowa City: University of Iowa, 1995).

3. Data from the ACCION study are drawn from:

Cristina Himes and Lisa Servon, *Measuring Client Success: An Evaluation of ACCION's Impact on Microenterprises in the United States* (Somerville, Mass.: ACCION International, 1998).

Candace Nelson, *Microenterprise Development Works! Outcomes for Clients*, Microenterprise Fact Sheet Series, Fall 2000 (Washington, D.C.: The Aspen Institute, 2000).

4. Data from the Welfare to Work study are drawn from:

Joyce Klein and Amy Kays, *Microenterprise As a Welfare to Work Strategy: Client Characteristics* (Washington, D.C.: The Aspen Institute, 2001).

5. Data from MicroTest are drawn from:

Karen Doyle, Jerry Black, and Tamra Thetford, "Performance Measurement for U.S. Microenterprise Programs," *Journal of Microfinance* 3, no. 1 (spring 2001).

6. CPR-Series P70–42, "Dynamics of Economic Well-Being: Poverty, 1990 to 1992," quoted in Peggy Clark and Amy Kays, *Microenterprise and the Poor*.

7. U.S. Small Business Administration, *Small Business Indicators* (Washington, D.C.: 1996), quoted in John Else et al., *The Role of Microenterprise Development in the United States* (Geneva, Switzerland: International Labor Organization, 2001), 55.

# Appendix B: Microenterprise Resources

For readers who want to learn more about microenterprise, here is contact information for organizations working with the women profiled in *Kitchen Table Entrepreneurs* and for national organizations involved in microenterprise development. Selected articles, books, and videos on the subject are also listed.

## Organizations Supporting the Women Profiled in *Kitchen Table Entrepreneurs*

Acre Family Day Care Corporation, 14 Kirk St., Lowell, MA 01852; (978) 937-5899; www.acrefamily.org

Appalachian By Design, 208 South Court St., Lewisburg, WV 24901; (304) 647-3455; www.abd.org

Colorado Enterprise Fund, 1888 Sherman St., #530, Denver, CO 80203; (303) 860-0242, ext. 17; www.coloradoenterprisefund.org

Detroit Enterprise Institute, 455 W. Fort St., 4th Floor, Detroit, MI 48226; (313) 961-8426; www.deibus.org

Good Faith Fund, 2304 West 29th St., Pine Bluff, AR 71603; (870) 535-6233; www.arenterprise.org

The Lakota Fund, P.O. Box 340, Kyle, SD 57752; (605) 455-2500; www.lakotafund.org

West Company, 367 N. State St., Suite 208, Ukiah, CA 95482; (707) 468-3553; www.westcompany.org

Women's Initiative for Self-Employment, 1390 Market St., #113, San Francisco, CA 94102; (415) 826-5090; www.womensinitiative.org

Women's Self-Employment Project, 20 North Clark, Suite 400, Chicago, IL; (312) 606-8255; www.wsep.com

**National Organizations**

Association for Enterprise Opportunity, 1601 N. Kent St., #1101, Arlington, VA 22209; (703) 841-7760; www.microenterpriseworks.org. Visit the AEO website for policy updates, fact sheets, a directory of local microenterprise programs, and information on state microenterprise associations.

Center on Law and Social Policy, 1616 P St. NW, Washington, DC 20036; (202) 328-5140; www.clasp.org. CLASP's website includes papers on a wide range of issues affecting the poor.

Corporation for Enterprise Development, 777 North Capitol St. NE, Washington, DC 20002; (202) 408-9788; www.cfed.org. A resource for information on microenterprise development and individual development accounts.

Count Me In for Women's Economic Independence, 22 West 26th Street, Suite 9H, New York, NY 10010; (212) 691-6380; www.count-me-in.org. Count Me In provides small business loans and scholarships for business training to qualifying women.

Microenterprise Fund for Innovation, Effectiveness, Learning and Dissemination (FIELD), The Aspen Institute, One Dupont Circle, #700, Washington, DC 20036; (202) 736-5807; www.fieldus.org. Visit FIELD's website for the latest research on microenterprise development.

Ms. Foundation for Women, 120 Wall Street, 33rd Floor, New York, NY 10005; (212) 742-2300; www.ms.foundation.org. The Ms. Foundation provides grants and technical assistance to women's economic development and economic justice organizations. Visit the website for the latest grant guidelines, publications, and information on training events. The Ms. Foundation does not provide direct support to women business owners.

National Association of Women Business Owners (NAWBO), 1411 K Street NW, Suite 1300, Washington, DC 20005; (202) 347-8686; www.nawbo.org. NAWBO is a membership organization representing the interests of women business owners around the country.

RESULTS, 440 First Street NW, Suite 450, Washington, DC 20001; (202) 783-7100; www.results.action.org. RESULTS is a nonprofit grassroots citizen's lobby that advocates for solutions to hunger and poverty.

Wider Opportunities for Women (WOW), 815 15th Street NW, Suite 916, Washington, DC 20005; (202) 638-3153; www.wowonline.org. WOW provides training to local organizations and advocates for economic independence and equality of opportunity for women and girls.

## Federal Agencies

For a complete listing of federal programs, see *Crossing the Bridge to Self-Employment: A Federal Microenterprise Resource Guide*, available online at www.ustreas.gov/cdfi/programs/micro/pdf/crossing_the_bridge.pdf.

Community Development Financial Institutions (CDFI) Fund, U.S. Department of the Treasury, 601 13th Street NW, Suite 200 South, Washington, DC 20005; (202) 622-8662; www.treas.gov/cdfi. The CDFI fund aims to expand the availability of credit, investment capital, and financial services in distressed urban and rural communities.

Office of Community Service (OCS), Administration for Children and Families, U.S. Department of Health and Human Services, 370 L'Enfant Promenade SW, 5th Floor West, Washington, DC 20447; (202) 401-5282; www.acf.dhhs.gov/programs/ocs. OCS administers the Job Opportunities for Low-Income Individuals (JOLI) program that supports efforts to create new employment and business opportunities for low-income individuals.

Office of Financial Assistance, Microenterprise Development Branch, U.S. Small Business Administration, 409 3rd Street SW, Washington, DC 20016; (202) 205-6490; www.sba.gov. The Microenterprise Development Branch administers several programs that enable local organizations to provide training and loans to microentrepreneurs, such as the Microloan Program and the Program for Investment in Microenterprise (PRIME).

Office of Refugee Resettlement (ORR), Administration for Children and Families, U.S. Department of Health and Human Services, 370 L'Enfant Promenade SW, 6th Floor East, Washington, DC 20447, (202) 205-3589; www.acf.dhhs.gov/programs/orr. ORR awards grants to nonprofit organizations carrying out microenterprise programs for refugees.

Office of Women's Business Ownership, Small Business Administration, 409 Third St. SW, Washington, DC 20416; (202) 205-7287; www.sba.gov/womeninbusiness. Through this office, the SBA supports Women's Business Centers throughout the country providing assistance to women-owned businesses. The SBA also supports the On-line Women's Business Center, www.onlinewbc.gov, which provides comprehensive information on how to start a business.

## Selected Articles, Books, and Videos

*Overviews of the Microenterprise Field*

Counts, Alex. 1996. *Give Us Credit: How Muhammad Yunus's Micro-Lending Revolution Is Empowering Women from Bangladesh to Chicago.* New York: Times Books.

Else, John, Karen Doyle, Lisa Servon, and Jon Messenger. 2001. *The Role of Microenterprise Development in the United States.* Geneva, Switzerland: International Labor Organization.

Langer, J., J. Orwick, and A. Kays, eds. 1999. *1999 Directory of U.S. Microenterprise Programs.* Washington, D.C.: The Aspen Institute.

Microenterprise Fund for Innovation, Effectiveness, Learning and Dissemination (FIELD) of The Aspen Institute and the Association for Enterprise Opportunity. 2000. *Microenterprise Fact Sheet Series:*

1. "Microenterprise Development in the United States: An Overview"
2. "Program Design for Microenterprise Development"
3. "Business Capital for Microentrepreneurs: Providing Microloans"
4. "Fostering Entrepreneurship Through Training and Technical Assistance"
5. "Sources of Public Funding"
6. "Microenterprise Development Works! Outcomes for Clients"

Servon, Lisa. 1999. *Bootstrap Capital: Microenterprise and the American Poor.* Washington, D.C.: Brookings Institution Press.

*To Our Credit: Part 1: Bootstrap Banking and the World* and *To Our Credit, Part 2: Bootstrap Banking in America,* two one-hour documentaries about microenterprise development. Rooy Media and the Access to Credit Media Project, 1998.

*Research Reports and Papers*

Clark, Peggy, and Amy Kays. 1999. *Microenterprise and the Poor: Findings from the Self-Employment Learning Project Five Year Survey of Microentrepreneurs.* Washington, D.C.: The Aspen Institute.

Doyle, Karen, Jerry Black, and Tamra Thetford. 2001. "Performance Measurement for U.S. Microenterprise Programs," *Journal of Microfinance* 3, no. 1 (spring).

Himes, Cristina, and Lisa Servon. 1998. *Measuring Client Success: An Evaluation of ACCION's Impact on Microenterprises in the United States*. Somerville, Mass.: ACCION International. (www.accion.org)

Klein, Joyce, and Amy Kays. 2001. "Microenterprise As a Welfare to Work Strategy: Client Characteristics." Available at www.fieldus.org.

*Best Practice Studies*

Bonavoglia, Angela, and Anna Wadia. 2001. *Building Businesses, Rebuilding Lives: Microenterprise and Welfare Reform*. New York: Ms. Foundation for Women.

Edgcomb, Elaine, Joyce Klein, and Peggy Clark. 1996. *The Practice of Microenterprise in the U.S.* Washington, D.C.: The Aspen Institute.

Holley, June, and Anna Wadia. 2001. *Accessing Lucrative Markets: Growing Women's Businesses in Low-Income Communities*. New York: Ms. Foundation for Women.

*Public Policy Papers*

Boshara, Ray, Robert Friedman, and Barbara Anderson. 1997. *Realizing the Promise of Microenterprise Development in Welfare Reform*. Washington, D.C.: Corporation for Enterprise Development.

Greenberg, Mark. 1999. *Developing Policies to Support Microenterprise in the TANF Structure: A Guide to the Law*. Washington, D.C.: Center for Law and Social Policy. (www.clasp.org)

Holland, Michael. 2001. *Your Savings or Your Health: How Asset Limitations Harm Low Income People*. Albany, N.Y.: Public Policy Education Fund of New York. (www.citizenactionny.org/ppef-index.html)

Plimton, Lisa, and Mark Greenberg. 1999. *TANF Policies in Nine States: Implications for Microenterprise Initiatives*. Washington, D.C.: Center for Law and Social Policy. (www.clasp.org)

Wider Opportunities for Women. 1996. *Six Strategies for Self-Sufficiency*. Washington, D.C.: Wider Opportunities for Women.

# References

Center for Policy Alternatives and Lifetime Television. 2000. *Women's Voices 2000*. Washington, D.C.: Center for Policy Alternatives.

Clark, Peggy, and Amy Kays. 1999. *Microenterprise and the Poor: Findings from the Self-Employment Learning Project Five Year Survey of Microentrepreneurs*. Washington, D.C.: The Aspen Institute.

Doyle, Karen, Jerry Black, and Tamra Thetford. 2001. "Performance Measurement for U.S. Microenterprise Programs," *Journal of Microfinance* 3, no. 1 (spring).

Else, John, Karen Doyle, Lisa Servon, and Jon Messenger. 2001. *The Role of Microenterprise Development in the United States*. Geneva, Switzerland: International Labor Organization.

Friedman, Robert, Brian Grossman, and Puchka Sahay. 1995. *Building Assets: Self Employment for Welfare Recipients*. Washington, D.C.: Corporation for Enterprise Development.

Himes, Cristina, and Lisa Servon. 1998. *Measuring Client Success: An Evaluation of ACCION's Impact on Microenterprises in the United States*. Somerville, Mass.: ACCION International. (www.accion.org)

Kaiser Commission on Medicaid and the Uninsured. 2001. *The Uninsured: A Primer*. Washington, D.C.: Henry J. Kaiser Family Foundation.

Klein, Joyce, and Amy Kays. 2001. "Microenterprise As a Welfare to Work Strategy: Client Characteristics." Available at www.fieldus.org.

Langer, J., J. Orwick, and A. Kays, eds. 1999. *1999 Directory of U.S. Microenterprise Programs*. Washington, D.C.: The Aspen Institute.

Nelson, Candace. 2000. *Microenterprise Development Works! Outcomes for Clients*. Microenterprise Fact Sheet Series (Fall). Washington, D.C.: The Aspen Institute.

Plimton, Lisa, and Mark Greenberg. 1999. *TANF Policies in Nine States: Implications for Microenterprise Initiatives*. Washington, D.C.: Center for Law and Social Policy. (www.clasp.org)

Raheim, Salome, and Catherine Foster Alter. 1995. *Self-Employment Investment Demonstration Final Evaluation Report, Part I: Participant Survey*. Iowa City: University of Iowa.

Self-Employment Learning Project. 1998. *SELP Longitudinal Survey of Microentrepreneurs: Major Findings over Time*. Washington, D.C.: The Aspen Institute.

Sklar, H., L. Mykyta, and S. Wefald. 2001. *Raise the Floor: Wages and Policies That Work*. New York: Ms. Foundation for Women.

# Index

# About the Authors

Martha Shirk is a freelance writer in Palo Alto, California. She is coauthor of *Lives on the Line: American Families and the Struggle to Make Ends Meet* (Westview Press, 1999 and 2000.) She reported for the *St. Louis Post-Dispatch* for twenty-three years, earning numerous awards for her reporting on women's and children's issues. Her mother, the late Mildred Shirk, of Slatington, Pa., was a kitchen table entrepreneur.

Anna S. Wadia directs the Ms. Foundation for Women's Economic Security Program. She oversees the Collaborative Fund for Women's Economic Development, a nationally acclaimed fund that has raised over $10 million to create jobs for low-income women. Author of several papers on best practices in microenterprise development, Ms. Wadia previously worked on economic development in Africa for the Ford Foundation and Catholic Relief Services.

Marie C. Wilson became president of the Ms. Foundation for Women in 1984. Under her leadership, the foundation has created groundbreaking national programs such as Take Our Daughters to Work® Day and has contributed millions of dollars to organizations serving women and girls. Coauthor of *Mother Daughter Revolution* (1993, Bantam Books), Ms. Wilson has received the Robert W. Scrivner Award for Creative Grantmaking and the Women & Philanthropy's Leadership for Equity and Diversity (LEAD) Award.

Sara K. Gould, executive director of the Ms. Foundation for Women, has more than twenty years' experience pioneering programs that create economic opportunities for women and their families. A leader in the microenterprise field, Ms. Gould founded the award-winning Collaborative Fund for Women's Economic Development and has written and spoken extensively on women's economic issues. She serves on the board of her family's 128-year-old company, the Challenge Machinery Company.

Earl Dotter has photographed people at work for more than thirty years. In 1998, he published *The Quiet Sickness: A Photographic Chronicle of Hazardous Work in America*, documenting not only the satisfactions of work but also its dangerous and dehumanizing aspects (AIHA Press). He was the recipient of an Alicia Patterson Fellowship in 2000 and was featured on the Newseum's website as Photojournalist of the Month in April 2001.